They're Playing Our Songs

Women Talk about Feminist Rock Music

ANN M. SAVAGE

Westport, Connecticut
London

Library of Congress Cataloging-in-Publication Data

Savage, Ann M.
   They're playing our songs : women talk about feminist rock music / Ann M. Savage.
      p. cm.
   Includes discography and bibliographical references.
   ISBN 0-275-97356-5 (alk. paper)
   1. Rock music—United States—1991-2000—History and criticism.
2. Feminist music—United States—History and criticism. 3. Women rock musicians. 4. Rock music fans—United States—Interviews. 5. Women rock music fans—United States—Interviews. I. Title.
ML3534.3.S28 2003
781.66'082'0973—dc21   2003045790

British Library Cataloguing in Publication Data is available.

Copyright © 2003 by Ann M. Savage

All rights reserved. No portion of this book may be reproduced, by any process or technique, without the express written consent of the publisher.

Library of Congress Catalog Card Number: 2003045790
ISBN: 0-275-97356-5

First published in 2003

Praeger Publishers, 88 Post Road West, Westport, CT 06881
An imprint of Greenwood Publishing Group, Inc.
www.praeger.com

Printed in the United States of America

The paper used in this book complies with the
Permanent Paper Standard issued by the National
Information Standards Organization (Z39.48-1984).

10 9 8 7 6 5 4 3 2 1

Copyright Acknowledgments

The author and publisher are grateful for permission to reproduce material from the following:

Tori Amos: "Father Lucifer," © 1996 Sword and Stone Publishing Incorporated. Used by Permission; "Hey Jupiter," © 1996 Sword and Stone Publishing Incorporated. Used by Permission; "Precious Things," © 1992 Sword and Stone Publishing Incorporated. Used by Permission; and "Silent All These Years," © 1992 Sword and Stone Publishing Incorporated. Used by Permission.

"Beautiful Red Dress" by Laurie Anderson. © 1989 Difficult Music. Reprinted with the permission of the author.

"The Christians and the Pagans," written by Dar Williams. © 1996 Burning Field Music (ASCAP)/Administered by Bug Music. All Rights Reserved. Used by Permission.

Ani DiFranco: "Blood in the Boardroom," © 1993 Righteous Babe Music. Used by Permission; "I'm No Heroine," © 1992 Righteous Babe Music. Used by Permission; "In or Out," © Righteous Babe Records. Used by Permission; "Lost Woman Song," © 1990 Righteous Babe Music. Used by Permission; "Make Me Stay," © 1991 Righteous Babe Music. Used by Permission; "The Million You Never Made," © 1995 Righteous Babe Records. Used by Permission; "Rush Hour," © 1990 Righteous Babe Music. Used by Permission; "The Slant," © 1990 Righteous Babe Music. Used by Permission; and "What If No One's Watching," © 1992 Righteous Babe Music. Used by Permission.

"Do You Take This Man." Lyrics by Diamanda Galas. © 1994 Mute Song Ltd. Used by Permission.

Everything But the Girl, "Missing," by Ben Watt and Tracy Thorn. © 1994 Complete Music Ltd. All Rights administered by Warner-Tamerlane Publishing Corp. All Rights Reserved. Used by Permission. Warner Bros. Publications U.S. Inc., Miami, FL 33014.

Everything But the Girl, "Politics Aside," by Ben Watt. © 1991 Warner Chappell Music Ltd. All Rights in U.S. and Canada administered by WB Music Corp. All Rights Reserved. Used by Permission. Warner Bros. Publications U.S. Inc., Miami, FL 33014.

Nanci Griffith, "Down 'N' Outer," words and music by Nanci Griffith. © Copyright Irving Music, Inc. on behalf of itself and Wing and Wheel Music (BMI). International Copyright Secured. All Rights Reserved.

"I Am So Ordinary" and "Where Have All the Cowboys Gone" by Paula Cole. © 1995. Used by Permission.

Indigo Girls: "Get Out the Map," words and music by Emily Saliers. © 1997 EMI Virgin Songs. Inc. and Godhap Music. All Rights Controlled and Administered by EMI Virgin Songs, Inc. All Rights Reserved. International Copyright Secured. Used by Permission; "It's Alright," words and music by Emily Saliers. © 1997 EMI

Virgin Songs. Inc. and Godhap Music. All Rights Controlled and Administered by EMI Virgin Songs, Inc. All Rights Reserved. International Copyright Secured. Used by Permission; "Love Will Come to You," words and music by Emily Saliers. © 1992 EMI Virgin Songs. Inc. and Godhap Music. All Rights Controlled and Administered by EMI Virgin Songs, Inc. All Rights Reserved. International Copyright Secured. Used by Permission.

"Lucystoners" by Amy Ray. © 2001 Daemon Records. Used by Permission.

Sarah McLachlan, "Black," words and music by Sarah McLachlan. © Copyright Songs of Universal, Inc. on behalf of Music Corp. of America, Inc. (BMI). 100.00% International Copyright Secured. All Rights Reserved.

Sarah McLachlan, "Good Enough," "Hold On" and "Ice Cream," copyright 1993 Sony/ATV Songs LLC and Tyde Music. All rights administered by SONY/ATV Music Publishing, 8 Music Square West, Nashville, TN 37203. All rights reserved. Used by permission.

"Nirvana" by Juliana Hatfield. © 1992 juliana hatfield music. All rights administered by Zomba Songs Inc. All Rights Reserved. Used by Permission. Warner Bros. Publications U.S. Inc., Miami, FL 33014.

Liz Phair, "Fuck and Run," copyright 1993 Sony/ATV Tunes LLC and Civil War Days Music. All rights administered by SONY/ATV Music Publishing, 8 Music Square West, Nashville, TN 37203. All rights reserved. Used by permission.

"Song of Sand" by Suzanne Vega. © 1992 Waifersongs Ltd. Used by Permission.

"Suicide Alley" by Shawn Colvin and John Leventhal. © 1996 WB Music Corp., Scred Songs and Lev-A-Tunes. All Rights o/b/o Scred Songs administered by WB Music Corp. All Rights Reserved. Used by Permission. Warner Bros. Publications U.S. Inc., Miami, FL 33014.

Pam Tillis, "All the Good Ones Are Gone," copyright 1997 Acuff Rose Music, Inc. and Polygram Int'l Pub./Ranger Bob. All rights on behalf of Acuff Rose Music, Inc. administered by Sony/ATV Music Publishing, 8 Music Square West, Nashville, TN 37203. All rights reserved. Used by permission; and "All the Good Ones Are Gone," words and music by Bob McDill and Dean Dillon. © Copyright Universal-Polygram Int. Publ., Inc. on behalf of itself and Ranger Bob Music (ASCAP). 50.00% International Copyright Secured. All Rights Reserved.

*This book is dedicated to my
mother and father,
Sophie and Len,
with love.*

Contents

Preface	xi
Acknowledgments	xvii
Introduction	1
1. Women's Attraction to Artists	23
2. "I'm Not the Only One Who Has Felt Like This": Identification and Appropriation	69
3. Finding Voice: Expression and Connection	115
4. The Industry, Society and Self	149
5. Conclusions	173
Appendix A: Participant Profiles	187
Appendix B: List of Artists Appealing to Respondents	191
Select Discography	195
References	199
Index	207

Preface

I was five years old as I stared over one of my sister's shoulders and onto the 45 RPM record player singing to the Jackson 5's 1970s hits "ABC" and "I Want You Back." At eight my sisters taught me every single word to Lynyrd Skynyrd's 1973 single "Gimme Three Steps." To my mother's dismay, we would jump up and down on our beds, singing our hearts out to all the hits of the day. With just one quick review of the songs, I could probably pick the words up again easily. I hear the songs bang around in my head as I write this preface. At least this is how I remember it; my sisters, all four of them, might have different accounts.

My sisters were my musical influence. All older and always seeming cooler than me, I listened to what they listened to. As young children, I remember Bonnie liking Donnie Osmond; Cindy's choice was Bobby Sherman; while I was left with Jimmy Osmond to adore. In later years Debbie was keen on Chicago, Bachman Turner Overdrive and Three Dog Night, and still to this day my oldest sister Cathy remains a big Steely Dan fan. I remember driving around in her car on hot sunny summer days with the windows rolled all the way down and Steely Dan blaring out of the tinny, auto-factory speakers. As we got older, Debbie and Cindy became big fans and in fact groupies of a Buffalo, New York, cover band, the Little Trolls; they looked like their name implies—long hair, beards, very much like lanky ZZTop members. Often I tagged along. All through high school my interest in music remained strong. Jethro Tull became my favorite band. I had even drawn an outline sketch of Ian Anderson playing his flute on the back of one of my jean jackets that my oldest sister Cathy embroidered for me. Another featured a sewn-on Pink Floyd emblem.

I remained a big fan of rock; although some are now embarrassing to admit, I went to concerts regularly including Deep Purple, Van Morrison, Ted Nugent, Rush, Triumph, the Rolling Stones, U2 and *so* many more. I collected records and made mix tapes that included Sugar Loaf's "Green Eyed Lady" and Shocking Blue's "Venus." People would compliment me often upon hearing them. Such a variety of songs and all the rock hits. Bad audio quality as compared to today's compact disc (CD) superiority, they remain on a shelf in a closet ignored for over 10 years now, never listened to again.

I was a big fan. I even remembered my mom saying to me when I was 16, "Why do you keep wasting your money on records, concert tickets and t-shirts? You're not going to be wearing t-shirts and listening to rock music all of your life!" It's a funny comment to think back on now, especially for myself and those who know me, because probably somewhat to my mother's disappointment and also perhaps because of my unconscious inclination to rebel against authority, I still buy lots of CDs, go to concerts and wear t-shirts sharing the names of my favorite music groups. Although these elements have stayed the same, the gender of the music artists and the stories told through the lyrics have changed dramatically.

When growing up, in some ways I felt I wasn't quite considered "knowing" of music and artists, as some of my male friends were. Decades removed from those years, I see things more clearly—that because I was a female, I never quite got the credit of knowing what I was talking about. When it came to music discussions in a mixed-gender group, attention was more commonly paid to the boys and men who talked. Sadly, I still sense this today.

The story I'm telling here has really come to mind because of working on this project. The research project that resulted in this book was very personal for me and provoked me to think about my own musical tastes. I've always loved music. Always from the outside looking in. After two sisters didn't follow through on guitar lessons, my parents weren't about to pay for the drum lessons I wanted as a kid. They were probably right. As an adult I took up guitar lessons but never did stick with it. I have never been a musician; I'm not a musicologist—always just a fan.

I loved and had a good time with all the rock music of my teenage years, but something was decidedly missing. I figured out what it was in the late 1980s. Those were some of the best discovery years in music for me. Michelle Shocked, Indigo Girls, Melissa Etheridge, Sinead O'Connor, Tanita Tikaram and Toni Childs released their first CDs. And there were so many others—Suzanne Vega, Tracy Chapman, Ani DiFranco, Tori Amos and Shawn Colvin. I was so drawn to these artists. They spoke to me in a very real way. I know that before these female artists there were other great female rockers like Pat Benatar, Heart, Chrissie Hynde, Blondie and even others before them. But for some reason the artists that debuted in the late 1980s and early 1990s rang truer to me in some kind of way—maybe because I felt like they were my musical discovery and not that of my sisters, or because the numbers were greater or because I just related more to this new generation of female singer/songwriter-rockers. Whatever the case, this was a musical and personal turning point for me.

I still listen to a lot of female artists. In fact, it was only when beginning this project in the mid-1990s that I first realized I listen almost exclusively to female artists. It occurred to me that I hadn't bought a lot of CDs recently by male artists—I'd pick up an occasional Van Morrison, Lenny Kravitz or Nirvana, but that was about it. My increased interest in music by women intensified and ran parallel to my maturation as a feminist. It was gratifying to hear women sing about the challenges, the pain and the frustration of being a woman in a patriarchal world.

The importance of music by women in my life coupled with the seemingly increased mainstream acceptance of female artists in the 1990s had me wondering what female artists' music meant in the everyday lives of women. So as a feminist media studies scholar, I set out on this project wanting to talk to women who were primarily interested in female artists that had a political and/or feminist sensibility. To keep the scope of the project manageable I chose to limit the study to fans of artists that generally fell within the broad-based rock genre including pop/rock, folk/rock, alternative/rock and singer-songwriter/rock. The focus was also on artists with substance: artists who use musical expression to give "voice [to] . . . personal politics as well as a means of affecting change in society more generally" (Pratt, 1990, p. 143). And as Tetzlaff (1994) wrote about authentic rock, they are artists whose lyrics and music "locates its truth either in the lived experience of a community it aims to represent, or in the unique creative vision of the musician. It has political or poetic significance; it is an object of commitment, not just consumption" (p. 98). These were my guideposts in defining the type and style of music I wanted to consider when identifying participants to interview. However, the women I interviewed were free to occasionally mention artists outside of rock, and they did, including country (Pam Tillis), rap (Salt 'n Pepa), disco (Sister Sledge) and jazz (Sarah Vaughn) artists, among others.

Narrowing and specifically defining the criteria of feminist and/or politically themed was difficult. Qualities of feminist and/or political sensibilities shift and are judged differently by every individual. Generally speaking, I wanted to consider fans of artists who, in one way or another, challenge gender roles and seek equality, respect and choice for women. Even though artists may not outwardly define themselves as political and/or feminist, the artists' work is critical of some aspect of women's subordination. They lend their names to, volunteer for or are activists for political and/or feminist causes, such as environmental causes, women's issues and children's issues. And even if artists are predominantly concerned about relationships and emotions, it is important to note that "these areas [are] of central concern to women and important sources of women's oppression" (Roberts, 1996, p. 137). Finally, the artists within the style of music considered for this project are, in essence, more so than less so political and/or feminist. I wanted to talk to women who were fans of politically conscious female rockers.

The interviews took place in 1997. All of the women were excited to talk about their favorite female artists and take part in this project. They all in their own way had interesting stories to tell. The best time I have ever had doing research was talking to these women in their kitchens, living rooms, bedrooms and offices. Over the past several years as I worked on this manuscript, I realized I am a lot like the respondents who share their stories in the pages of this book. Honestly, it wasn't until my friend Marie was reading through a very early draft of this book when she said to me, "You should put your story in here—you are these women." Another friend said the same, so I felt compelled to share some bits and pieces of my life here—in some way to reciprocate the generosity of the women who share their stories through these pages. In some ways, maybe their stories are my stories.

There are two common characteristics among the women interviewed for this study that some readers might find troublesome. First, 14 of the 15 women interviewed here are white; there is only 1 woman of color—an African American. Second, all of the female respondents are from lower-middle-class- to upper-class-income levels. In some ways, I don't consider the lack of racial and economic diversity as a shortcoming of this study—but more as a finding and symptomatic of the framework in which this study was conducted. As discussed in more detail later, music is largely racialized, and rock is a white music genre. It logically follows that because most rock performers are white, then most rock fans and respondents for this study are Caucasian. These numbers simply mirror the racial breakdown of the completed questionnaires I received identifying women interested and willing to be interviewed for this study. Conversely, because lesbians have a higher propensity to be drawn to female artists, 5 of the 15 women interviewed identified as lesbian.

Furthermore, although a few of the respondents self-identified as lower class economically, my observation was that none of the respondents were close to poverty in any real way. Often they had familial financial support in various forms whether monetary support from parents (especially with the younger respondents), cohabitating with family members as an adult, or attending college and the low-income status was a temporary sacrifice. Moreover, I was interested in talking to women who are invested listeners, people who seriously attend to music. Therefore, it logically follows that the respondents would not come from economically impoverished households because of the necessity of disposable income to divert to buying CDs, going to concerts and attending to music press. I concede that a more accurate subtitle for *They're Playing Our Songs* would be: "Fourteen White and One African American 'Middle-Class' Women (Five of Which Are Lesbian) Talk Mostly about Rock Music But Also Mention the Occasional Rap, Country or Jazz Artist."

Whatever the case, the focus is the women's heart-wrenching and moving stories present in the pages of this book. The respondents talk about why they are primarily drawn to female artists, how they appropriate music to cope with life's troubles, how they share a connection through music with family and friends, their criticisms of the music industry and finally recognizing the importance of the mainstream acceptance of female artists.

This book is primarily intended for academics with a scholarly interest in popular music, popular culture, fandom, media, feminism, gender studies, women's studies and audience studies. Secondarily, I think the general reader with an interest in music, female rockers or feminism will find the academic jargon kept to a minimum so that they too may enjoy a read as well. My hope is that this book will serve as a vehicle for women's voices to be heard—voices often dismissed by the larger culture as well as the music industry. I hope it helps to chip away at the continued dismissal of female fans of music. Perhaps some readers will even see themselves in the pages of this book, as I have.

Acknowledgments

Thanks go to a lot of people who in different ways and at different times helped me see this project to fruition. I would like to thank my dissertation committee, Peter Shields, Jack Santino, Dean Crystal, Radhika Gajjala, Gene Trantham and Vickie Rutledge Shields (chair), for their guidance as a graduate student at Bowling Green State University. Thanks to Vickie in particular for her advice and encouragement in bringing my work to book form. Readers of a very early draft of this book helped me to think that maybe I really could do this and include Caroline Huck, Emily Pettigrew and Marie Jones. Special thanks go to Marie who read my introduction more than once and located the name of a song that I couldn't place. Media studies scholars Robin Means-Coleman and Cynthia Lont offered expert advice and encouragement that this was indeed a worthwhile pursuit. Cynthia, in particular, was especially supportive and generous with her time and advice. Special thanks go to Butler University and in particular Kenneth Creech and Peter Alexander. Their support of this project helped me get it into print.

I would also like to thank all of the artists who allowed me to reprint entire song lyrics free of charge or for a nominal fee. Special thanks also go to all of the generous respondents who gave me time out of their day to talk about their musical interests. I enjoyed talking with all of you immensely.

I would like to thank all of my friends who endured phone calls of doubt, fear and frustration. Thanks to my sisters Cathy, Debbie,

Cindy and Bonnie just for being my big sisters and for influencing me in all the ways you have—especially musically—and making Buffalo always fun to go home to. Thanks to my nephews Kyle, Corey, Justin, Gabriel and Elliott and my niece Julie—you add color and joy to my life.

Most important, I am incredibly appreciative of my parents, to whom I have dedicated this book. They have always let me be me. And without them, all of this would have been so much more impossible. This is for you, Mom and Dad! I am so proud to be your daughter. I love you.

Introduction

i sing what i wish i could say
and i hope somewhere
some woman hears my music
and it helps her through her day

—Ani DiFranco, "I'm No Heroine," 1992

Well . . . Janny Wenner Janny Wenner—Rolling Stone's most
  fearless leader—gave the boys what they deserve, but with
  the girls he lost his nerve.
Testing 1, 2, 3 in the marketplace—it's just a demographic-
  based disgrace,
and a stupid, secret, whiteboy handshake that we'll never be
  part of.

—Amy Ray, "Lucystoners," 2001

In the mid-1990s there was unprecedented mainstream acceptance (in terms of record sales, concert attendance and chart hits) of female rock artists including the various subgenres of pop/rock, singer/songwriters, folk rock and alternative. In 1997 there were "more women on *Billboard*'s Top 100 charts than in any period in history" (Anderman, 2000, sec. 2). These were take-charge women who told of the pleasures and struggles of living in a patriarchal world. An altogether new role had evolved for women, a role outside the more traditional one allowed in the music industry.[1] Female artists executed control over their image, music and careers. Many embodied a feminist and/or political sensibility including Tracy Chapman, Tori Amos, Melissa Etheridge, Hole, P.J. Harvey, Liz Phair, Indigo Girls, Ani DiFranco and Sarah McLachlan, among many others. This newfound mainstream acceptance peaked with the advent of McLachlan's all-female Lilith Fair—an all-day concert sparked by the industrywide contention that two female acts couldn't successfully share the same stage. Female fans flocked to the fair and proved otherwise.

The fair consistently outsold male-dominated concert festivals such as the Horizons of Rock Developing Everywhere Festival (more commonly known as HORDE) and Lollapalooza. Certainly, the Lilith Fair was not a perfect manifestation of idealized feminism; it was plagued with corporate sponsorship and lacked diversity. Furthermore, devoted fans of female artists' music since the 1970s know Lilith was not the first all-female music festival, as was frequently touted by the mainstream media. The well-attended Michigan Womyn's Music Festival had been going on for 25 years, not to mention countless small women's festivals around the country. Nevertheless, Lilith Fair was an unprecedented feminist event that received an unheard of level of mainstream acceptance and brought a feminist consciousness (although mild by some feminist standards and too popularized for others) to the forefront. Clearly, Sarah McLachlan and the artists who participated were agents of social change. It appeared as though "the times they were a'changing." But progress came slowly, and the struggle was long.

THE RISE OF WOMEN IN ROCK

Throughout Western history women worked long and hard, fighting many battles, in an effort to develop a presence in music. The fact that women had to fight patriarchy to gain entry into music is especially disheartening considering that music was historically considered a feminine art form. But men making up the patriarchy of the church and state sought to lay claim to music; in doing so, they systematically excluded women from public participation in the writing and performing of most forms of music. Women were considered physically, mentally and creatively incapable of producing music and encouraged to limit their musical activities to the home.[2]

Women's exclusion from music corresponds to and is congruent with the exclusion and subordination of women as second-class citizens in all realms of Western culture.

With the advent of rock and roll in the 1950s, women's subordinated position persisted as objectified subjects in rock lyrics and as the "passive" bystander of groupie. Considering that popular music was male dominated, it is not all that peculiar that women became the subject of many a rock song. Rock and roll became a way for men to remasculate themselves, and in so doing, women often became the victims. Throughout rock and roll imagery there's a persistent theme of using women, hating women or blaming the mother. Women are often described in disparaging terms. There's the ever-present and persistent notion that if a woman participates in sex acts, she's a slut; if she doesn't, she's a prude. As exemplified in the music of Nick Cave and Jimi Hendrix's "Hey Joe," the theme of men killing women plays with very little outright objection to such imagery. Sadly, blatant misogyny in rock music continues. The critically acclaimed techno band the Prodigy had commercial success with their 1997 release *The Fat of the Land* that included the single "Smack My Bitch Up." Rap star Eminem reached the top of the charts with explicit lyrics of violence toward women and gays. On his Grammy-winning *Marshall Mathers* release, Eminem violently sings "bleed, bitch, bleed" in a song that shares the same name of his wife, Kim.[3]

Historically excluded from the creation and production of music, one of the few ways women could become involved was as ardent fan, a role that was and is frequently viewed as inconsequential. Although women were main supporters of early rock and roll, and men in the industry should have valued female fans' economic support, quite the opposite happened—at least on the musical appreciation side of the coin. Not only were women often relegated to the position of fan, but often when an artist's predominant fan base was made up of women, the music was perceived to lack authenticity or credibility. The group was considered bland, a sellout, and the music dismissed.

One of the first styles of rock music in which women began to have a role as performer began in the 1960s. Beginning with the Shirelles' 1960 hit written by Brill Building songwriters Carole King and Gerry Goffin, "Will You Love Me Tomorrow," in what came to be known as "girl group" music, female artists found themselves at the top of the charts through much of the decade. Although often dismissed by musical critics as a mediocre period, girl groups created music girls and young women could relate to and were empowered by. Often in this genre, girls or women were no longer the objectified subject in the lyrics but rather the protagonist. Through a song like the Shirelles' "Will You Love Me Tomorrow," young women contemplated the possible outcomes of having or not having sexual relations with boys (Douglas, 1993, 1994). Teenage girls, for the first time, experienced music from their point of view. Although many of the songs were still relegated to solely heterosexual romance and the perceived necessity of a man in a woman's life, such as the Shangri-Las' "Leader of the Pack," the Angels' "My Boyfriend's Back" or Dusty Springfield's "I Only Want to Be with You," they were nonetheless from a female perspective detailing female experiences. Despite many critics' view of this genre as a feminization of rock and roll, Douglas credited the girl groups, along with other media fare, as precipitating the 1970s women's movement.

The 1970s women's liberation movement, now referred to as the second wave of feminism, demanded social change and equality. Singer/songwriter folk music with feminist- and lesbian-themed lyrics developed intertwined with and in support of feminism. Commonly referred to as "women's music," lesbian and women-identified folk artists emerged with a focus on "music for, about and by women." Although women sounded a collective sigh of relief, woman-identified folk artists were relegated to the margins. Holly Near, Cris Williamson and Meg Christian were some of the best-known performers of "women's music"; however, they never reached popular fame. With their albums released on small, women-oriented independent labels, they could not compete with the sales and promotional push many artists, mostly male, received as part of their major label record deals. In turn, their sales and exposure lagged. Women-identified artists suffered from other people's ignorance. Because they were singular female performers with a feminist message, early recordings were relegated to an obscure bin far removed from the traffic created by the record-buying public, literally left to a world of marginality. But the artists inspired by the women's movement cultivated a community that provided a great deal of support. Women-identified music, although apart from the mainstream, developed a following that literally became the lifeblood that kept women's involvement in music going. The strength, persistence and dedication of both the performers and the fans kept women's active participation in music alive and no doubt contributed to women's more prominent place on the popular music charts in the 1990s.

There were other female artists making an impact in the 1970s. Separate from, yet similar to, the sound and tradition of "women's music," folk artists Joni Mitchell, Joan Armatrading and Joan Baez garnered critical acclaim and widespread attention and reached the top of the charts. Breakthrough artists at the time included Brill Building–era songwriter Carole King with her megaplatinum 1971 album *Tapestry*, and Helen Reddy's 1971 hit "I Am Woman" unintentionally became the "theme song" of the 1970s women's liberation movement. In rock, women tended to play the role of female singers backed by male musicians, with only a few gaining popular success, such as Janis Joplin and Grace Slick. The role of singer was considered appropriate for a woman, but the position of the talented instrumentalist was still considered a position *naturally* best suited for men. Regardless, female rockers cut against the grain, presenting themselves as women who were seemingly in control of themselves—sexually, creatively and professionally. These artists helped raise people's awareness that women can successfully be a part of the music scene. Moving away from their musical role as an objectified subject in the past, women were now able to present a more realistic presentation of women's diverse and complex lives. It was through these doors that women began to make a marked impression in the music industry in terms of pure numbers, creative control and appropriation of their material. Unfortunately, the success gained by these female artists was more the exception than the rule.

Punk was another music scene that opened its doors to women. Punk provided a countercultural outlet that women were allowed to explore. Although punk culture was a misogynistic one at that, the "anything goes" atmosphere provided women—Patti Smith, the Slits, the Raincoats and others—an opportunity to express themselves sexually, politically, and stylistically in an alternative fashion like never before. While singer/songwriter folk music opened the door, punk blew it open, and female artists in this genre played music on their own terms.

Still later, and as Lewis (1993, 1995) argued, MTV provided a new outlet in the 1980s that allowed pop-oriented female performers to gain exposure and break through to the mainstream. Madonna,

Cyndi Lauper and Tina Turner were regularly touted as exemplifying the new role of women in rock and roll. No longer relegated to the margins, these artists and others—Pat Benatar, Chrissie Hynde, Joan Jett—exerted a new kind of assertiveness and gained mainstream acceptance. Madonna, in particular, was and still is frequently acknowledged as an artist who made a unique and significant impact on women's roles in music. Madonna not only broke artistic ground in terms of both music and music video; she also made an impact on the business side of the music industry in terms of management and marketing.

The female artists who were a part of this subculture of women's folk music and the punk movement and others who gained more popular success did much more than create music with a feminist sensibility or provide a women's perspective. These artists successfully rebelled against what Frith and McRobbie (1978/1990) called gender-assigned roles of males as active participants and females as passive consumers.[4] In so doing, these artists of the 1960s, 1970s and 1980s provided a vision and a dream merely through their presence on a stage once dominated by men. The young girls and women in the audience saw possibilities laid out before them. Having grown up with rock and roll, this generation would reap the benefits of the strides made by the generations before.

Although the music industry generally undervalued these artists, young women and girls who were musically inclined saw them as valuable role models. Just as the blues, gospel and country artists before them influenced early rock and roll performers, contemporary female artists were influenced by the artists of the past. Today's artists heard Janis Joplin belt out, Joan Baez introspectively doubt and Grace Slick psychedelically question. In fact, Melissa Etheridge cites Janis Joplin as a major influence, and Emily Sailers of the Indigo Girls thanked Joni Mitchell "for inspiration" in their self-titled major label debut's liner notes. Because of their strength, talent, uniqueness and mere presence, things changed. Girls and young women listening to these artists with their defiant lyrics and oppositional style during their impressionable youth, began to believe in opportunity and possibility that had not existed before.

WOMEN AND ROCK IN THE 1990s

Many of the young women who were influenced by earlier female performers' success, talent and politics contributed to the unique presence that developed in the 1990s. Many of the artists who surfaced were politically conscious, had direct control of their work and career and received unprecedented recognition for their efforts. Examples include Indigo Girls, Melissa Etheridge, Tori Amos, Ani DiFranco and Sarah McLachlan.[5] As is the case with much of rock music, a lot of their songwriting focuses on love and relationships. But these artists also uniquely tell stories with political and/or feminist themes. Topics include abortion, domestic violence and hate crimes. These artists also contribute much more than their art in an effort to effect change. They are politically active, giving of their time, image and money.

Indigo Girls regularly involve themselves with pro-choice activities (i.e., Rock for Choice), environmental issues (i.e., Greenpeace) and Native American causes (i.e., Honor the Earth Campaign), among many others. Self-described feminist Melissa Etheridge is a champion of gay and women's rights. Tori Amos has done benefit shows for and acts as a public figure representing the Rape, Abuse and Incest National Network (RAINN), an organization that provides information and assistance for victims/survivors and was the first to establish a nationwide crisis 800-number.

Ani DiFranco is the most demonstrative in terms of being politically conscious. A self-described feminist, Ani DiFranco's political activism is most evident through the intentions of her art—her music and lyrics—and her label Righteous Babe Records in her hometown of Buffalo, New York. The decision to keep the label in Buffalo was deliberate in an effort to provide economic benefits to what some would characterize as a "depressed steel town." DiFranco views Righteous Babe Records as an opportunity to "give stimulating business to local printers and manufacturers and to employ the services of independent distributors, promoters, booking agents and publicists" (DiFranco, 1997). DiFranco contends the label is a space where "[p]eople who [work there] incorporate and coordinate politics, art and media everyday into a people-friendly, sub-corporate, woman-informed, queer-happy small business that puts music before rock stardom and ideology before profit" (DiFranco, 1997).[6] In line with DiFranco's political philosophy, Righteous Babe Records is a conscious effort to rebel against the corporatization of America.

Sarah McLachlan's most high-profile political effort has been the staging of the all-female Lilith Fair. The fair successfully destroyed the mainstream contention that two women couldn't successfully share the same stage. Although there have been, and continue to be, other (more feminist and less commercial) all-female festivals (e.g., Michigan Womyn's Music Festival, National Women's Music Festival—Indiana), Lilith Fair was the first accepted within mainstream industry circles. In its debut year of 1997, the Lilith Fair was the most touted summer tour, outperforming the male-dominated Lollapalooza and HORDE festivals. Ticket sales were brisk as well for the 1998 and 1999 tours. Although year one was predominantly made up of singer/songwriters with musical stylings that blended folk, rock and pop, the lineups improved in years two and three, with more artists spanning across other more diverse genres. Artists included Suzanne Vega, the Pretenders (with front-woman Chrissie Hynde), Liz Phair, Queen Latifah, Sinead O'Connor, Indigo Girls, Angelique Kidjo, Patti Smith, Aimee Mann, Mary Chapin Carpenter, Neneh Cherry, Fiona Apple, Lisa Loeb, Victoria Williams, Erykah Badu, Missy Elliott, Bonnie Raitt, Luscious Jackson and Autour De Lucie, among many others. By all accounts, the Lilith Fair was a milestone for women and the music industry.

The Lilith Fair was a success on many levels, but many feminists, as is customary with critical theory, lodged valid complaints against the fair. Feminism is not monolithic and encourages divergent voices in the seemingly ever-present push toward cultural change. Therefore, these criticisms are not entirely negative but are worthy, collective counsel. The fair and the coinciding mainstream acceptance of female artists during the 1990s were at the same time limited and contained within a dominant ideological framework the resulting function of *white supremacist capitalist patriarchy* (as coined by cultural critic bell hooks [2000]). Although there was a predominantly feminist and political message sung by these artists, most of the artists who did reach the stage and rotation on the radio playlists were white, thin, heterosexual and able-bodied, and their appearance fit within the hegemonic masculinist prescription of "attractive." Although the Lilith lineup improved in years two and three, year one was an exceedingly white one and not as diverse musically as it should have been. The "successful 1997 Lilith Fair concert tour, which, although touted by organizer Sarah McLachlan as a 'celebration of women in music,' was in fact primarily a celebration of white female singer-songwriters" (Wald, 1998, p. 589). However, from the very beginning McLachlan wanted to recruit as diverse a lineup as possible, and invitations followed, but many artists outside the (her) genre were unfamiliar with her and had no sense of what Lilith was about and were in turn reluctant to sign on (Tayler, 1998).

Another criticism of the fair was its reliance on corporate sponsorship. Although some might find this commercial investment a blockade to a stronger feminist message, it is important to remember that corporate sponsors do help to keep costs down (and sometimes even ticket prices down). Most Lilith performers took pay cuts in comparison to what they would have made on a solo tour. There were high costs involved in staging a project of this magnitude. Further, McLachlan and tour organizers selected corporate sponsors they believed to be "clean"—"no child labor, no animal testing [and also] community oriented" (Wall Street Journal, 1997, sec. 9). According to a 1999 fair press release, sponsors had to share in the fair commitment "to entertain, benefit and contribute." Lilith Fair turned down national marketers in favor of more socially conscious and charitable ones. The sponsors made substantial donations to national women's nonprofits, resulting in over $2 million of donations. Recipients included Planned Parenthood, the Breast Cancer Fund, LIFEbeat (an HIV/AIDS resource and awareness organization), Rape, Abuse and Incest National Network (RAINN), the National Coalition against Domestic Violence, and Amnesty International. These organizations were the beneficiaries of this corporate sponsorship and also had information booths set up on-site at each Lilith Fair staging.

McLachlan and the fair are both feminist and political. McLachlan identifies as feminist[7] (Vaziri, 1999) and conducts herself in feminist ways. During the years prior to Lilith, McLachlan made concerted efforts to support female artists. Nine out of 10 of her support acts in the years prior to Lilith were purposely female. Moreover, the fair donated $1 from each ticket sale to a local charity (in most cases a domestic violence shelter) at each city they visited. McLachlan also made concerted efforts to have as large a female crew and staff as she could. Although not enough for some critics—40 percent of Lilith workers were women, "from riggers to lighters to sound crews" (Tayler, 1998, sec. 22), This percentage far exceeds any mainstream tour previously. In 1998 and 1999, McLachlan dedicated the opening slots of each show to local female artists. In years two and three and at each city the fair visited, McLachlan invited local, independent (often feminist and/or gay/lesbian) bookstores or shops to set up vendor booths.

Although not perfection by some feminist standards, there were more positives than negatives when the whole of the fair is considered. As feminists and allies, we need to accept a variety of forms and manifestations of feminism in exchange for real social change. As Carla DeSantis, editor and publisher of *ROCKRGRL* magazine says, "there aren't a lot of festivals that give money back to charity. If donating money to rape crisis centers and battered women's shelters isn't political, I don't know what is" (Tayler, 1998, sec. 21).

The 1990s also witnessed female artists exerting more control over their "product"—with Madonna leading the way in the 1980s. Although women were first credited with writing lyrics in popular music in the 1960s, they more likely than not worked with male producers. And although women still employ male producers, today many females have moved into the role of producer, either in cooperation with male partners (Melissa Etheridge and Hugh Padgham, Tracy Chapman and Don Gehman, Queen Latifah [Dana E. Owens] and Lancelot H. Owens, Liz Phair and Brad Wood) or alone (Tori Amos, Rickie Lee Jones, Jane Siberry, Paula Cole). Achieving both commercial success and critical acclaim, Missy Elliott is a renowned performer and music producer. In keeping with the spirit of 1970s feminist labels Olivia Records and Redwood Records, others have even stepped up their control to free themselves from typical record label hassle and constraints. Ani DiFranco has released all of her work on her own Righteous Babe Records label. More recently, DiFranco has been supporting other critically acclaimed but lesser-known artists such as bassist Sara Lee and Bitch and Animal. Michelle Shocked has ventured out on her own after having fought against her label for the right to create music on her own terms. Amy Ray, in an effort to support lesser-known artists, started Daemon Records in 1990. Melissa Ferrick, having left both major and independent support, has released her most recent albums on her own Right On Records label. Jonatha Brooke achieved great success with *Steady Pull* (2001) on her own Bad Dog Records. More women take a more active part in the production and promotion of their music releases.

The Grammy Awards in the 1990s were another indication of acceptance of women into the mainstream music industry. In 1996, although critics and scholars alike question her credibility, authenticity and even talent, Alanis Morissette swept the Grammy's with her chart-topping album *Jagged Little Pill*. Her release clearly resonated with female listeners and won four trophies including the highly prized Best Rock Song, Best Rock Album and Album of the Year. In 1997, four of the five best new artist nominees were female performers or female-fronted bands and included No Doubt, Jewel, Garbage, LeAnn Rimes—along with the only male nominee, Tony Rich. Winners for 1997 included Tracy Chapman's "Give Me One Reason" for Best Rock Song, and Sheryl Crow's self-titled, self-produced release won Best Rock Album. In 1998 Shawn Colvin garnered three nominations, winning one each for Record and Song of the Year. Paula Cole, with seven nominations including the first ever for a woman for Best Producer, walked away with a Grammy for Best New Artist, while Sarah McLachlan took away two for Best Pop Female Vocal and Best Instrumental. In 1999 there were an unprecedented number of women nominated for top prizes—including Lauryn Hill garnering ten nominations and Crow with six and both were nominated as producers. Madonna, Ani DiFranco, Lucinda Williams and Tori Amos also had nominations.

Despite the peaks women experienced in the past with girl groups of the 1960s, the folk music scene that coincided with the feminist movement of the 1970s and the rise of Madonna and other female pop artists that used MTV as a vehicle for exposure in the 1980s, the rise and mainstream acceptance in the 1990s appeared exceptional and seemed to have staying power. It appeared as though women with an interest in rock, whether as artists or as fans, had crossed the final hurdle of breaking into the music industry and were merely destined to have an ever-increasing level of acceptance and success in this masculinized popular culture form. I was convinced real social change was built brick by brick, and the success of the 1990s was just one step in that direction. I believed real permanent progress was being made.

I wasn't alone with my optimistic thoughts; plenty of media attention and industry talk was paid to this newfound acceptance of women's presence in rock (Atkinson, 1997; Hinckley, 1996; Howard & Cerio, 1994; Potter, 1998; Powers, 1994; Shuster, 1995; Udovitch, 1994; Zach, 1996). *Toronto Star*'s Mitch Potter wrote in 1998, "The phenomenon of women claiming high positions in the Billboard charts is no fad, but rather the emergence of a brave new balance in pop culture" (sec. 5). But as I sit and write in 2002, I reluctantly have to admit to myself, "I was wrong." What I thought to be just the beginning of women's move and acceptance into this male-dominated industry has now become a snapshot of a moment in time. It looked as though female artists couldn't be stopped. But they were stopped. Perhaps the old saying is true: Looks CAN be deceiving.

What is even more disappointing as a feminist and music fan is that this heightened mainstream attention female artists enjoyed wasn't all that *equal* in the first place. At the peak, the percentage of debut singles by female acts for 1992, 1994 and 1995 was around 20 percent, with 1993 at almost 15 percent—all still far below any sort of egalitarian, 50–50 gender split. And in 1999 and 2000, these percentages took a drastic dive to a dismal 6 and 3 percent, respectively (Pesselnick & Caulfield, 2000). I can only hope that we return to the record high (yet still unequal) 20 percent range.

I should have seen it coming when the Spice Girls, with superficiality and scantily clad sex appeal taking precedence over substance, became incredibly popular with their self-titled release in 1996.[8] Perhaps this was the beginning of the end to what appeared to be a transformative feminist momentum in popular music. This short-lived rise has seemed to have disappointingly slipped away. *Billboard*'s Pesselnick and Caulfield (2000) report, "[I]n 1995, there were 34 female debuts on the Modern Rock Track Charts, yet in 2000, there were merely four." (sec. 3). According to program director Oedipus, "[W]omen make up less than ten percent of [Boston Rock Station] WBCN's play list" (Anderman, 2000, sec. 21). The music pendulum has dramatically (and purposefully?) shifted away from female music artists with an empowering message.

As we entered the twenty-first century, the top of the music charts were crowded with boy bands such as 'N Sync, the Backstreet Boys and 98 Degrees; teen-pop sensations Britney Spears, Christina Aguilera and Jessica Simpson; and male rap and hip-hop metal bands with their misogynistic-laden lyrics such as Eminem, Kid Rock and Limp Bizkit. Some would argue, in particular when considering the hard hip-hop and metal bands, that we are suffering a Lilith Fair backlash. Perhaps the male-dominated industry and disenfranchised male music listeners felt threatened by the success of the Lilith Fair and female artists in general and have responded with hard, angry rock. Woodstock 1999, plagued with assaults and reported rapes against women, with its violent and riotlike atmosphere that resulted in fires and extensive property damage, is overwhelming, tangible evidence of this dramatic shift in music. At 1999's disastrous Woodstock,

Jewel, Sheryl Crow and Alanis Morissette were faced with constant taunts from the audience of "show us your tits." Not only are listeners saturated with aggressive sexist music, but this shift also results in female musical artists with a feminist and/or political sensibility pushed further to the margins.

As a fan of female artists regardless of popular trends, I know they're still out there—there have been new releases and touring by female rock artists such as No Doubt (with front-woman Gwen Stefani), P.J. Harvey, Poe, Tori Amos, Indigo Girls, Ani DiFranco and Joan Osborne, among many others. Female rock artists are just not getting the attention they enjoyed in the 1990s. In the *Boston Globe*, Anderman (2000) reports that longtime publicist for Ani DiFranco, Tracy Mann, "is inundated with calls from women, both signed and unsigned, soliciting her services" (sec. 24). Newer artists such as the all-female punk rock Butchies, hard rock Skunk Anansie with front-woman Skin, and metal rock band Kittie have emerged, but they're not getting nearly the radio play nor the media attention that was lauded on rock acts in the mid- to latter 1990s.[9]

On modern rock stations in 2001, not only were female artists not even added to the mix, but record labels were hardly even pitching female artists to the stations. Mike Peer, music director for New York's WXRK (K-Rock), is quoted in *Billboard* as saying "that less than 5% of the singles that are pitched to his station are from female artists or bands . . . [with the] probability that a chosen song is female is minuscule" (Pesselnick & Caulfield, 2000, sec. 5). Labels are deliberately steering away from female bands. In fact, Indianapolis pop/rock recording artist Jennie DeVoe (2000) suggests, based on her experience, labels don't even want to consider adult women, instead preferring teenage or even preteen girls in the vein of Britney Spears or Christina Aguilera. In a July 2001 *Rolling Stone* magazine interview with Mim Udovitch, Melissa Etheridge concedes she too would be having difficulties maintaining major label support if it weren't for her dedicated and loyal following. And Amy Ray of the Indigo Girls is quoted in a 2001 *U.S. News & World Report* as saying that "outside of country and top 40, women aren't even on radio playlists right now" (Gilgoff, 2001, sec. 8). The claim that we are suffering a Lilith Fair backlash is convincing. Even though the fair shook up the industry and female artists were able to exert more control over their individual careers and work, perhaps, as coauthor of *Manifesta: Young Women, Feminism and the Future* Jennifer

Baumgardner says in a 2000 *Boston Globe* article, "women have never controlled any aspect of the music industry [in the first place] ... the power was never theirs" (Anderman 2000, sec. 22). At the very least, they never had enough power to cause real permanent change.

However, despite this disappointing shift to hypermasculinized rock (or even perhaps because of it), the 1990s rise of female artists with a political and/or feminist sensibility is significant to document and recognize. Although the 1990s rise of female artists did not demolish the wall of male control, it certainly served another moment in chipping away at it. Much of the music that reached the top of the charts was feminist inclined, and the Lilith Fair was the first time the staging of an all-female lineup achieved such mainstream success. Women's voices and stories were being heard and validated at a major level.

FEMALE FANS' VOICES

Female music artists made a convincing impact on the music scene in the 1990s. More noteworthy was that many of these artists gained mainstream acceptance despite their political and/or feminist sensibility. Noting these changes, I wondered what meaning this had in the daily lives of female listeners. Why were women attracted to these artists? What did women think of the changes in the music industry? I wanted to talk with women who listened to artists who challenge gender roles and seek equality, justice and choice for women—artists that are critical of women's subordination and dedicated to political and/or feminist issues through their personal and professional involvement. My intention was to create a venue in which women's often-silenced voices and views about rock music, a popular culture arena where women are all too commonly kept to the sidelines or discounted in terms of having anything of value to say, could be heard.

They're Playing Our Songs was driven by this general research question: *What does female artists' music with a political and/or feminist sensibility mean in the lives of invested female fans?* A question largely left unanswered by both popular and academic presses. Barbara Bradby (1993) comes closest to what this book sets out to do with her 1993 article "Does It Matter Who Is Singing?" exploring how one bisexual and five lesbian, Irish women in Dublin gauged the relevance and/or importance of singers' sexual identity in terms of their appreciation of women's music and the appropriation of mainstream, heterosexual music. Bradby (1994) has also done similar work exploring five 11-year-old girls' "reception" of Madonna's music. More generally, there has indeed been an increase in attention paid to the broader topic of women rockers in the last decade (Bayton, 1998; Burns & Lafrance, 2002; S. Cooper, 1996; McClary, 1991; McDonnell & Powers, 1995; Morris, 1999; Raphael, 1995; Reynolds & Press, 1995; Whiteley, 1997, 2000). There have also been many historical journalistic accounts (Gaar, 1992; Hirshey, 2001; O'Brien, 1995; O'Dair, 1997). Much of the recent research and analysis (and in some cases commentary) on the broader topic of women and music has focused on riot grrrl bands (Driscoll, 1999; Gottlieb & Wald, 1994; Kearney, 1997; Leonard, 1997; Riordan, 2001; Wald, 1998), rap artists (Berry, 1994; Forman, 1994; Gaunt, 1995; Kolawole, 1996; Rose, 1994) and the Spice Girls (Dibben, 1999; Douglas, 1997; Driscoll, 1999). All of these works made valuable contributions to this growing body of literature, yet there remains a dearth in the number of empirical investigations on women and rock music. The amount pales in comparison to the volumes written about rock in general (in which authors are really writing about *male* rock, yet they commonly fail to acknowledge that).

They're Playing Our Songs also contributes to the understanding of women's relationship with media. Most female audience–based studies have focused on romance novels (Radway, 1984), soap operas (Hobson, 1996; Seiter et al., 1996) and daytime television (Modleski, 1996). Many sought to reevaluate women's reception of media, discovering that women experienced resistant or oppositional readings to the dominant ideological text. This study differs, in part, because it concentrates on music that is politically and/or feminist minded—text that often challenges dominant ideology. Women's experience with this style of music differs from the resistant and oppositional readings that women experience with women's magazines, soap operas or romance novels. To this end, this book helps to answer the call put forth by feminist media scholars Lont (1993), Bayton (1992), Hollows (2000) and Van Zoonen (1994) for an examination of women's engagement with feminist texts.

The mainstream acceptance of female music artists with a political and/or feminist sensibility is worthy of note, and the exploration of the relationship between these artists and their female listenership is valid, legitimate and primary to this book—but it is important to recognize the lack of diversity among the female artists that attained mainstream success in pop/rock in the 1990s. Therefore, this book is framed within the context of who is *not* represented. Although there are exceptions, a majority of the female pop/rock artists who have enjoyed a notable level of mainstream acceptance are heterosexual, white, thin, able-bodied women who are often perceived as *attractive* per society's standards. Alternatively, if the women profiled in this book find meaning in the type of artists talked about here, then what might the lack of representation mean for women whose voices are not accepted by the mainstream? Similarly, because of the arguable demise of female artists at the top of the charts at the time of this writing, this book is also an empirical examination of a snapshot in time as opposed to an analysis of a musical form that was sustained. Therefore, this study lends insight into the women in this study's interaction and experience with this form of music but also clearly dramatizes the magnitude of the absence of those who are not represented or who are underrepresented and women in the past, present or future who did not have the opportunity to engage with the heightened acceptance of female music artists with a feminist and/or political sensibility in the 1990s.

I wanted to talk to women that were passionate and invested in female music artists with a political and/or feminist consciousness. As voices that are often dismissed, I wanted to explore why women are attracted to particular artists and what impact, if any, the music has on their lives. To identify appropriate candidates I first used a filtering questionnaire asking women to identify their favorite artists and what they liked about them. I sought out women who were purposeful, selective, active and discriminating in their music choices. They (more so than less so) regularly listen to female artists' music in the home or automobile, attend club shows or concerts and pay attention to the popular music press. They also had to have a stronger interest, even if only slight, in female artists over male artists. In an effort to reach women who were invested in feminist and/or politically minded artists, I made questionnaires available at women's bookstores (which also sold music selections) and concerts in Ohio and Michigan.

Approximately 130 questionnaires were distributed, with 42 completed and returned and 30 respondents indicating they would be willing to participate in an in-depth interview. From the information provided by the screening questionnaire, 15 women were selected based on the following: (1) They indicated they listened to female artists at least 50 percent of the time; (2) those artists embodied a feminist and/or political sensibility; (3) on a scale from 1 to 10, they rated music from at least a 7 to 10 in terms of importance; (4) they were within a three-hour driving distance of where I was living at the time, Bowling Green, Ohio; (5) they wrote answers that were indicative of an invested listener (i.e., in comparison to the others, they were written in-depth and in detail; (6) and final consideration was given to achieving as much diversity as possible.

In spite of this final effort, this project fell short in succeeding in the recruitment of as diverse a group as had been hoped for in terms of race. Of the 15 women interviewed, only 1 was a woman of color (African American). Arguably, this is in part due to the marked and continued culturally and self-imposed segregation that can still be evidenced in musical genres and audiences in the United States. Music is racialized. Furthermore, it logically follows that if female artists who have been allowed access to the stage are predominantly Caucasian (in part because of racism and racial pigeonholing), then those who attend to these artists are also more commonly or likely to be white. Similar to what Bayton (1998) argues in her book on female rock artists, generally speaking, rock is a music genre that attracts mostly whites, whether as performer or fan. Consequently, Caucasian singer/songwriter Michelle Shocked has been known to publicly express disappointment over the lack of diversity in her audiences (Guzman, 2001). In fact, I don't necessarily view this as a study "limitation" because it is simply symptomatic of the industry's and society's imposed racialization of music. Lack of integration is a failure of our society. Therefore, this study lends insight into the ramifications of the music industry's exclusion of more diversity, especially in terms of race.

The next four chapters are the women's narratives. Chapter 1 focuses on women's preference for female artists over male artists and reviews the qualities they find attractive in particular female artists. The respondents tended to prefer artists who wrote their own songs with substantive lyrics, had complex and interesting music and unique vocal abilities and exemplified skilled musicianship. They were also interested in artists who were politically involved and maintained a marked level of control over their work.

Chapter 2 focuses on female listeners' discussions of identifying with female artists and their appropriation of female artists' music into their everyday lives. As women, the respondents could identify with the artists, and they shared experiences of validation, affirmation and empowerment. They also appropriated music to cope with a variety of transitions and challenges in their everyday lives; among others, these included personal relationships, fighting depression, coming to terms with past experiences of abuse and dealing with their sexuality.

Chapter 3 focuses on discussions of women finding voice through female artists, actually utilizing female artists' music to communicate and bond with others. These women talked about using female artists' music as a tool of personal expression: to communicate, to bond and to connect with both family and friends. The women also talked about the soothing, uplifting sense of security experienced at female artists' rock concerts with a predominantly female crowd. These respondents marked their lives with music and associated music with particular memories.

Chapter 4, the final chapter to center on respondent narratives, focuses on the respondents' declarations of the importance of female artists' music and expresses their views of the music industry. The respondents were acutely aware that the industry largely viewed female artists and their fans as "angry" or "silly." They were also very cognizant that the main reason female artists were allowed access was because of the potential for profits. These women had no doubt that the presence of female music artists with a political and/or feminist sensibility provided an important presence and discourse, not only personally but also socially and culturally.

Chapter 5, the conclusion, reviews the previous chapters as a whole and theorizes about the possibility of cultural transformation through women's relationships with female music artists with a political and/or feminist sensibility. This final chapter also considers the contributions this study makes to feminist-media studies and offers suggestions for future research.

Appendix A lists alphabetically (by their pseudonyms) the women who participated in this project, along with a brief biographical statement that includes their age, race, occupation and favorite artists. Appendix B lists the artists mentioned by the respondents in a favorable way. The artists may not be their favorites, but the participants referred to them positively and complimentarily.

The lyrics chosen for inclusion in this book are quoted or mentioned by the respondents (more often quoted). I chose to provide them for clarification and context for the reader. However, all the lyrics I would have liked to use are not included because of prohibitive costs to reprint. Words are by the performing artist unless otherwise noted.

NOTES

1. For further discussion on a comparison of the new roles, see Stewart (1995) where he compared Whitney Houston's "The Greatest Love of All" (traditional role) to Janet Jackson's "Control" (new role).

2. Readers interested in reading more about women's exclusion from the production and/or performance of music should refer to Longhurst (1995), McClary (1991) and Pendle (1991).

3. For more on sexism and misogyny in rock music refer to Butruille and Taylor (1987), V.W. Cooper (1985, 1992), Meade (1972), Reynolds and Press (1995), and Sloat (1998).

4. In fairness, it is important to note that Frith and McRobbie (1978/1990) made this initial claim in 1978. Frith has since noted the weaknesses of the piece, including confusing "issues of sex and issues of gender" (1985/1990, p. 420). Nevertheless, the gender roles declared in the original piece are still widely believed today.

5. The choice to use the Indigo Girls, Melissa Etheridge, Tori Amos, Ani DiFranco and Sarah McLachlan as exemplars here was completely driven by the respondents' interviews. The women I interviewed mentioned these five artists most often.

6. Disappointed in a *Ms. Magazine* article that focused on the financial success of Ani DiFranco's Righteous Babe Records as part of a feature on "Twenty-One Feminists for the 21st Century," DiFranco wrote a letter to the editor. Although published in the January–February 1998 *Ms. Magazine* issue, the letter was edited. The remarks used here come from an unedited version of DiFranco's letter widely posted on the Web.

7. At the onset of Lilith Fair, Sarah McLachlan responded defensively toward press questions that called the Lilith "feminist" or "man hating" or questioned its exclusion of men. In fact, McLachlan even considered adding male artists in future lineups. However, as the tour progressed, McLachlan became less defensive about the use of the word *feminist* in attachment to the fair. McLachlan self-identifies as feminist and views the fair as feminist as well (Childerhose, 1998).

8. Although some scholars have argued that the Spice Girls are a positive representation of "girl power," especially for teenagers and young women, I contend the Spice Girls are a step backward for feminist causes and gender

abolition. For readers interested in this debate, see Dibben (1999), Douglas (1997), Driscoll (1999), Parmar (1998) and Whiteley (2000).

9. Fortunately, there's been an exception to this trend with a refreshing surge of success by crossover rhythm and blues artists such as Alicia Keys, Macy Gray, India.Arie and Jill Scott.

SONG LYRICS

Ani DiFranco, "i'm no heroine"

you think i wouldn't have him
unless i could have him by the balls
you think i just dish it out
you don't think i take it at all
you think i am stronger
you think i walk taller than the rest
you think i'm usually wearing the pants
just 'cause i rarely wear a dress
well . . .

when you look at me
you see my purpose you see my pride
you think i just saddle up my anger
and ride and ride and ride
you think i stand so firm
you think i sit so high on my trusty steed
let me tell you
i'm usually face down on the ground
when there's a stampede

i'm no heroine
least not last time i checked
i'm too easy to roll over
i'm too easy to wreck
i just write about what i
should have done
i sing what i wish i could say
and I hope somewhere
some woman hears my music
and it helps her through her day

some guy designed
these shoes i use to walk around
some big man's business

turns a profit every time
i lay my money down
some guy designed this room
i'm standing in
another one built it
with his own tools
who says i like right angles
these are not my laws
these are not my rules

i'm no heroine
i still answer to the other half
of the race
i don't fool myself like i fool you
i don't have the power
we just don't run this place

Amy Ray, "Lucystoners"

We were talking ticket slump, trying to put our finger on it.
Quantify the undoing . . .
of each little step-its just a lack of press.
The refrigerator down at the boys club
with its little magnets of poetry,
finding one hundred different ways to say blow me . . .

Well . . . Janny Wenner Janny Wenner—Rolling Stone's most
 fearless leader—
gave the boys what they deserve, but with the girls he lost his
 nerve.

In every post punk bar there's a dressing room wall
where the rockboy band will make its mark—
one hundred different pictures of private parts and some girl going
 down.
And all the faggot bashing poetry but the boys are just saying,
"love me please."
In every hate filled phrase they just give it away . . .
ah boys, you give yourselves away . . .

You know . . . Janny Wenner Janny Wenner—Rolling Stone's most
 fearless leader—
gave the boys what they deserve, but with the girls he lost his
 nerve.

Testing 1, 2, 3 in the marketplace—it's just a demographic-based disgrace,
and a stupid, secret, whiteboy handshake that we'll never be part of.
So when its DJ Blow and the morning show,
I'll give you one hundred reasons to just say no . . .
Come on girls, lets go, right now . . .

Cause Lucy Stoners don't need boners, ain't no man could ever own her,
with the boys she had the nerve to give the girls what they deserve.

Chapter 1

Women's Attraction to Artists

Terri has been singing her own songs since she was 3 years old. Of course nothing was written down; they were just songs about what she was doing: cleaning her room, walking to the kitchen or getting cookies out of the cupboard. For her it was better than talking. She has always had a particular affection toward music and was particularly fond of singing along to female voices. Now, far removed from those years at 29, she remains a music enthusiast with a particular penchant for female artists. Terri had a sometimes-troubled childhood that included the divorce of her parents and a mother and stepfather who took her regularly to the bar they frequented. Her adult life dealt her difficult times as well, problematic relationships with men and navigating a sometimes-fragile self-esteem. Those who don't know her well wouldn't guess the latter; she's tall, beautiful and bright. A great personality, someone people enjoy having around for the laughter and conversation.

When she was eight years old the bars her mother frequented became her playground. For children there were only three choices to make for entertainment: billiards, pinball and playing the jukebox. Terri chose the jukebox and begged for quarters to hear the music play. Her favorites included folk group Peter, Paul & Mary's version of "Leaving on a Jet Plane" and country artist Lynn Anderson's 1971 crossover hit "(I Never Promised You a) Rose Garden." She danced and twirled to the music, all the while singing along. Her interest in music continued as she grew. In grammar and high school she took choir and singing lessons with the hope of some day being a rock star. As she grew older her musical tastes twisted and turned from matching her voice to Olivia Newton John's "I Honestly Love You" to screaming at the top of her lungs to heavy metal Quiet Riot's "Cum on Feel the Noize" and rocker Sammy Hagar's "Dick in the Dirt" while getting ready to go clubbing as a college student, to being a feminist and relying on Tori Amos, Ani DiFranco and Indigo Girls to put into words what she's convinced she can't. Music has always been there for Terri.

Music is a pervasive and powerful art form. As the soundtrack of our lives, we tie our memories, pleasures and dreams to music as well as our sadness, struggles and failures. For all intents and purposes and as in all other media forms, women were symbolically annihilated, left without diverse, realistic and in-depth representations. Portrayals of women created from a patriarchal perspective fell short in characterizing the diversity and realities of women's lives. Controlling mediated forms is power, and by denying women access in the creation and production of media, it perpetuates women's marginalization and oppression. Throughout the second half of the twentieth century more diverse views of women's lives began to emerge as more and more women gained access to the writing, production and performing of music.

Artists came to the music scene in an effort to, consciously and unconsciously, create and provide their own symbolic representation. Female audiences, starved for more realistic and diverse representation, rushed to support a women's musical scene. In fact, in 1998, the Recording Industry Association of America reported that women purchased more music than men for the second year in a row. This heightened sense of connection between songs, lyrics and female audiences reached an unprecedented and qualitative peak in the 1990s. Many artists who garnered audience attention embodied a feminist and/or political sensibility. Through the process of interpellation, the songs hailed women. Women were drawn to particular artists because of similar ideological and gender positioning between artists and listeners.

When women attend to music, they bring their history and life experiences and are attracted to particular artists and songs because of the relevancy the text (the lyrics, music and performer) has to their lives. Women hold certain social allegiances with the artists, the lyrics and even other fans and will act upon certain discursive practices, which results in a heightened experience. Although all women's life experiences are varied and multiple, there are some commonalities in the experience of living as a woman in a patriarchal society. Arguably, an artist's life experience influences her songwriting and performance style. In turn, a female artist's music is bound to ring true for, and be relevant to, other women's lives. Female audience members are drawn to female artists' music because of similar lived experiences. The music, lyrics and the artist become relevant to the listener's life.[1]

This book explores 15 women's experiences and allegiances with female artists' music that embodies a political and/or feminist sensibility. Generally speaking, I was interested in talking to fans of artists that use their music to effect change—artists that are critical of women's subordination and dedicated to political and/or feminist issues through their art and personal and professional involvement. This chapter focuses specifically on characteristics women find appealing about female artists and women's attraction to particular artists.

THE MUSIC FANS

I talked with 15 women: 5 lesbians, 7 heterosexuals, 2 bisexual women and another woman who was ambiguous about her sexual orientation, writing "heterosexual or bisexual?" on the questionnaire (see Appendix A for individual participant profiles). Only one person of color was interviewed, an African American. All of the other women were Caucasians of European decent. Their economic backgrounds and current status varied. Individual incomes ranged from $15,000 to $90,000. Considering some of the younger respondents still relied on parental income, their actual income (i.e., $4,000 or $5,000) was less telling. However, most of the respondents identified as lower middle to upper class. Ages ranged from 19 to 42. All of the women, although they indicated that they did not listen exclusively to female artists, listened to music by women at least 50 percent of the time as compared to male artists, with most listening predominantly to female artists' music. The individual interviews lasted anywhere from one to three hours.

Almost all of the respondents tended to listen to prerecorded music more frequently than the radio. Many indicated the lack of music by female artists that they liked being played on the radio as one of the primary reasons. The repetitiveness of radio was another reason cited for listening to prerecorded music more than the radio. More than half of the women also indicated that they had a musical background, most of which was playing an instrument as a child or young adult. Some continue to play. Interestingly, when asked why they never pursued a career in the musical arts, most of the women felt they lacked the talent to do so. Those who do not play an instrument currently or in their past usually indicated that they had a familial or nonrelation musical influence. Only a few women did not clearly identify an early influence.

Women approached their individual interviews with enthusiasm and interest; all were curious about the project and its purpose. All of the women regularly referred to their favorite artists by their first name, even if they were a group or duo, suggesting that they felt a certain amount of intimacy and closeness toward the artists. Furthermore, it was interesting to observe that most of the women (all perhaps except two) were regularly able and willing to cite lyrics off the top of their heads and knew names of albums and song titles. These women closely attend to the music and lyrics of female artists. In total, over 160 female artists were mentioned during the course of the 15 interviews (see Appendix B). Pseudonyms are used to maintain each respondent's anonymity.

As the women tell their stories, it is important to remember female artists' subordinate position in the music industry throughout Western history. Having an understanding of context provides a foundation to better appreciate women's often-dismissed views about music in general. There were, and continue to be, commonly held false beliefs that women, as dictated by their gender, were incapable of being discriminating musical connoisseurs and practitioners. There is no doubt that the industry—although there have been improvements—continues to hold condescending and dismissive views about women as fans and artists. This book provides a much-needed venue for the voices of women to dispute these false, untenable claims and myths. These women clearly demonstrated discriminating taste and were articulate and specific in their explanations. At the very least, their critiques as laypeople are quite comparable to and rival critic print reviews. Women deserve much more than being monolithically seen as "superficial, hysterical, idolatrous, at once fickle and blindly loyal" (Reynolds & Press, 1995, p. 5). Their testimonies are also a strong endorsement of music by women—music that is often dismissed by the male-dominated music industry.

This chapter and the next three discuss variations on women's relationship with music. This chapter focuses first on women's preference for female artists over male artists and second on their attraction toward particular female artists. These women were very specifically drawn to female artists, although at times it appears as though they talk in "essentialist" terms—their attraction toward female artists is more socially or culturally focused rather than biologically centered. Each respondent, in her own way, is hailed specifically by music of female artists because of shared experiences of living as a woman in a patriarchal world. Because I was purposeful in selecting women who are interested in female artists with a feminist and/or political sensibility, the findings detailed in this chapter are not revelatory but, of course, naturally follow. Nonetheless, the women's stories in their words remain compelling and informative.[2]

AFFINITY: WOMEN'S PREFERENCE FOR FEMALE MUSICAL ARTISTS

Frequently, when women talked about their attraction toward female artists, they often spoke about it in terms of comparison to male artists and their music. A number of points of comparison emerged. All of the women felt as though they could identify with and relate to female artists more; some note one place they locate this affinity is through lyrics. Whether just listening to or singing along, many of the respondents indicated that they identified with the female singing voice, finding female voices, in general, more pleasing than male voices. Women felt that female artists were better able to capture the nuances of relationships, emotions and feelings. Some respondents found their interest in music by women paralleled their developing interest in women's studies or feminism. Similar to Bradby's 1993 findings, lesbians in particular described a unique connection to female artists' music because they were woman-identified or a part of a larger women's community. And still other women are attracted to female artists because they recognize the courage that it takes to succeed in a male-dominated industry, appreciate artists' struggles, recognize their political efforts and choose to consciously support female artists. All of the women cited a combination of the explanations above. Furthermore, it is important to note that some of these same reasons (i.e., identification, politics, professional standing) specific to female artists and respondents' personal stories (without the comparison to male artists) are explored in further detail in the following chapters.

Overwhelmingly, female listeners' ability to relate to or identify with female artists' music was one of the primary explanations when discussing why they were interested in music by women as opposed to men. Many respondents felt female artists were better able to speak to their own experience because of the general commonalities of experiencing life as a woman. Female artists are more likely and much less monolithically able to express the varied experiences of living as a female in a world that values masculinity far more than femininity. Women sensed an affinity with female artists through their lyrics and the sound of female voices.

[I have always listened] more [to] female artists [as opposed to male artists]. I think I always have leaned that way. In part, because I can sing along. Because my voice matches, and when I sing along, I'm always singing, even now.... Plus their lyrics, I can identify with them. They sometimes sing my life. (Terri)

In addition to the preference for a woman's voice and the relevancy of the lyrics to women's lives, many women felt that their own increased interest in music by women has paralleled their developing interest in women's issues and/or feminism. As Paige explains for herself, "[I've become more interested] because I found more of an interest in women's studies, feminism and stuff like [that], that's pulled me closer to women's music" (Paige).

Elisabeth, a lesbian, talks about being particularly interested in an artist because of her dedication to politics. This is another attribute of female artists that listeners describe as a positive characteristic of the artists and their music. This will be explored in further detail later in this chapter:

[I] probably [listen to] more female artists [than male artists].... I think some of it's just the sensibility. Like women you know are lesbians you think, "Wow, I really like that," and you kind of get into that and some of it is just like Sarah McLachlan who has this incredible voice and

"Wow," or Tracy Chapman. You know, I guess it's just a sound. I don't necessarily dislike male artists; there aren't as many that I seem to be as fond of.... But, I guess in general, especially when you are talking about artists, it just seems to be more of the female artists that I like.... I think part of it is because I know where they come from. I think that's definitely part of it. And I don't know if I just like the sound of the voices better, or if men write songs that I'm not particularly interested in.... It seems to [also have something to do with] people who have a political agenda like Sweet Honey in the Rock, and some of the stuff that they do that's kind of political, and women-centered and stuff, I guess that's part of it.... Because as I get older, the lyrics are a lot more important to me than they used to be. (Elisabeth)

Many of the respondents were also very aware of the potential barriers that a female artist might encounter working in a male-dominated industry. They express a certain sense of admiration, an appreciation for the artists' struggles, and they make conscientious efforts to support women. The reasons detailed in the following excerpts were not exclusive to the others already detailed previously. Terri is clear that she appreciates female artists' courage and also contends that female artists are better able to tap into feelings. "I prefer female over male artists . . . mostly because I admire them for their abilities and courage to perform. Female artists also are able to capture and express certain feelings and thoughts that I am unable to" (Terri).

Jill, a singer/songwriter and sometime-performer herself, recognizes struggles made by female artists and clearly seeks to support them:

[I] definitely [listen to] female [artists more than male].... There's very few male artists that I like ... I like women artists for the fact that they are women artists.... If they're female in the first place I'm going to give them a second look.... Female music in my opinion is just so connected to my experience.... [I] relate better to female artists as a performer [myself] because of the whole female experience. The whole struggle of being a female musician—the constant struggle [against] oppression and not being taken seriously. (Jill)

Deirdre, a politically active lesbian who identifies herself as a radical feminist, is frustrated by the music industry's lack of broader acceptance of women and cites this as one of her reasons for deliberately listening to female artists. Concurring with themes drawn out earlier, Deirdre is attracted to female artists because she senses an affinity with female artists over male artists, is attracted to those who incorporate politics into their art and is drawn to women's voices.

[Female artists' music] is still different [from the majority of music played on the radio]. [I turn to female artists' music] because it's different and because it's the music that I enjoy. It's the music that is more likely to speak to me in some way and I mean there are male groups I enjoy or there are male groups that I listen to because they are on the radio, but it's not what I buy and it's not what I necessarily would choose to listen to first certainly. . . . [I like these female artists because of] some of the politics of it, just the sound—hearing the women's voices. And because that's what I am. And as a feminist I feel like that informs my musical choices and tastes—and it's hard to separate that. I choose to read women authors for the most part too. Also it's because the whole rest of my life until I was probably twenty-five—that's not what I was doing. And now I can choose and that's what I would choose to do. Before I was twenty-five—it's like, comparing [female authors] . . . to male authors [is the same as comparing female musicians to] male musicians. In school these are the books I had to read and they were by male authors. And on the radio these were the musicians you had to listen to because that's what's being played. So when I have a choice—I will choose women artists and also to support them. That's important to me too. I feel like that's all tied up in it also. (Deirdre)

These women have a preference for listening to female artists as opposed to male artists for myriad reasons. The interviews I conducted support Bradby's (1993) contention that it does matter to women who is singing. Bradby interviewed six Dublin women (five lesbians, one bisexual identified) to explore women's talk about popular music—including the question, "Is she or isn't she a dyke?" (p. 151). Among other things, Bradby established "that it does matter to lesbians who is singing, but not in any one straightforward way" (p. 169). Bradby's informants did not listen to a particular artist solely because she was a lesbian, but the women in her study clearly placed a level of importance on the performer's identity. The women also appropriated, "enjoyed and used in a lesbian context" (p. 170) what is understood as mainstream and heterosexual music. Questioning, creating or knowing the identity of the singer—that is, categorizing singers—becomes a part of lesbian discourse as a means to " 'cementing a common identity' " (p. 170). Bradby concludes that this practice "can be seen as radical, and as an important component in the ongoing process of constructing lesbian identities in everyday life" (p. 171). It makes sense that some women, as well as those I interviewed and regardless of sexuality, would have an attraction toward female artists because of the shared social allegiances (whether real or perceived) and the relevancy of the music and artists to the listener's life. My respondents were interested in female artists, not at the exclusion of men but with a preference for women.

The question remains, however, What attracts or draws women to particular female artists as opposed to other female artists? These women not only share similarities in their reasons for listening to female artists as opposed to male artists, but they also share commonalities in their reasons for their attraction to particular female artists. In the next passage, provided in length, Sandi not only contemplates the issue of taste when comparing female artists' music as opposed to men's but also provides an appropriate and insightful transition into further exploring women's musical tastes within the broader array of music by women. Sandi also suggests that she experiences a connection among fans of similar artists and describes this as being in on a "secret." The theme of connecting to others through female artists' music is discussed in more detail in Chapter 3.

A college English major, 23-year-old Sandi is clever and sharply funny. Witty and thoughtful, she had strong jazz influences through her dad, and Sarah Vaughn remains one of her favorites. In response to a question about whether she wanted to be a rock star, part of her response included, "I wanted to be a cat burglar." A neat original woman, Sandi, provides our transition to the next section.

I have a little metaphor. There's a guy who teaches here at [my university] in creative writing. He had this saying that, "The house of poetry has many rooms." And really it applies to everything. "The house of color has many rooms." So it's the same thing with women's music—it's like the house of women's music has so many rooms. And it's just nice because as soon as you open the front door there's like all these rooms and you can kind of check them out and you can kind of wander around. There are rooms that I really don't like to go to. I got this CD that was like women's ska—it was really not good. And it might have just been—like some compilations are just not that good. So they might have just picked poor groups or there might just not be that many. Or maybe my ear for ska is sort of waning. So I'm probably not going to be going in that room very much. But, there are these other rooms that are like—the folk room is huge! Ya know what I mean? And the jazz room is just like—as far as vocal jazz—it's really, it's a neat room. There's all these nooks and crannies. And it's that feeling of like I'm walking through and I know where the doors are but other people don't necessarily know. Ya know, I guess it's the "secret" again. I don't know. It's not that they don't know—I don't know. There's some feeling of like—this isn't just a random communication. Something is really being said. And I know what it means, I understand what it means—and other people can hear the same thing—and they'll get something—I guess that's true for all music though. But somehow it feels different with women's music. Men's music, it's like, "ya know, I don't know." But in general it's like—"okay, well it's Blues Traveler, okay we all know, [their song] '100 Years.' Yeah, we got it." But especially if it is something that like reflects something I've seen or somewhere I've been. It reflects it more [in women's music] than even, like, James Taylor—or ya know, Beastie Boys could reflect. It's a stronger connection somehow. Not all of the time. It just seems like certain people are, more than others. (Sandi)

ARTIST QUALITIES WOMEN ARE ATTRACTED TO

Women described a variety of qualities when discussing what attracts them to particular female artists. When I asked women about what they liked about female artists they were drawn to, I did not ask with the concept of authenticity in mind. However, as I reflect on the respondents' answers now, the qualities described here are often referenced in debates about authenticity. For sometime now, scholars and music critics have fallen short in coming to a widely accepted consensus of criteria to identify a musical form or artist's authenticity (or credibility).

Authors and critics have questioned what authenticity *is, what it means* and *how to define it*. There are competing definitions and debates about whether authenticity even exists. There have been deliberations about different musical styles—with the most common comparison that *rock* is authentic, but *pop* is not. Authenticity debates continue to shift and change with the debut of each new music style from disco to rap to techno. Arguments are further complicated with every new form of technology, from basic recording to multitrack to synthesizers to sampling. With the use of each technological development, the music is labeled as artifice or cooked (technologically infused) versus the authenticity of raw, natural sounds (whatever those might be argued as at that time). When Bob Dylan first went electric and amplified live in England in 1966, many contended he had abandoned the authenticity (pureness, realness) of folk. If a band used synthesizers, their authenticity was questioned. Even with the advent of MTV and music videos, lip-synching came into question of whether it was authentic or not.[3] What is perceived as authentic or inauthentic changes not only with genre and technology but with authors, critics, scholars and audience members as well. The what is or isn't authentic debate is never ending. But frankly the academic and press deliberations are quite useless for fans because, as Auslander (1998) writes, "the fact that the criteria for rock authenticity are imaginary has never prevented them from functioning in a very real way for rock fans" (p. 5).

Therefore, the authenticity debate conducted by critics and scholars, and keep in mind both are made up of mostly males, is not a core concern of this book, especially when you consider that, whether mere oversight or purposeful exclusion, authenticity is almost exclusively discussed in relation to male artists. What is important is what the respondents thought of as necessary qualities in the music they chose to listen to. These women collectively (though not in consultation with each other) established their own criteria for authenticity using adjectives such as "real," "pure," "committed" and "poetic." As Tetzlaff (1994) writes:

In the end, authenticity is not created by performers, nor embodied in their character. It is created by fan cultures and embodied in the sign systems they use to articulate their sense of the real. . . . The issue is . . . whether fans can use the performers' music and imagery to articulate their own authentic responses to their conditions. (p. 111)

I have left the defining of authenticity to the audience.

To this end, then, in addition to women feeling a certain sense of affinity with female artists as opposed to male artists, all of the women explained that they are interested in particular female artists whose work exemplifies a certain level of depth or substance. Women are drawn to artists that they felt had "something to say," provided a message in their music or had a story to tell. Furthermore, these women are attracted to female artists who seem to embody a certain amount of personal strength or courage, which is in turn reflected in their art. The respondents also put a lot of weight into whether the artists wrote their own songs and, at times, considered whether the artists themselves were involved in the production of their work. These women were also able to talk discriminatingly about the type of music they preferred and the artists' abilities as musicians. Just as the respondents described a preference for female vocal qualities over male vocal qualities, these women also tended to differentiate between female artists based on vocal qualities as well. Some participants also indicated a preference for artists who wrote their own songs from a political perspective, in particular feminism or gay rights.

Once again, when most of the women talked about their attraction to female artists, almost always a combination of the above explanations, and arguably even others that were less frequently talked about across all of the interviews, was given. There's no doubt that these women are discriminating listeners and embody some level of proficiency and ability to critique music. In fact, with many of the respondents having musical backgrounds, many were able to offer substantial critique.

Substantive Lyrics

Women are interested in music with substantive lyrics. Overwhelmingly, the respondents were interested in music that had a certain level of depth. The descriptors used by the participants when characterizing artists' songs and their lyrics included "meaningful," "storytelling," "dense," "depth," "thought-provoking" and "conveying a message." It should be noted, however, that certainly women also found less substantive qualities appealing and used such descriptors as "upbeat and happy," "fun," "beautiful," "little peppy tune," "hilarious" and "thumping." However, for each woman that mentioned perhaps a more lighthearted reason for being attracted to a particular artist or song, they had far many more examples and appeared to lend a great deal more of importance and weight to songs that were somehow more meaningful and substantive for their everyday lives. It is important to remember that what is critical here is that for so long women's stories (or issues women tend to be concerned about) were not being told. And even today stories of substantial relevance to women's struggle in the real world are left to the margins—

with much-lighter-subject pop songs rising to the fore. Therefore, the respondents' stories are all the more noteworthy and salient.

Julie declared that she listens to music across a broad range of genres, but what was most important to her was what was being said through the artist's lyrics. Julie, along with other respondents, believed recording and selling albums for a living is a privileged social position to be in. A position that should be taken seriously. The message should be meaningful and take priority over profit.

I listen to the music for the lyrics. I mean, I listen to it for the music, but I listen to it for the lyrics because if the lyrics don't mean anything then I think it's a big waste of time. You have an opportunity to say something and you're choosing not to. I don't understand why somebody would do that. (Julie)

Sandi's and Terri's comments ring true with Julie's, citing that they value songs that are dense and have some depth to them.

When I first heard her [Ani DiFranco]—I was like, "she's talking too fast, she's talking way too fast." But that is what's exciting about it—it's like you have to listen to it. Now that I got the sheet music, ya know, it's like, "Oh, wow." And I think her songs are very dense. A lot of songs—are like, refrain, refrain, refrain. Everything's the repeat. But [Ani's] are very dense. And then she does this stuff that is like poetry. Which I thought that was neat too. And Suzanne Vega does the same kind of thing. . . . But it's like storytelling—it is really neat. Ya know, it's, it's actually conveying something. . . . [W]ith Ani DiFranco it takes you a couple of times to catch what's going on. Then you have to think about it. (Sandi)

I like songs that have depth to them. [But] I don't know if I can articulate [what depth means necessarily]. Depth—mean[ing] that they're talking about something important, that I deem important. And that they say things in a way that I've never thought of. And there's some analysis there—that it's not just, "Oh, he dumped my ass, whatever." It's like, how does that feel, and what does that mean, and what are the implications of this, and how nutty are you gonna get or does it mean nothing, you know? (Terri)

Terri's reference to a personal heterosexual relationship and her emotions surrounding a breakup should not be quickly devalued, deemed unimportant or considered remarks merely about "romance." Relationships are indeed sights of women's oppression. The personal is political. These are sights of struggle that women fight to overcome. Terri appropriates music as an important tool of survival.[4]

Jane also keys in on the message of a song and regards music as an arena for people to reflect on issues and perhaps provoke some sort of action. This notion of provoking one to action moves music away from the concept of music as being merely pleasurable but toward the concept of music as a tool for social change. These women believed that musical artists hold powerful and important positions as contributors to media content and should take social responsibility seriously and use it to effect positive social change.

[I'm attracted to a performer] I guess just in general [because of] what their message is. I think a lot of what people do in music is to talk about things that are not right or good . . . [and] what are we going to do about it, or, I think that's just been the tradition of music and why people sing is to say, either "I care very much about the person or thing" or "I recognize this"—and it's a way to help make other people recognize it. . . . I guess I'm just naturally aware of what's the message here. Do I agree with it. There's a lot of music that I listen to; it's that I agree with the message. . . . I think probably a lot of different groups I really listen [to] and what is attracting me is because I really believe in what they are saying. (Jane)

Jill, a singer/songwriter and sometime-performer herself, is not only attracted to the message artists are trying to get across but also feels that this is in fact something relatively, although certainly not exclusively, unique to female artists. Placing a high level of importance on the message, Jill explains how she, similar to some of her favorite artists, actually takes the time to explain the meaning of a song when performing live. She refers specifically to independent folk singer Ani DiFranco and self-identified feminist Tori Amos. These are two artists the women refer to often.

[F]emale musicians that I am familiar with and myself included are more into getting a message across. . . . [Some female artists] stop after every song and explain what the next song is going to be about. I do that. Ani [DiFranco] does that sometimes. Tori [Amos] does that a lot. . . . I think that [female artists, myself included are] just more comfortable letting people know how we feel about stuff [more than male artists]. And being in a vulnerable position and just opening up and letting it go. (Jill)

These women place a value on artists and their songs that say something meaningful. Along with saying something substantive through their music, these respondents expressed an appreciation and respect for an artist's strength and ability to say what she, the artist, wants to say. Terri, Jo and Lynn speak specifically to this, with Ani DiFranco used most often as an example. These women actually benefit from the artists' outspokenness. Part of their consideration here is the recognition of women's subordinate position in society. Not being able to "beat the system" every day in their own lives, they at least take some satisfaction in female artists' ability to be aggressive and not passive, forward and not shy, outspoken and not quiet. As Terri declares, "Like Ani, like I said, the attitude, that she can say 'fuck you' when I can't say 'fuck you.' " Jo not only refers to Ani DiFranco but also mentions Tori Amos as having the same sort of quality. Jo sees DiFranco's willingness to be outspoken as a way in which DiFranco actually speaks for other women unable to exude that same sort of confidence.

[Ani DiFranco is] incredible, her words, she's so talented. I mean she's so tough and she says exactly what's on her mind and she doesn't apologize for it and I love that. . . . Ani's strong. She says what she means. She doesn't have to hold back, which we all want to do. . . . I admire that. . . . [And] Tori says things like "How's your Jesus hanging?" [in "Father Lucifer"]. How many of the mainstream people are not going to be offended by some of her lyrics, but she says them anyway. (Jo)

Lynn also describes this feature as a reason for her attraction to one artist over another. Lynn is an energetic 22-year-old. Some might even consider her high strung, especially when it comes to talking about her favorite female artists. A social policy and women's studies major and her arms flailing about as she talks, Lynn describes these artists' outspokenness as an effort to seek some sort of justice or to rectify inequality. Lynn identifies these characteristics in the work of Ani DiFranco and 1960s groundbreaking blues/rock singer Janis Joplin.

Ani [DiFranco] is just like, "Hey I'm mad. I'm really pissed off." And it's just great because she must be like, "ya know what, screw you!" And I love it, because she is so straightforward. . . . She's kinda like, "yeah, ya know what, fuck you." And I think that's great. Because I don't think people, women say that enough. So it's really exciting for me to hear her. . . . [S]he has this one song called "Untouchable Face" and she's just like, "Ya know, fuck you!" And I'm like, yeah!! Because I've been there! . . . I like [Janis Joplin because of] what she represented in that time. Where she came from and her background and how she wasn't the popular kid in school. And I think, not that I related to that in a way, but I think that parts of me do relate to that. You can just tell that she was in so much pain—I like women artists that are laying it all out on the line [like the Indigo Girls too]. . . . So, I think Janis [Joplin] is kind of the same way too. She's just kind of like, "Man, this sucks, ya know. What's going on with this." Ya know, and I love it! I think she's great! (Lynn)

Lynn also expressed an appreciation for the straightforwardness of alternative rock band Hole's front-woman Courtney Love. She talks about how Courtney Love "kicks ass" and finds a greater amount of satisfaction in that as opposed to if it was a man. Clearly, more gratification comes from a female artist who challenges the status quo and does so in an artistic form not often attributed to "females." Lynn appreciates Love's ability to rock against gender expectations.

I like [Hole's] "Miss World" song. The one that was played over and over again. I like it—because it's like—she's like kicks ass, ya know what I mean? You're just like, "Yeah!" You're like in the car driving with that song and you're like, "Alright!" . . . It's much more appealing to me that it's a woman that is kicking ass, because I don't really care if a man kicks ass. They've been kicking ass forever, ya know what I mean. It's just like—it just doesn't seem—there's nothing significant in them kicking ass. Because a lot of times it's kind of—violent, er, not violent—because women can be violent too. I mean that—they've just been doing it—and I don't know what they're [men] really kicking ass about. Ya know what I mean? (Lynn)

Lynn's very clear here that part of the enjoyment and empowerment of an artist's "kicking ass" is in fact that the artist is a woman. Recognizing the social status men—in particular, white heterosexual males—have held throughout American history and the music industry, she takes pleasure in women challenging gendered oppression. She experienced a sense of satisfaction in artists who perform loudly and raucously against dominant culture's gender expectations and norms.

These women clearly look for a certain amount of depth (as defined by them) within a song. They prefer music that has something to say and/or provokes a listener to ponder a situation or topic. Women's attraction to the "straightforwardness" of artists like Ani DiFranco, Tori Amos, Janis Joplin and Courtney Love is important to take special notice of. The attitude displayed by the artists is reflected in their lyrics and further substantiates the importance of their message-laden songs.

Authorship

These women were interested not only in artists whose songs were meaningful, as defined by the women themselves; many of the respondents also placed a high priority on artists who write their own songs. As Jo declares, "So the ones [artists] I've listed so far are the ones I like most lyric-wise and music [-wise]. All of them write their own stuff. They're not doing anyone else's stuff."

For the respondents, when an artist writes her own song, it adds to an artist's credibility (or authenticity). If the women relate to a song and the artist has written the song herself, it contributes to the attraction of an artist. The artist is perceived as more genuine or sincere, and if a fan identifies with the story told in the song, it further accentuates what the fan perceives as a connection to the artist. The artist appears as substantive rather than artifice.

Sandi not only explains that an artist's ability to write her own songs is important, but she also places a value on artists who "do their own thing" and are self-produced. Later in this chapter, the respondents' interest in artists with noted involvement in the production of their music and image is explored in further detail. Sandi's comment also harkens back to and supports the earlier contention that women have an interest in artists who have something meaningful to say.

I think I always had more respect, or more interest at least—in an artist who writes his or her own [songs]. I have a lot more respect for that. Or if they are like, Ani DiFranco started her own [record] company—ya know what I mean? . . . It means more. . . . Just that they [some of the female artists I tend to like] are doing their own thing and there's nobody [producing them]. They don't dress themselves up to play to a different audience. So it feels like what they're producing is what they really mean to say. I guess in general it just feels like, why would I want to listen to something that's not what somebody means to say. . . . It just seems more real. I don't know what the point is otherwise. (Sandi)

These women have a preference for artists whose songs are meaningful and display a certain amount of courage and who write their own music. Another way women differentiated between artists was based on sound.

"Dark Brown Satin Fabric": Music, Vocal Skills and Musicianship

Not only were these women selective in the type or style of music they were attracted to; they were also able to discuss music with a distinguishable level of knowledge or proficiency. These women described the sound they found appealing in a variety of ways; primarily women spoke of musical qualities, women's voices and musicianship.

This section focuses on what these women considered to be good music. Some critics and scholars might argue that determining what is so-called good music is close to impossible. However, still others would be quick to suggest that they could indeed do just that. Whatever the case, it is not important for the purpose of this project to debate and define what is *good* music. What's important in this in-depth audience study is that these women were able to define what they found, for them, to be good music and in turn were able to talk about music discriminatingly.

Take note that because many of these women are attracted to certain artists based on a combination of factors and in turn talk that way, many of the subthemes detailed earlier, such as meaningful and courageous lyrics and authorship, continue to be echoed in this section. Vivian, an amateur musician, describes a variety of sounds that attract her to particular female artists:

Well, I kind of like music that grooves. But then I also like music that is layered sometimes, with like a lot of band people in it. And then sometimes I just like something stripped down. Like [recording artist] Lois, sometimes she's stripped down, just like the guitar. Sometimes P.J. Harvey, she has a guitar, bass and drums. I don't know because I like things that are kind of weird and disjointed too—that wouldn't naturally go right together, but there is just something about it. I guess it's the creativity, and putting the songs together. (Vivian)

Sue, who studied piano as a child, also talks about sound that she finds attractive. Sue, along with Jane to follow, also continues to reinforce the level of importance of lyrics and artists' messages as detailed earlier in this chapter.

[I am attracted to artists because of]—in general, the quality of the music, the quality of the lyrics, the quality of the sounds. Just how it touches you. Some music you can put it on and say oh this is technically good, but it doesn't do anything for me. I've taken like 12 years of piano lessons and was in high school band and I know enough about music to know what's good and what isn't technically, but some of the Babes in Toyland music is still technically got a heart to it, it's got soul, it's got guts, something behind it. . . . [It's] just a gut feeling. (Sue)

Jane not only describes sound but also displays the facility to follow, comprehend and appreciate the progression and musical development of one artist in particular, Michelle Shocked.

I like a lot of acoustic artists even if they amplify their music. It just seems to be more pure than when you can hear the notes and you can hear the lyrics as compared with some of the rock n' roll where it just seems to be noise. You can't necessarily tell the difference between the bass or maybe the monitor doesn't hear it and you clearly can't tell what the lyrics are. But it has no appeal [for me]. Michelle Shocked is really interesting. She has such a range of music. . . . [A friend of mine] explained to me once that Michelle Shocked kind of had an evolution, she'll pick up some things and really pursue it [that style] and put an album out around that and one of her albums is kind of jazzy [*Captain Swing*] and another is clearly acoustic [*Short Sharp Shocked*] and she has a kind of bootleg one that is campfire songs [*The Texas Campfire Tapes*], just recorded with a tape player and she was doing whatever she felt like, and then she evolved into kind of a punk rocker. And even in all of those different styles, I found them all appealing, all interesting. It's almost as if you listen to them and went through them, you evolved with her to the point where she is now, which is fairly sophisticated. On the surface it seems simple, but I think it must be complex the way she puts it all together.[5] (Jane)

Similar to many other women, Deirdre also refers to the appeal of women's voices and, in particular, harmonies. Deirdre displays a fair amount of proficiency when critiquing music and expresses an interest in artists' level of talent as musicians:

[I] like any harmonies, like the Chenille Sisters—they do great harmonies. The Story [with Jennifer Kimball and Jonatha Brooke] who aren't together anymore—it was two women—do amazing harmonies also and I like their sound. So I think about voices primarily, but also the Indigo Girls would be another big one in terms of sound. I love their: Amy rocks, Emily's mild—kind of thing. But they also do each other's stuff. And that shows the diversity within that genre. Ya know, they can't exactly be pigeonholed entirely. So that's definitely a sound. It's just great to see them playing guitar. And they do amazing guitar things. I don't even know what they do, because I don't know, but I know anyone who's ever tried to learn are like—"they make up their own chords!" Ya know? And so it's somebody else who's like, they're good at it. And it's not like folk singers playing the same three chords or something. They care about the music. . . . They're good at it, and they enjoy it and they can do it loud. I love some of their [Indigo Girls] rocking songs and they can do it really mellow. It's all great. (Deirdre)

Julie is most attracted to certain qualities of female voices, Sarah McLachlan in particular. Julie also makes reference to sound and authorship. Julie finds the diversity of female artists particularly appealing—that two different female artists can play the same song with a different result and that two different female artists can play very different songs with the same effect.

I like voices that are clear and full and rich. I like voices that are just really rich. It reminds me of—the picture that I am creating in my mind, that's the only way I can figure to describe it—is really thick dark brown, like satin fabric; it's not real bright and shiny, it's solid and it's there and it's clean and it's smooth and it's just there. It's just really powerful. I like really rich, full voices, and I like women who take advantage of their vocal range and do all kinds of stuff with it but not like Mariah Carey and scream high notes. [The type of vocals I like in a song] seem more honest. It seems like they're not messing around with a lot of different techniques and a lot of different sounds. It's just clean and it's honest and that's what it is. . . . They just like lay it out. . . . Their voices are incredible. Sarah McLachlan's voice is absolutely incredible. She just blows me away. . . . The things she can do with her voice and the music that she writes and the lyrics that she writes, she can pack so much emotion and so many different emotions into a song. She's got every range of emotions from happiness, sadness, to anger, to depression, fear, I mean everything. She just runs the gamut. And there is just so much feeling in her voice and the way she says her words and the way she uses her words in what she writes to get across what she's trying to say.... And I like hearing how different women express the same thing in different ways, and different words, and different rhyme schemes and different, just everything you can hear one song played—two artists could sing the same song and you can get a totally different feel out of it. And two artists can sing songs that are way different and convey the same kind of meaning. Just the inspiration that there are phenomenal women out there. (Julie)

Jo, a onetime professional musician, touches on many areas focusing on musical qualities when describing what attracts her to particular artists. Jo provides a serious and credible critique about sound and an artist's talent. Interestingly, however, Jo expressed some difficulty describing sound, explaining that it is easier to play an example. In spite of what she perceived as an obstacle, Jo was still able to provide a worthwhile critique of music.

There's people like Tori Amos . . . I can admire the composition that she does. If you listen, very close to the background, there are violins, trumpets, she plays a harpsichord. The sound of her music, God. I can't describe the sound. It's just beautiful. I mean, she has this amazing ability to compose music. I can't describe the sound. Have you ever heard the song "Mother"? Somehow through her music, I get the whole feeling of that song. The way she does that music, and the way she whispers that, it's hard to describe sound. I never thought about it before but it's really tough. I hear classical constantly in [her] music. I mean, Jesus, she will be playing harpsichord, but it will still somehow be classical. You can tell she was obviously trained in classical. And, Ani [DiFranco]'s music, you can hear jazz. Her music changes constantly; it can be funk, it can be jazz, it can be blues. I mean, Ani changes with every CD. (Jo)

Jo not only describes the quality of music, as defined by her, she is attracted to but asserts that lyrics are of equal importance and is particularly intrigued when the lyrics seek to somehow match the music, that they somehow tell the story and convey the emotions simultaneously.

I think that the sound that I'm looking for, and here again I go with the lyrics, but the artists who are able to punch their lyrics with their sound, and these [artists I have been talking about] are all able to do it. The sound personifies the meaning. I don't like the three-chord crap. I like to hear more than that. I like to hear, gosh, I don't know how to describe it. I like to hear somebody with the understanding of composition. It's evident in pretty much all of the artists [I like]; they all write their own, but like Tori Amos, everything's synchronized and perfection, I mean it's like perfect. She's perfect. And then you hear violins in Suzanne Vegas's [music], the violins that sometimes—I keep thinking of that one song ["Song of Sand"] over and over, in fact through this whole conversation.... "If sound waves were sand waves," [*sic*] keeps going through my head. In that song, [there's this] thin violin sound that is almost like a lack of air. Like this thin, and there's this feeling that I get from this sound that I can't even describe, but it puts you in conflict with words again. And then Annie Lennox, I mean "Walking on Broken Glass" sounds like walking on broken glass. I mean it's like, and "The Little Bird," God I love that song. She wants to sit right down and cry, and it's another freeing song, but her music articulates the lyrics, but it's musicians who are able to articulate what they are saying through their music are the ones that impress me. Annie Lennox really does it too.... Somehow I look for lyrics to be backed up by the music. And both of them have to be equal. (Jo)

Sandi indicates that voices and musicianship are her priorities when considering music she is attracted to. Sandi also puts some weight on meaningful lyrics and whether the artist writes her own music.

As far as sound, I like voices or their own musicianship—like the Indigo Girls play their own music. Melissa Etheridge plays her own music. People play their own music are like automatically are like [puts her thumbs up].... They could have other people play it for them, they could have it all synthesized.... [When they write their own music] it just seems more real. I don't know what the point is otherwise. Ya know what I mean?... Otherwise maybe it's about money—And "I don't care about money! I'm not going to make any money off of it, so what do I care."... I think what I found is that with women's music, I find more women's music that is self produced. And maybe it's because like I've gotten interested in certain ones, and so I have access to [them]. (Sandi)

Paige clearly displays discriminating taste. She is able to recognize and determine what she considers to be good music. Paige cognizantly critiques music and finds an artist's voice particularly important. And like many of the other women's statements above, she also places a high level of importance on lyrics. Not only does Paige provide specific examples of what she finds appealing, but she also explains how she'll sometimes listen to music, breaking it down, listening to specific instruments through the course of the song. Certainly she is able to bring a critical eye and perspective to evaluating music and determining what music she considers being of quality for her. It's also interesting to note that Paige, like Jo and Vivian before her, indicates a particular attraction toward songs in which the lyrics and music complement each other so well that they are both able to convey the same emotion if separated from the other.

Probably just their [the artists I like] ability to combine all the elements that make a good song—well, in my eyes a good song—or in general. The style, the voice, the lyrics. And if they can place that all together well enough, then it's appealing. There's just something about it that just all clicks. . . . Well there are different things [that I like about music]. I find Jewel's music to be more simplistic. It's [just] her guitar—it's pretty much—I find it mostly her guitar. . . . It's mostly her guitar and I find that to be kind of soothing and her voice is very—is soft and intriguing. Sarah [McLachlan]'s and Fiona [Apples]'s I find their music to be more. . . . I think Sarah has gotten more lush over the years, you know between [1992's] "Solace" and [1994's] "Fumbling towards Ecstasy"—there is a huge difference. And Fiona—just the music itself is so full and all the instruments that play into that. I think—even if you didn't have any of the lyrics. I think it still creates a mood. . . . I think it's just the combination of the whole, of everything—their voice, their style, their music, their instruments. It's just the way it fits together, and that's what makes a good song. And that's when I kind of—like sooner or later—sometimes I will break them down. I listen to different parts—not probably intentionally. Just when I am listening to live music. I've wanted to try and break it down, but sometimes I will follow the bass. Sometimes I will follow the drumbeat. . . . I think that's given me more of an understanding of—the combination—the song as a whole just to better appreciate it. Better understand it. It just keeps you interested, because there's always something there that you haven't heard before. (Paige)

Terri values artists with the courage to speak out. The excerpt below also continues to support Terri's and others' earlier comments about being attracted to artists who are talented musicians and the sound of female voices:

I like good musicians. Tori Amos is an incredible piano player. I mean, she's great! And you just listen to her play, she doesn't even have to sing, and it gets to you. Amy [Ray] and Emily [Sailers, of Indigo Girls], the way they play the guitar. I mean, they can fucking kick ass. They are just great musicians. And it's just like, YES! And it's like, you know, I wanna go "pussy power!" You know what I mean? And it's just cool to see women do that, and to be strong, and play like that. (Terri)

These women clearly display an ability to critique music with a measurable amount of proficiency. Despite what some of the literature suggests, these women are discriminating listeners and are quite capable of evaluating music, vocal skills and musicianship.

"Music That Makes a Difference": Politics, Feminism and Gay Rights

Intertwined with many of the characteristics described above (substantive lyrics, authorship, sound, musicianship, voices), some women also described artists' ability to create music from a politically informed perspective or include political topics in their songs as another attractive feature. Many of the women indicated a preference for female artists who "try to do good" or "try to make a difference." The two political topics brought up the most were feminism/women's issues and gay/lesbian/bi issues.

When Deirdre considered what she found appealing about the artists she liked, she included an artist's political consciousness concurrent with her discussion of sound. And as detailed earlier, Deirdre's comment below further illustrates her interest in music that makes a difference, displays a capability to critique sound and places a heavy emphasis on meaningful lyrics.

I think there are things that they [the female artists I have mentioned] have in common—they're all primarily folksy, but they can also rock in their own way—and I think they all are powerful in some way and they all have political—ya know, not all of their songs are political, but they have political songs. Which makes me respect them more and also—makes me enjoy listening—it has meaning to listen, so those would be things they all have in common. And then there's things for each one individually—I like Cheryl Wheeler, Dar Williams and Nanci Griffith—[they all can] sometimes can be hilarious. They can be hilarious and political and powerful and have a great song all in the same song. I think those are all things that I like and look for. And Tracy Chapman doesn't—I don't think anyone would say she was funny—but she has some very political stuff.... [And it's appealing] I guess [because] I feel like it's music that makes a difference. It reflects things that I feel. So I enjoy listening to it for that reason. . . . I like that it's good music and it's political—you don't have to choose [between] them. (Deirdre)

Many of the women keyed into an artist's efforts to include political topics in her songs. Artists that are singled out here include Ani DiFranco, Indigo Girls and Emmylou Harris. Terri mentioned both the Indigo Girls and Ani DiFranco.

Amy and Emily [of the Indigo Girls] are cool, because they're activists. And so is Ani DiFranco, and Ani has this lyric in [her "The Million You Never Made" song something like,] If you don't live what you sing about, your mirror's gonna' fuck you. And, that's what I think. I think [it's about] that praxis thing, that live what you believe. Not that I always do, but I like to see artists do that.[6] (Terri)

Before the interview had begun, Patricia made a comment about how she was impressed with Emmylou Harris at the Lilith Fair she attended. Emmylou Harris had talked about land mines during her set and had encouraged people to participate in the cause to eliminate them. When the recorder was on I asked Patricia to talk about this incident and whether that plays a role in why she might like someone. Patricia indicated an artist's willingness to make a difference does play a role in her attraction toward a particular artist.

I think that if you do something positive, like when they [musical artists] were doing these Farm Aids and all of that and benefits for AIDS. I think that tells a lot about a person. And I believe they can use their music in a positive way to make a difference—regardless of what it is, I mean—you don't necessarily have to believe in their cause, but for me it shows integrity and it shows a motivation other than money to get up there and do something. I think [for me there] is a political element in music. (Patricia)

Beyond mentioning political involvement in general terms, many of the women actually associated specific causes with particular artists. For example, Patricia talked about Tracy Chapman songs that uncover the injustice and hardships of poverty. Jill refered to Buffy Sainte-Marie and her involvement with Native American causes. Sue describes the work Diamanda Galas has done for AIDS.

[Diamanda Galas] does a lot for the AIDS cause. Her brother died of AIDS, and she has her hands tattooed and she has like "HIV+" or something, and "We're all HIV positive"—because it's along the lines of "don't ask for whom the bell tolls, the bell tolls for thee" and that's very much her philosophy and she's very, very adamant and militant about the AIDS cause. (Sue)

Deirdre cites songs she likes in part because of their political message. The first is particular to Nanci Griffith and homelessness and issues of class, and the second focuses on Dar Williams and religious dogma. And once again, Deirdre refers to an artist's capabilities as a musical artist, the artist's voice and the general quality of the songs as appealing features:

There's this Nanci Griffith song "Down 'N' Outer." . . . The song is about a homeless man and it's actually from his perspective and [he's] talking to people from this [upper-class] neighborhood. He says, "I don't want a house there on your street, I don't want to hurt your family, I don't want a house there on your street, I just." And the chorus is like, "Can you spare a dime, can you spare the time, can you look me in the eye. I was once like you." And it said something about "Do you ever think of me on Sunday?" [*sic*] Which I think is cool—a church reference. And it's like powerful and subtle—it's not like this big political song. She doesn't say anything about homelessness or housing the homeless, but it's like class references. [And she does it] in an amazing way. She like plays a great guitar and this kind of freaky but great voice. And it feels like she wouldn't have written it or be singing it if she didn't feel it too. And it seems like it can be reflected in her voice also. Because sometimes it'll be like this angry—like it's still this beautiful melody but there's like a different tone that she's singing in. . . . Dar Williams has a song that I love [called] . . . "Christians and the Pagans." And it's just this poppy little peppy tune. It's about this lesbian couple going to one [of the] woman's uncle's house for Christmas. And at the same time the women are celebrating solstice. And then they're explaining solstice to the family. And then the kid in the family is like, "[Dad] can I be a Pagan [too]?" It's funny and it's political in its own way and it's a great tune. (Deirdre)

Not only do women recognize and appreciate politically conscious artists, but they also recognize the power in an artist's ability to shed light on a political cause. Although the excerpts focusing on politics above did not refer to this explicitly, it's certainly implied. For example, when talking about artists' political actions, Jane specifically mentions how an artist's involvement with certain causes does prompt people, herself included, to think twice about a certain issue. Jane talks about Michelle Shocked and two of her songs. She refers to Shocked's "Graffiti Limbo" about the killing of graffiti artist Michael Stewart by New York City transit cops and the cryptic "(Don't You Mess Around With) My Little Sister" with its veiled critique of relations between the United States and Central and South America:

If you really listen to what [Michelle Shocked] says, it can fit with a person evolving; when she was into punk rock she was defending and supporting the artists, graffiti artists because that was important to her, injustices in the world and putting it with music that was lively and upbeat and on one hand you could just listen to it and not pay attention to the lyrics and not realize there was a message there about the injustice to one man who was killed by the police because he was a graffiti artist or another song on the same album that talks about the relationship of the United States to Central and South America and that they're really overpowering them economically. I think if you listen to it on more than one level. It's music, it's nice, you're doing the dusting or whatever; on the other hand you can listen to it and you might understand what they are talking about. (Jane)

Feminism/Women's Issues

One of the political topics brought up most frequently by the respondents was related to women's issues. Although the respondents did not always indicate this specifically with definitive words such as "feminism" or "women's issues" throughout this chapter, nonetheless this sensibility is implied. In this particular section, references to issues surrounding women are more clear and succinct. Some women made general statements about women's issues, while others spoke about specific examples. Sue certainly finds Sister Sledge's "We Are Family" appealing because of what she reads as a feminist-themed message.

[I d]efinitely [like] Sister Sledge, "We Are Family." . . . [Sister Sledge] was cool. It was great. They seemed like unified. And they seemed strong. And there was nothing about meeting a man that I remember. And it's like, yeah, we're together, we can do it, we're having a good time and it was like upbeat and encouraging and positive and a solidarity thing. (Sue)

Jane, a professional businesswoman, describes Laurie Anderson's "Beautiful Red Dress" which mentions the disparity between the average woman's wage and the average man's.

Laurie Anderson has a song about [what] women make in wage and she said, "At the rate we're going," something like "we should be in the equality so far in the future, it's absurd;" it's like 2800 or whatever. I know we make some progress, we always make some progress because I wouldn't be in the position I am without things changing, but I think it's slow progress. (Jane)

Paige talks about an Ani DiFranco song that focuses on abortion. "[In terms of social issues] Ani DiFranco is probably the most in the forefront of that just because she is so blatant with it. [There's the "Lost Woman Song" on her self-titled debut], it's about abortion. ... [O]ne time I was reading the lyrics—I always grab the lyrics—I love reading lyrics—and I read it and I was like WOW!" (Paige).

Patricia talks about the Tracy Chapman song "Behind the Wall" that focuses on the unheard and ignored cries for help of battered women:

[Sometimes] the music doesn't do much for me, but the lyrics are so—[for example] Tracy Chapman's song about women and their abuse and being abused. There's absolutely no musical interest; it's just her voice—it's very, very powerful for me. . . . I think [I relate to that song] just because it's by a woman, about women and how no one [is] listening or no one [is] hearing the cries for help. The neighbor calls the police, but they don't come and when they do come they don't do anything, and then they eventually come and it's too late; she has already died. And it's just, her voice is just like a rock solid, deep voice and it's just very poignant. (Patricia)

Sandi provides a number of examples of different artists' focus on women's issues. She refers to Ani DiFranco's and Salt 'n Pepa's representation of sexuality and how they fight against feminine beauty norms, such as wearing so-called feminine attire like high heels, shaving body hair and even going against society's expectation that women should be passive when it comes to sexual relations and desire. Sandi suggests there is power exemplified in these artists' strength and courage to sing openly, perform openly and dress openly. She finds these recording artists particularly appealing because they take advantage of a forum and say things that all too frequently other women are unable to or won't say. Sandi then segues into a discussion that includes Melissa Etheridge, suggesting that these three artists include topics of abuse and social justice into their music.

I think that Madonna's portrayal of sexuality is based on victimization. It's all about power and control. And a lot of people feel that way, and that's okay. Except it is always about power and control. And it is always about being on top or bottom. It is very extreme. To me it is not very attractive. Or at least it is not very positive. When I listen to it, I don't go, "Yeah, beat me up." Ya know? It is just really kind of creepy if I listen to it too much. Whereas, Ani DiFranco and Salt 'n Pepa [in their mid-to late 80s work] are like, "Ya know, we are not cute, we are not pretty, we're not—we don't all wear high heels"—it's changed [since Salt 'n Pepa's earlier work—but they were saying] "We don't dress up, we wear sweats, we cut our hair off." But at the same time they're like, "We like sex, I love sex." And even more than that it is sort of this "If you don't like it, fuck you" attitude which is—like my mother has that attitude and that's about it. There are just not many women that I've known who are, who first of all have the forum to be able to say [that], even if they want to. And then there's not as many who want to. Or who seem to want to. It's just nice. It's like—"Yeah, I don't have to scrape myself with razors or whatever to be attractive, or just to be a sexual thing, being, an emotional being." And emotions don't mean crying. They also mean anger—like Melissa Etheridge—is the same kind of thing. . . . And then they bring up things that aren't brought up in men's music or in other forums. Like abuse, or I don't know if you want to say, like social justice. But different ways of looking at social interaction. [Singing about] sexuality that's not "oh I want to be with you forever" or "I want to hit you around—I wanna push down." . . . I just think [Salt 'n Pepa and Ani DiFranco] are fab. (Sandi)

Not only do these women focus on the content of songs, but they also value an artist who becomes actively involved in certain causes. Jo, although a big fan of Tori Amos's musical abilities, is also attracted to Tori Amos because of her contributions to and leadership in RAINN.

Tori Amos, god, look at her personality, she's working on RAINN and helping young girls who have been sexually abused or boys or whatever, but that is not only reflected in her music, but here she is actually committed to this organization, which I think is cool; so yeah, that has a big part with why I like her. (Jo)

Jo also talked about Sarah McLachlan's feminist efforts and in particular the Lilith Fair. Jo was not the only one to make specific mention of Lilith Fair. The interviews were conducted during the course of Lilith's first-year run in 1997. Not only the women who attended (which included 9 of 15 of them: Deirdre, Jill, Lisa, Lynn, Julie, Mary, Patricia, Terri and Paige) but even some women who did not attend (Jo and Elisabeth) recognized the importance of artists' involvement in Lilith Fair.

Elisabeth indicates that Sarah McLachlan's work with the Lilith Fair is certainly one of the things she finds appealing about her. Elisabeth also feels a certain amount of satisfaction when choosing to economically support female artists.

I really like what Sarah McLachlan writes and the more I find out about her, like the Lilith thing this summer, and I just think that's just cool. It seems to me that the more I know about an artist, I tend to look for their music, listen to their music, buy their music because if you respect them or think they are doing neat stuff in their life or in music you tend to respond to that. . . . I think it's just a kind of respect issue. If you respect what someone is doing and if you are impressed with what they are doing in the world, that's the kind of thing that would make you seek out what they're doing. And almost economically you are saying, here I'm supporting what you're doing. It's almost that. And it kind of makes me feel good, to think that she's out there, this is what she's doing, and I think I really respond to that. I read this whole long article when I was working out the other day, on the festival [Lilith Fair] that she started, and I thought, Man that's a cool thing. (Elisabeth)

Mary finds particular importance in the Lilith Fair. She admires Sarah McLachlan for creating the Lilith Fair and in Chapter 2 shares a remarkable story about how the Lilith Fair actually aided her in becoming a feminist and enabled her to become more outspoken within her family circle. "I just admire her for putting Lilith Fair together, for finally stepping out and making people aware that female artists are out there" (Mary).

Lesbian/Gay/Bisexual Issues

In addition to political issues in general and women's issues, some also admired artists who write from a lesbian or bisexual position.

Jill, who indicated some ambiguity about her sexuality, writing "heterosexual, bisexual?" on the filtering questionnaire, was pleased to see the Indigo Girls, two lesbians, be more open about their own sexuality in their lyrics.

I think . . . it's really pretty cool that they're [Indigo Girls] getting more bold with some of their lyrics now. Like on this new one—that lyric—[in "It's Alright"] "hate me cause I'm different, hate me cause I'm gay."[sic] [I think] that is really cool that they're getting more bold, feel more comfortable getting more bold. I just think it's cool that they are strong women and they're out there sharing their music. (Jill)

Elisabeth, a lesbian, is excited when artists include the topic of lesbian relationships in their songs. "[I think I like female artists] just [because of] the sensibility. Like women you know are lesbians you think, 'Wow, I really like that,' and you kind of get into that. . . . I think that's part of it and when you know that there's one woman singing about another woman, that's exciting" (Elisabeth).

Some women were not only interested in female artists' inclusion of lesbian topics within their songs but also admired female artists' courage to be out of the closet and the effects of that public statement in changing society's perceptions of lesbianism. Jane talks about the Indigo Girls in particular. Along with talking about the Indigo Girls being out as lesbians, Jane's comments also harken back to artists who are politically conscious, making reference to the Indigo Girls' exploration of such topics as religion and institutionalized learning.

The Indigo Girls, you really have to look at their lyrics if you want to hear all their complexities because they are very intelligent women and if you can hear it in their vocabulary and they talk about the Bible and they're well-educated. . . . At the same time they're fun. They just seem to really have a fun-ness about them. And they are just so strongly woman identified. They were one of the first groups of women to come out, to openly come out as lesbians and not really care about what anyone thought about that because they were doing what they liked to do. (Jane)

Jo has a great deal of respect for artists who are publicly honest about their sexual orientation. Jo, in line with her comments cited earlier about Melissa Etheridge, refers to Melissa Etheridge again in terms of what she's accomplished for gay rights.

I see women like Melissa Etheridge, she came out to the public as incredibly strong and that just makes me more and more attracted to her as a person because she was able to be that strong. . . . I think [coming out] definitely makes me more attracted to them [out artists]. I can't help but see it as a positive. I can't help but see anyone who turns—to being themselves without letting the public stop them, and that makes me more attracted to them as people, period. Because they have the strength to do that. . . . Being open about their sexual orientation in the face of adversity makes me more attracted to them. . . . I admire them more if they're willing to say, "Hey, this is how it is and I don't give a shit how you people think." Just because it has to be done. It has to be done for perceptions of change. So I admire them for that. . . . The fact that [Melissa Etheridge] came out was a huge step in courage . . . to actually get out there and do what they have to do to make changes in the world and that's something that I really admire about her and anyone who gets the opportunity to do it on such a grand scale. (Jo)

At another moment in the interview, Jo talked specifically about Melissa Etheridge's and her partner's [at the time, Julie Cypher] courage to be open about the first child they had together.

I admire [Melissa Etheridge] for coming out to the whole world and saying [that she's a lesbian], especially now that she had a kid. I think that's really cool. . . . I think her personality, being able to do that, and then going so far as to actually being the first people publicized to do that as far as I know, in the mainstream, have a child together, I think that that's really cool. (Jo)

These women are clearly interested in artists who try to make a difference. These women described a particular appeal in artists who write from a political perspective and try to effect change. Although many indicated a variety of causes, these respondents were more likely to make mention of women's issues and gay rights.

"She's Just Doing It by Herself, Making It by Herself": Professional Autonomy

Many of the women disclosed a preference for artists who display some sort of autonomy or control over their career and performance personae. Female listeners recognize and appreciate female artists' struggle for success in a male-dominated industry. And similar to women's attraction toward artists who write their own songs, some of the women expressed a preference for artists who produce their own work. Finally, some women made reference to an attraction for artists who are their own person when it comes to performance and style.

Sandi is appreciative of female artists' determination and in particular recognizes the obstacles they face, unique only to women. "It's just that I appreciate that they [female artists] have to fight harder" (Sandi). Sandi applauds and refers specifically to rap artists Salt 'n Pepa and Queen Latifah. "Another reason why I like Salt 'n Pepa is because they went into rap which is all male, pretty rough—at the time it was not even big news. It [rap music] was still in the street. They were IT. And Queen Latifah. Just like riding at the edge of this wave" (Sandi). These female listeners want women to have as much control as possible over their art.

Several women, including Jo, Sandi and Jill, referred specifically to Ani DiFranco's achievements through her own record company, Righteous Babe Records.

Jo: [A]nother thing I really respect about Ani [DiFranco] is that she opened her own record company [Righteous Babe Records]. She didn't let anyone else produce her.

Sandi: I think I always had more respect, or more interest at least, in artists who write their own or perform their own [music]. I have a lot more respect for that. Or if they are like, Ani DiFranco started her own company.... It means more.

Jill, a sometimes-professional singer/songwriter herself, makes particular mention of Ani DiFranco for handling her career on her own terms. Jill has a fondness for Ani DiFranco and the success she's had with her independent label without relying on, and in fact even rejecting, the traditional and patriarchal means of the industry:

She has all these old white men in suits knocking at her door and she's just like, "Fuck you. I am doing this fine by myself. What do I need with you?" And she has a such a huge fan base and she is not even on the radio. She's not even hardly on MTV. I think that is really cool.... [T]hat somehow through the underground she got out there to so many people.... [S]he's just doing it by herself, making it by herself and not having to prescribe to any male dominated way of doing things. She's just kind of like, "This is the way I want it to be and so this is the way it's going to be." And nobody can take her down on that because she's got the power in her arena and I think that is wonderful. (Jill)

In the following excerpt, Jane talks about the Indigo Girls' support for other artists as a display of autonomy and independence. Often the Indigo Girls pick lesser-known artists to open for them when performing and in turn provide these artists with exposure they may have never received. Furthermore, and although Jane does not mention it specifically, Amy Ray of the Indigo Girls owns her own record company, which showcases unknown artists. Putting these unknowns on their bill is a continuation of support and reaching out into the musical community.

Another thing I really like about the Indigo Girls is that they seem to be very, very supportive of other artists, both men and women, and it shows in some of the actions that they take and some of their concerts that they'll have, the back-up bands, that they really truly are trying to promote [artists] that they think are worthwhile and they're getting ready to give them a chance or they'll have people come up stage for a song or two and play with them, so there's, to me, a down to earthiness about the Indigo Girls, which seems so genuine. They have a true love for it and I just think it comes off in everything they do. (Jane)

Finally, similar to the respondents' mention of appreciating artists who can "kick ass" (Lynn, Terri), some of the respondents found the independent nature of certain artists' performance style and dress, and the attitude that comes through that, to be appealing.

Lynn: The women at the Lilith Fair—I think it was great that like Paula Cole came out—she like had her hair back in a pony tail. She's just kind of like, "Yeah, I was wearing this all day. I just came out here to do this." And I was like, "That's alright."

Jill: Ani just puts on a damn rockin' show. She's such a performer. She's up there laughing and dancing around and doing her own thing up there—and I think that is really entertaining. . . . Tori [Amos] is quite a performer [too]. I've never seen anyone interact with the piano like she does.

Paige: Sarah McLachlan was just phenomenal. After seeing her in concert, I have so much more like—I just love the woman. I am like WOW! Paula Cole—she's very strong in her music and on stage—all full front.

Sue: Babes in Toyland are totally awesome. . . . Lori [Barbero, the drummer] is awesome. I can't keep my eyes off her when she's drumming. She's got these awesome arm muscles. She wails on those things. She looks like a female Bam-Bam or something. She's got this dreadlock hair like piled up. She's so cool. And they [Babes in Toyland] do have like this really great persona on stage. She's [Barbero] so tough, like Hell's Angels on the stage.

CONCLUSION

This chapter suggests that women are capable of discerning musical taste and should be recognized as such. Although this may be a given to many feminists or female fans of music, sadly, for most of the mainstream and what I've come across as a music fan myself, this is not how women are perceived. The industry and the mainstream population in general do not consider women connoisseurs of music. When women are informed and selective music fans, it is still perceived as an anomaly, and when a mixed-gender discussion turns to music, attention is usually paid to the men who speak. Similarly, ask any women who have walked into a music store to buy an instrument or an electronics store to buy stereo equipment, and they too will likely be able to share stories of being "technologically" dismissed by the (usually) male staff. When it comes to music, women as a gender are often discounted. In fact, during their individual interviews, both Sue and Jill shared experiences similar to this. Sue talked about her own husband being dismissive about her musical tastes and the artists themselves. Jill, a semiprofessional singer/songwriter, talked about not being taken seriously when walking into a music store or recording studio. More so and similar to what other female musicians have stated in various editions of *ROCKRGRL* magazine, even chart-topping Grammy winner Shawn Colvin stated that she "hated going into music stores" because of the overwhelming and intimidating atmosphere (DeSantis, 2001, p. 24).

Hopefully, the respondents' stories help to challenge these widely assumed false beliefs. Women are capable of discerning listenership, and any mind-sets to the contrary are in part because women are marginalized and don't have a great deal of influence in the industry or the outlets that contribute to the public definition of what is "good" music. Despite this, these women have overcome these obstacles—for some, because they're part of a larger women's community or had familial musical influences; for others, out of pure tenacity.

These women clearly demonstrated that they have discriminating taste and have a marked level of proficiency to evaluate music. They delineated their own set of criteria in relation to the concept of authenticity, citing depth, authorship, quality sound, a political perspective and professional autonomy as factors they deemed important. Moreover, they are purposeful and selective consumers of music and look for and seek to support artists with the qualities detailed here, qualities they find attractive. Their attraction toward female artists, and for those who consciously choose to support female artists, helps to get feminist messages out and stories heard. Furthermore, the respondents' acknowledgment of interest in artists who take on political issues suggests that music can be a vehicle toward social change. Although music does not always provoke an outward revolution, perhaps it speeds up the evolution. At the very least, it creates awareness and consciousness raising, which is never enough but better than nothing.

Finally, it is also interesting to note the feminist sensibility of these women at a time when many rightfully claim a backlash against feminism (Faludi, 1991) or many women's purposeful disassociation from it. Of course, this study was specific to artists with a feminist and/or political sensibility, so this is no surprise, but I think it does help to suggest that feminism is not entirely dead outside of the academy. Some, having experienced a sort of raised consciousness about feminism in the college classroom, have remained cognizant of women's oppression and subordination. So, for myself, as an educator and feminist, it is encouraging to learn that what happens inside my classroom can make a difference outside of it. More so, those artists who embody a feminist and/or political sensibility have made the classroom much larger.

NOTES

1. For more on relevancy, see Fiske (1988) and Cohen (1991). For more on interpellation, see Bobo (1988).

2. As the following themes and subthemes that emerged are fleshed out in this and the next three chapters, it is important to note that none of the themes are mutually exclusive of the others. The overlap and combination

of reasons for women's attraction to female artists and their music are seemingly endless. For instance, talk surrounding the themes of sound, lyrics, feminism/women's issues or gay/lesbian/bi issues resonates with other themes throughout all four analyses chapters. Similar sensibilities of these multiple themes are echoed throughout these four chapters and therefore support the emergent nature of each individual theme. Finally, the complementing nature of these various themes—which results in themes resonating with other themes—more clearly exemplifies and profiles the artists and music that these women talked about.

3. For more on authenticity, see Auslander (1998), Frith (1996), Grossberg (1994), Jones (1992), Pattie (1999) and Tetzlaff (1994).

4. Women's response to music that is romantic-relation focused should not be dismissed as nonfeminist or unimportant. "[T]hese areas [are] of central concern to women and important sources of women's oppression" (Roberts, 1996, p. 137). Approaches to feminism take various forms. Roberts (1996) makes this argument when weighing the feminist qualities in female country artists' videos, writing that "issues of purity are quite simply irrelevant" (p. 140) and what is important is that a feminist message has the potential to reach a wider audience.

5. Michelle Shocked gained popularity in the late 1980s with her *Short Sharp Shocked* release on Mercury Records. As Jane indicates, Michelle experimented with different music genres with each new album she released. Mercury Records was not always approving of the genre changes. Shocked eventually sued and won her way out of Mercury's control and was awarded the rights to her songs. Although some *Short Sharp Shocked* songs have a punk attitude, Shocked never released a pure punk album. She does, however, reference herself as a "skateboard punk rocker" in "Anchorage" and did for a period of time display a punk aesthetic in her style of dress and her New York City squatting lifestyle.

6. The correct lyrics to Ani DiFranco's "The Million You Never Made" are "if you don't live what you sing about your mirror is going to find out."

SONG LYRICS

Tori Amos, "Father Lucifer"

Father Lucifer
You never looked so sane
You always did prefer the drizzle to the rain

How's the Lizzies
How's your Jesus Christ been hanging

Nothings gonna stop me from floating
Nothings gonna stop me from floating

He says he reckons I'm a watercolour stain
He says I run and then I run from him
And then I run
He didn't see me watching
From the aeroplane
He wiped a tear
And then he threw away our appleseed

Nothings gonna stop me from floating
Nothings gonna stop me from floating

Everyday's my wedding day
Though baby's still in his comatose state
I'll die my own Easter eggs
Don't go yet
Just don't go
And Beenie lost the sunset but that's OK
Does Joe bring flowers to Marilyn's grave
And girls that eat pizza and never gain weight
Never gain weight
Never gain weight
Father Lucifer you never looked so sane
You always did prefer the drizzle to the rain
Tell me that you're still in love with that milkmaid
How's the Lizzies
How's your Jesus Christ been hanging

Laurie Anderson, "Beautiful Red Dress"

Well I was down at the Zig Zag
That's the Zig Zag Bar & Grill
And everybody was talking at once
and it was getting real shrill.
And I've been around the block
But I don't care I'm on a roll—I'm on a wild ride
Cause the moon is full and look out baby—
I'm at high tide.

I've got a beautiful red dress
And you'd look really good
standing beside it..
I've got some beautiful new red shoes
and they look so fine
I've got a hundred and five fever
and it's high tide.

Well just the other day I won the lottery
I mean lots of money
I got so excited I ran into my place and i said:
HEY! Is anybody home?
Nobody answered but I guess that's not too weird
Since I live alone.

I've got a beautiful red dress
And you'd look really good
standing beside it..
Girls?
We can take it And if we can't
we're gonna fake it
We're gonna save ourselves
We're gonna make it And if we don't
we're gonna take it
We're gonna save ourselves
Save ourselves

Well they say women shouldn't be
the president
Cause we go crazy from time to time
Well push my button baby here I come
Yeah look out baby
I'm at high tide

I've got a beatiful red dress
and you'd look really good
standing beside it..
I've got a little jug of red sangria wine
and we could take little sips
from time to time
I've got some bright red drop dead lips
I've got a little red card
and mechanical hips
I've got a hundred and five fever!!!

OK! OK! Hold it!
I just want to say something.
You know, for every dollar a man makes
a woman makes 63 cents.
Now, fifty years ago that was 62 cents.
So, with that kind of luck, it'll be the year 3,888
before we make a buck. But hey, girls?

We can take it And if we can't
we're gonna fake it
We're gonna save ourselves
save ourselves
(Yeah tell it to the judge)
We're gonna make it And if we don't
we're gonna take it
We're gonna save ourselves
save ourselves
We've got a fever of a hundred and five
and look baby
It's high tide.

Well I could just go on and on and on . . .
But tonight
I've got a headache

Ani DiFranco, "lost woman song"

i opened a bank account
when i was nine years old
i closed it when i was eighteen
i gave them every penny that i'd saved
and they gave my blood and my urine a number
now i'm sitting in this waiting room
playing with the toys
and i am here to exercise my freedom of choice
i passed their hand held signs
went through their picket lines
they gathered when they saw me coming
they shouted when they saw me cross
i said why don't you go home
just leave me alone
i'm just another woman lost
you are like fish in the water
who don't know that they are wet

but as far as i can tell
the world isn't perfect yet
his bored eyes were obscene
on his denimed thighs a magazine
i wish he'd never come here with me
in fact i wish he'd never come near me
i wish his shoulder wasn't touching mine
i am growing older waiting in this line
but some of life's best lessons
are learned at the worst times
under the fierce flourescent
she offered her hand for me to hold
she offered stability and calm
and i was crushing her palm
through the pinch pull wincing
my smile unconvincing
on that sterile battlefield that sees
only casualties
never heros
my heart hit absolute zero
lucille, your voice still sounds in me
mine was a relatively easy tragedy
the profile of our country
looks a little less hard-nosed
but that picket line persisted
and that clinic has since been closed
they keep pounding their fists on reality
hoping it will break
but i don't think there's a one of them
who leads a life free of mistakes

Ani DiFranco, "the million you never made"

the air comes off the ocean
the city smells fishy
the air is full of fish and mystery
whispering who? what? when?
i'm warning you i'm weightless
and the wind is always shifting
so don't hang anything on me
if you ever want to see it again
i'm telling you i'm different
than you think i am

and you can dangle your carrot
but i ain't gonna reach for it
'cuz i need both my hands
to play my guitar
and life is a sleazy stranger
who looks vaguely familiar
flirting with a bimbo named disaster
at the end of the bar
and i'm telling you that i'm different
than you are

at night when you're asleep
self hatred's going to creep in
you can blame it on the devil
(the one who's bed you sleep in)
don't tell me what they did to you
as though you had no choice
isn't that your picture?
isn't that your voice?
if you don't live what you sing about
your mirror is going to find out

yeah, i'd like to go to all the pretty parties
where all the pretty people go
and i ain't really all that pretty
but nobody will know
'cuz everybody loves you
when you're a star
and nobody questions
what it takes to go that far
life is a sleazy stranger
and this is his favorite bar

and no i don't prefer obscurity
but i'm an idealistic girl
and i wouldn't work for you
no matter what you paid
i may not be able
to change the whole fucking world
but i can be the million
that you never made

yeah i could be the million
that you never made

you're looking at the million
that you never made

Nanci Griffith, "Down 'N' Outer"

I once was a lot like you
We share a dream I couldn't make come true
I was a child who wrote my name
across a frosted window pane

And there are jobs that I might hold
if they'd just let me through the door
without a shower and new clothes
that I can ill afford

(Chorus)
Can you spare the time?
Can you spare a dime?
Can you look me in the eye?
I'm down 'n' out
and I am lonely
Do you ever think of me on
Sunday?
No. I don't live
across the water
Hey, I live right here
on this corner
. . . just a bank account away from
America
I won't hurt your family
I don't want a house there on your street
And I know you think that I'm . . .
as lazy as a hobo's sigh
Now, you call me down 'n' outer
if there's a way out . . .
I've not found 'er
I only want to earn my piece of America

I'm just a bank account away from
America

Indigo Girls, "It's Alright"
Written by Emily Saliers

it's alright forty days of rain
my skin stretched out from the growing pain

it'd be nice to have an explanation
but it's alright

and it's alright if you hate that way
hate me cause i'm different
you hate me cause i'm gay
truth of the matter come around one day
so it's alright

i look at this lifeline stretched way all across my hand
i look at the burned out empty like a plague across the land
and for everything i learn there are two i don't understand
that's while i'm still on a search
through the weather strewn church
i'm doing the best that i can
and it's alright

and it's alright though we worry and fuss
(alright)
we can't get over the hump or get over us
(we can't get over us)
it seems easier to push than to let go and trust
(alright)
but it's alright

when we get a little distance some things get clearer
yeah give em the space some hearts grow nearer
i ran as hard as i could i still ended up here
but it's alright

as i look at this lifeline stretched way all across my hand
(lifeline all across my hand)
i look at the fires of hatred
(fire)
burning up the bounty of this beautiful land
(burning up the land)
i know that i'm small in a way but i know i'm strong
and it's my thirst that brought me to the water
well i give it all up then she carries me on
it's alright

yeah

and it's alright if i feel afraid
my plans in pieces
my plans mislaid

it's the will of the way
(the will of the way)
the will of the way
(it's the will of the way)
the will of the only way that could have brought me here today
and it's alright

and it's alright

Suzanne Vega, "Song of Sand"

If sand waves were sound waves
What song would be in the air now
What stinging tune
Could split this endless noon
And make the sky swell with rain

If war were a game that a man or a child
Could think of winning
What kind of rule
Can overthrow a fool
And leave the land with no stain.

Chapter 2

"I'm Not the Only One Who Has Felt Like This": Identification and Appropriation

Nineteen-year-old Mary is of slender build, timid and speaks with a slight lisp. She conveyed several moving stories that are present in the pages of this book. Interestingly, Mary often responded with a quick "I don't know" to questions during the course of the interview. Almost as a lack of confidence or as though she were searching for some sort of "right" answers. It took a little more prodding and asking similar questions in different ways to get her to share her stories. Fortunately, she opened up and she divulged some telling stories. An elementary education major, Mary's piqued interest in female artists' music had only commenced a year before the interview. She latched onto music her first semester at college, spending a lot of time in her room alone. Music was her friend, maybe her only one on campus. Her CD purchases were on the rise. She studied the lyrics, trying to decipher the underlying meaning and mapping them on to her life. Her list comprised the most Top 40, pop and country artists when compared to the other respondents, yet she was also one of the few who used the adjective "feminist" when describing the type of artists she was drawn to. McLachlan and Lilith Fair changed her life—made her stronger—and she expected only more of the same, as she grew older, more independent and less reliant on parental permission.

Journalist Victoria Brownsworth (1995/1999) writes about Jill Sobule's 1995 hit "I Kissed a Girl" in the *Philadelphia Daily News*, "It no doubt will change the lives of thousands of young lesbian and bisexual girls. . . . The positive affirming message would have helped me and my queer friends when we were teens" (p. 287). This quote concisely illustrates exactly what this chapter is about: music affirming women's lives. Music can act as a great resource for women, particularly music that is feminist or politically inclined. Considering women's experiences have, and continue to be, largely dismissed in the broader culture, music by women, telling stories about women's lives, provides a release and validation for female fans. The experience of engaging with the music is only heightened when specific lyrics ring particularly true for the female fan. And the respondents' excerpts below certainly attest to this. These women clearly identified with female artists and reveled in the more representative and diverse portrayal they provided as opposed to the more patriarchal-dominated attempts. The respondents' reactions are arguably similar to what Douglas (1993, 1994) argued about the Shirelles' 1960 hit "Will You Love Me Tomorrow." With a woman as the protagonist, songs provide an opportunity for women to identify with a song as opposed to merely being the subject of a song from a male perspective. The inspired 1970s women's movement folk scene, with "music by, for and about women," also provided moments of heightened experiences for female listeners. In all of these instances, women are drawn to the text because it is more representative of women's lives. And with music that embodies a feminist sensibility, the experience is further intensified for some women.

The women who participated in this study clearly identified with the music of female artists. They felt their experiences as women were affirmed and validated. Some women have even used music to help form their own sense of identity. Similar to what Tetzlaff (1994) writes, rock is a "vehicle by which fans and artists have attempted to work against their institutionalized position" (p. 113). These women appropriate music to help them cope with life, whether in intimate relationships, fighting depression, working through past abuse or dealing with their sexual orientation. Women felt empowered and their lives strengthened. Female artists' music, music that privileges the stories of women, acts as a tool for women to resist cultural hegemony. More so, not only does music by women provide a space for women to engage and celebrate in narratives about women, but music also works in a very real way for these women in the formation of identity. As Frith (1997) writes in "Music and Identity," "[M]usic seems to be a key to identity because it offers, so intensely, a sense of self and others" (p. 110). "Our experience of music . . . is best understood as an experience of this *self-in-process*" (p. 109).

Women's descriptions of identifying with and their appropriation of female artists' music emerged into several delineated categories. All of these themes serve to answer the research question, "What does female artists' music mean in women's lives?" As you continue to read and as I have mentioned previously, by the very nature of talk, one will find many sections that harken back to themes drawn out previously or that may even foreshadow themes to be detailed later in this chapter. This is pointed out in most instances.

The following pages detail some in-depth, moving and intimate stories of the way respondents appropriate music into their lives. With this in mind, it is important to take note that women use music in simpler terms than is presented in the bulk of this chapter. For example, women use music to create or enhance a particular mood:

Patricia: I'm a marathon runner, so the *Rocky* theme song will get me pumped.

Julie: [My roommate and I] woke up and we put in Deana Carter and that was just because it was upbeat and we needed to get going and get motivated for morning.

Terri: I listen to music based on my mood. . . . And if it's mellow, then sometimes I'll look at it, I'm like, "oh, that's too mellow," I'm feeling more upbeat, I want like the partying kind of mood, and then I'll stick in Hole, and some more dudes. So it's mood-dependent.

Paige: [I like] Sade—her *Love Deluxe* CD. There's some songs on Fiona [Apple]'s that just—they'll put you in the mood for sex.

Elisabeth: [I]f you're in a romantic mood . . . well, we [my partner and I] really like that new k.d. lang CD, *Drag*. That's really good. And if I'm cleaning house I want to put Melissa Etheridge on or something like that. It just kinda depends on what mood you're in and what mood you want to be in. . . . I definitely use [music] to create a different mood.

Although the way women use music to create a romantic or upbeat mood is germane information, this project is an effort to look further than these more surface constructions by women about their relationship to music. This project focuses on ponderous stories and life experiences that are told in-depth.

"YES!" IDENTIFICATION, AFFIRMATION, VALIDATION AND EMPOWERMENT

Women certainly talk about having a strong connection to female artists' music. Women are attracted to artists because they can identify with them or relate to particular artists. These women shared very detailed stories about how they apply, depend on and appropriate music by women into their everyday lives. Again, certainly not every woman's sense of identifying with an artist contained a great deal of depth. Sometimes women described simple reasons for identifying with a particular artist. For example, Lisa talked about relating to Melissa Etheridge and the Indigo Girls because they are all in relationships and their individual jobs entail a lot of traveling:

I'd like to talk to [Melissa's life-partner] Julie [Cypher] and find out how she handles Melissa traveling. I'd like to know how the Indigo Girls handle traveling all the time. Because I [travel]. And they've been in and out of the relationships, so how do they do it? . . . [I]f I'm going to hang out with somebody, it's going to be somebody I can relate to. (Lisa)

And Sandi, a short person herself, finds a certain satisfaction in Cheryl "Salt" James's (of female rap duo Salt 'n Pepa) and Ani DiFranco's similar limited stature. "I just think [Salt and Ani DiFranco] are fab. They're like five foot two. So being a short person [myself]—it was like, 'Yeah!' Not everybody is six feet tall" (Sandi).

Beyond this sort of more obvious oriented way of women identifying with or relating to artists, one critical area that emerged was that women's experience with artists and/or their music provided a certain amount of support for invested listeners. Women talked about feeling less alone in their emotions and life experiences. These women declared that female artists' music helped them to feel validated, justified, affirmed and empowered. Jane's explanation is somewhat comprehensive of this theme. "[When I identify with a song I feel a sense of s]elf-affirmation. 'Oh, you felt that way also.' That it just gives you a justification that your emotions have validation" (Jane). These same sentiments resonate in the examples below from Sandi, Lisa, Jill and Patricia.

Identification and Appropriation

Sandi talks about feeling a sense of affirmation through a Salt 'n Pepa song—feeling reaffirmed in her desire to challenge men. "I always feel like I'm argumentative with men—then to hear songs, where it's like, 'yeah I am, so what.' It's not like, 'I'm picking a fight with you.' It's like, 'I'm just not gonna take it.' So it was kind of reaffirming" (Sandi). Strong, assertive women are erroneously often labeled as pushy or bitchy. They are a threat to patriarchy, and in part because of this labeling, some women tend to avoid standing up for themselves. But through Salt 'n Pepa's music, personae and attitude, Sandi draws strength from their forwardness and strength to stand up for herself despite the potential for her to be labeled "bitch."

When Lisa talks about the importance of music in her life, she expresses a certain amount of validation when she feels an affinity with a song and therefore less alone in the experience of her feelings. "[Music] validates what you're thinking. To know I'm not the only one who has felt like this.... [It's] kinda letting you know you're not alone, other people have felt like this, whether it's good or bad or anything in between. You see? I'm not the first one to go through this. It's okay" (Lisa).

Similarly, Jill talks about the relief she feels at an Ani DiFranco concert because she perceives a sense of validation in who she is and what she feels and experiences. Feeling at times outside of the dominant culture or oppressed by it, Jill enjoys an Ani DiFranco concert because it provides a space for her own self-expression around and with people "who are like her." She feels a sense of freedom to express herself without the risk of social ramifications. In Chapter 3, I write more about the concert scene.

Ani [DiFranco]'s shows are so full of energy. I mean we're on our feet the entire time dancing around and screaming and singing along. It gets back to that whole freedom thing. "Ahhh, finally yes." I can let loose and someone hears my pain here. Someone hears what I am talking about and understands and I can scream about it and jump up and down and won't get this look like "where are you coming from." Because they all get it. (Jill)

Similarly, Patricia feels a certain affinity with some of her favorite female artists, experiencing both power and a certain amount of relief when discovering she must be "pretty normal" when comparing the multiple facets she views as a part of her personality and comparing that to some of her favorite artists.

Melissa Etheridge . . . Tracy Chapman . . . I love Paula Cole and of course Sarah McLachlan and Jewel. Kate Bush, I really like her music. . . . Sheryl Crow, Tori Amos . . . [And] I think [I'm attracted to them because] . . . in my mind they're emotionally strong—just listening to the music is very powerful. . . . [And] they're really diverse. They're on both sides of the spectrum. And I guess it reminds me of me. That on any given day the pendulum can swing [from] bitch! [to] bad mood [to] unhappy [to] mad [to] crying. [There's a] huge pendulum swing. And it's so neat, "Wow, I must be pretty normal." That other people can experience that too. (Patricia)

Similar to Patricia, Lisa and Terri also talk about feeling empowered through female artists and their music. Lisa is a busy, upper-class, 40-year-old business professional. She's serious and to the point. Lisa reflects back 20 years and cites Helen Reddy's 1970s hit "I Am Woman" as complementing her first taste of independence.

[My earliest meaningful memory of listening to a female artist is] Helen Reddy, "I Am Woman." . . . I was in college, probably about nineteen years old and kind of flapping my wings for the first time and having some sense of independence because I went away to school. [And] that song was YES! I got that album and I was home for the summer and my brothers would tease me all the time because I'd be playing it, and the more they teased me the louder I turned it up. (Lisa)

Helen Reddy's "I Am Woman" gave Lisa an extra boost and incited her exploration of self and looking beyond what the mainstream, traditional media and even familial outlets were encouraging. Her courage and revelry to play the song even louder within her home clarified for her that the political is indeed personal.

In the following two excerpts, Terri's comments complement many of the sentiments detailed earlier. First, similar to both Patricia and Lisa, Terri talks about how she feels empowered by some of her favorite artists and their music because of their in-your-face attitude.

[Some of my favorites are] Indigo Girls, Tori Amos. I like Liz Phair for like, the attitude. Millions of them. Ani DiFranco, too, for the attitude, and lyrics, and [the] "fuck you" kind of attitude. And maybe it's because I don't necessarily feel it all the time, and it just feels empowering to listen to some of her songs. (Terri)

Terri, often feeling contained by the dominant culture and wanting to disrupt the dominant perceptions of normalcy, prefers artists that appear braver because in some instances they've fought against the gender boundaries of rock and roll and society in general and have succeeded.

In this second excerpt, and similar to Patricia, Terri identifies with an Alanis Morissette song because it is exemplary of a multitude of sides to one's personality. Through this song, Terri feels a sense of relief and affirmation for being a person with what she views as many sides to her personality.

But I do like [Alanis Morissette's] "Hand in My Pocket." I love that song. . . . I can identify with [the lyrics]. She's talking about contradictions within herself. And I am a walking contradiction. And the multiple personalities—I heard that song, the first time, it just made me smile, because, it's like, yes! Why do you have to be one thing? Why can't you be a million things rolled into one? And not even be consistent about it. (Terri)

Similar to feeling a sense of empowerment through music by women, some women, including Terri, Sandi, Jo and Mary, even describe having used music, usually songs in particular, as an agent in their own personal development of self. The music becomes a tool for these women in the formation of their identity. The songs are positioned in such a way that invites listeners to map their experiences onto a song. Terri, Jo and Mary talk specifically about instances of using music at relatively critical times in the development of their individual identities.

Terri spoke specifically about how Tori Amos's "Silent All These Years" and "Precious Things" helped her to find her voice, independence and autonomy as a young woman.

Tori Amos, when she first came out with hers [Amos's first album] . . . "Silent All These Years" was one [song]. And it was when I was struggling to find my voice, and I still didn't have one. And then there was that line [in "Precious Things"]—I love lyrics. "So you can make me cum, that doesn't make you Jesus." And I was just like, you know, fuck those guys! I don't need a man in my life. And it was like, a time trying to find my autonomy, my independence, and the lyrics really helped me. (Terri)

Similar to both Patricia and Terri, Sandi also contends that there are many attributes to her personality and discovers empowerment by finding various, complementary characteristics in some of her favorite female artists. She even describes it in terms of actually "add[ing] this other sense of identity" (Sandi). In fact, as the excerpt below suggests, Sandi actually sees these artists as an extension of her own identity.

It's a little bit of an empowerment thing. A little bit like—"well there, okay"—like Ani DiFranco is sort of quirky and feisty and whatever. So it's like, okay—so that gives me that sense of—I can be quirky and I can be feisty—and that's something that we can share. Maybe not really but, ya know, "I understand—it's okay—that's part of who people are." And then Nanci Griffith is mellow and pensive. Just thinking about life and time and telling stories. And it's all—"ya know I can be pensive and think about stories." I can have part of that. And then—Sarah Vaughan—I can be beautiful and I can be—I don't even know what the words are—like, "smooth." Whatever that feeling is. They all add this other sense of identity—that you could have all of these things. (Sandi)

Sandi derives satisfaction from the availability of different styles of female artists. She identifies with elements of each that validate who she is.

These women derive a sense of validation, affirmation and empowerment from female artists, their lyrical narratives, their style and their music. For them, the artists justify who they are—all of the sides of their personality. In a few instances the impact that music by women has on female listeners' lives is quite considerable. Jo and Mary shared some exemplary life stories in depth.

Jo first recognized a connection to female artists' music during her early twenties when she was drawn to the Indigo Girls in particular. It was at this time that Jo was dealing with issues surrounding relationships and becoming independent. Through the Indigo Girls' music, Jo gained a sense of validation and a sense of feeling less alone. Furthermore, Jo's comment about "feeling free" echoes comments earlier in this chapter made by Jill and her experience of "letting loose" at an Ani DiFranco concert.

The Indigo Girls, just the whole period of what was going on in my life at the time. [Their music] just helped me kind of get through everything. It seemed like every time they came out with something it just helped—it

Identification and Appropriation

spoke right to whatever was going on in my life. So that was very helpful. . . . [It was during my early twenties when] I was dealing with relationship stuff, the way I was feeling, becoming independent. [Listening to the music and] feeling free and beginning to feel like who I am now and beginning to [become] . . . who I am now. [The Indigo Girls] were the beginning of—making, feeling free and . . . becoming who I am now. [Their music and that they] were strong women . . . I [began to] realize other women were out there that were somewhat like me. And I was like, "cool." Which kind of validated who I was and I kind of thought, "oh it's okay to be this weird." Cool, there are other people like me, I'm not a freak. They kind of validated my feelings. (Jo)

Mary's use of music in forming her own identity is quite unique. Nineteen-year-old Mary talks about two different occasions in which music really influenced her in the development of her self-esteem and identity. The first example that Mary describes is focused on issues of self-esteem. Mary felt that she wasn't good enough to be treated well. Yet in Sarah McLachlan's song "Good Enough," she negotiated the song in such a way as to help her realize that she is good enough to be treated well.

I guess a big one would be Sarah McLachlan's "Good Enough." I don't know if I can even explain this. I don't know if I can put it into words—what [the song] means [to me]. I guess all through junior high and high school—I never had a lot of friends all through high school. And the self-esteem thing had been kind of low until I got out of school. And before I started dating my boyfriend, we had tried dating—it just didn't work out. . . . I guess I never felt like I was ever good enough—and it makes me think about how—either I wasn't good enough, good to other people, or they haven't been good enough to treat me better. . . . ["Good Enough"] just relaxes me, it makes me feel good. It makes me realize I am good enough, people are good to me. Like, me and my boyfriend—people are good enough to treat me right and I treat them right. (Mary)

Although McLachlan's "Good Enough" centers on spousal abuse, Mary appropriates the song, perhaps unknowingly, in such a way that it is specifically meaningful for her. Through the song, she derives the courage to noticeably improve her self-esteem and demand that others treat her "good enough." Mary's second exemplar is also framed around Sarah McLachlan. Mary talks about actually changing her family's perception of her for one of the first times. During a family get-together, people took notice of her Lilith Fair concert t-shirt and questioned her about it. In response, Mary talked about her interest in female artists' music, her experience at the all-female Lilith Fair concert and the meaning behind both. Right before her family's eyes she exerted her individuality, described herself as a feminist and displayed her independence—to family members who had not seen this side of her ever before. Toward the end of this extended excerpt and similar to Jill's comments about attending a DiFranco concert and Jo's remarks about the Indigo Girls' music, Mary also describes her attendance at the Lilith Fair as experiencing a sense of freedom.

I haven't really talked to my family about it [my interest in music by women], but a couple of weeks ago I had a party at my aunt's house and I wore my Lilith Fair t-shirt. And I think I really astonished everyone. They asked me about it and I think it shocked them how much I knew. How I portrayed my feelings about women's music. How I believe in equality. I was explaining all this to them. I think they saw that I really am an adult now and I'm not just some silly teenage girl who loves music, that I actually can understand it, that it's more than just songs. . . . It started when they asked me [about the] picture of Lilith on [my t-shirt]. They asked me what it was. And they asked me who Lilith was and I explained it to them. And they were all like, "Okay—she's turning into some women's lib person"— and I have to admit, I am, after . . . [attending] the Lilith Fair. Realizing the urge for equality for women—that's all the Lilith Fair. And then I started telling them more about Sarah McLachlan and how she is an absolutely phenomenal talent. . . . And they were just really impressed because everyone in my family is musical. . . . And I think it just really astonished [them]—because I've always been the one to just hold back from music, because I'm not the most musically talented person in the world. But I think when I was telling them about Lilith Fair and telling them about Lilith and Sarah McLachlan—I think they saw a different person, which I'm really glad they finally got, get to see. They would be surprised at what a different person I am. And I think music has a lot to do with it. Especially the Lilith Fair. . . . And it just really made me think and realize that I do—even though I've never really thought about it before—but women really do need to be treated equal. . . . But, the Lilith Fair, I don't know, it just made me think actually. [And] I told them, that according to mythology—Lilith was Adam's first wife and she wanted to be treated equal to him and he didn't like it so he basically left her behind and then, Eve came along. [And I told them that the Lilith Fair] was a concert of all female artists—celebrating women in music and [to] make a point about the fact that female artists are just as good and equal to male artists even though they seem to get less [support or] get lost in the shuffle—they're not as well known.... [That whole experience kind of] means independence and freedom [to me], because my parents did let me go to this concert in ... [a city three hours away, without an adult being with us]. They realized I am an adult. I can do these things and be okay. (Mary)

Although the fair's corporate sponsorship and lack of diversity was problematic, it is important to take careful note of the transformative feminist power the fair had on this young woman. Sarah McLachlan and many of the artists mentioned in this book involve themselves in feminist causes and more so than less so write, record and perform music that embodies a feminist and/or political sensibility. When their music becomes popularized, in part because of the success of Lilith Fair, the audience is broadened, and more people are exposed to feminist-themed music. Many may not have and may never have any exposure to feminist theory or literature, but because of the popularity of music by women, the number of people exposed to feminist messages multiplies. Although limited, for some women, attending Lilith Fair was transformative in very real and positive ways.

COPING THROUGH APPROPRIATION

The respondents not only identify with and feel empowered by music by women; they also use the artists' music as a coping mechanism, a tool for survival. Music is in fact a way of making sense of the world including our life conditions and ourselves. In efforts to make sense of their world, these women described various stories revolving around transitions and changes in their lives, including personal intimate relationships, fighting depression, working through past abuse and dealing with sexual orientation. Some of the women's stories are hopeful and encouraging; at the same time some of the stories are quite sad. Music helps women deal with sadness in their lives. This section of Chapter 2 details specific individual examples of how women actually apply and appropriate music to cope with life. The themes of women identifying with music and feeling a sense of validation, affirmation and empowerment and the formation of one's identity are not exclusive to the section above. These topics will recur in other forms and as supportive comments in the themes detailed below.

Women appropriate music in a variety of ways to help them cope. As Terri commented, "I listen to songs to help me get through what I'm going through.... I want to stick in my CDs, I want to cry about them, I want to jam to them, I want to work out to them, and I want them to mean that to me, for me, all the time" (Terri).

Jo describes how she uses particular artists for different reasons. To vent she uses Melissa Etheridge; she finds comfort in Sarah McLachlan's music, and she uses Tori Amos's music to deal with "emotional stuff," particularly from her childhood.

[When] I need to vent—[Melissa Etheridge] helps me do it. I don't even just sit and listen to her. I have to be screaming along with her. So she helps me get through emotional stuff.... Sarah [McLachlan] I turn her on to console myself. Tori Amos definitely when I'm going through emotional stuff. When I'm re-living, when I'm working on something from my childhood, I usually turn on Tori Amos because it's all about digging all that crap up. And I think I turn her on when I really want to, when I'm working on me, I turn Tori Amos on. When I'm really working on figuring out something about me or something that I feel needs work, Tori Amos is the one I turn on. (Jo)

Vivian cites specific songs to indicate how she uses music to deal with the pressures of life. She refers to Juliana Hatfield's "Nirvana" and Sleater-Kinney's "Call the Doctor" as providing her with support when dealing with life issues. Soft-spoken yet confident, Vivian is clear that these female artists' ability to share their experiences helps her to cope with hers.

There's a particular song by Juliana Hatfield—it's called "Nirvana" and I guess she's having a bad day or something, but then she's like—into the song—"I am so glad I am not dead" or whatever. I am like, "yeah, me too." And, sometimes like dealing with society. There's a song by Sleater-Kinney called "Call the Doctor." [They sing about being socialized.] I am like "Yeah, I know about that too."... [Sometimes] I'm like—"that's exactly how I feel."... And also, like the problems that I go through and that other people go through, them expressing it to me kind of helps me—they express that and it helps them. (Vivian)

Despite life's challenges, Hatfield's "Nirvana" helps Vivian to embrace life, while her use of Sleater-Kinney's "Call the Doctor" is a clear attempt of hers, and with help from the song, to be resistant toward dominant culture. Vivian referred repetitively to the descriptor "pro-girl" as the type of artists that she's drawn to, including P.J. Harvey. All have empowered her politically and emotionally. Music by women is important to these female listeners. They very specifically identify with particular songs and/or artists and use the music as a tool to get through troubles in their daily lives.

"We Do Not Grow Up with a Cinderella Life": Negotiating Intimate Relationships

One of the areas women talked most about was identifying with a song or using music to help them deal with particular relationship issues. Generally speaking, when women associate with music (as well as films or novels, for that matter), sometimes it is in reference to love relationships, a very much perceived "feminine" topic and therefore also often dismissed. Some may wish to still perceive it this way, but there is a difference between "dreamy idyllic romance" and women's real relational struggles in their everyday lives. Certainly, the women shared some stories of their enjoyment in this idyllic presentation of romance in some of the songs, but many more of the stories are about the toil and negotiation involved with relationships. Regardless and, as I noted earlier, even if an artist is predominantly concerned about relationships and emotions, it is important to note that "these areas [are] of central concern to women and important sources of women's oppression" (Roberts, 1996, p. 137).

Although the majority of the stories told by the women are about empowerment and latching onto a feminist message, many struggle with the dominant culture's prescription of romance, finding love and living happily ever after. Women straddle and work to negotiate the line between being an independent woman and falling in love with a man. Patricia, 34 years old and heterosexual, sensing familial and social pressure to have a family, talked about how Pam Tillis's "All the Good Ones Are Gone" genuinely reflects what she was experiencing in her life at the time. Her life story in relation to this song is within the context of her talking to a friend about music. Her friend Janice is sympathetic to her situation. Patricia's sharing of this experience with Janice foreshadows a later section in Chapter 3 that focuses on women's connection with friends and music.

My girlfriend [female friend] Janice and I talk about [female artists' music] a lot.... "You've got to hear this song. It's [this] 'push, go away, no wait a minute, stay here' thing.' It's so us." And there's a country song about a woman who's 34 and she goes out with her girlfriends for the weekend to drink and celebrate her birthday and her mother calls the morning of her birthday and wishes that she had a family of her own. And she says, "Mom it's not that easy." The song starts with [something like] "I turned thirty-four today or this weekend" [sic] and [the song] ended that way—there's nothing resolved; that's just the way it is. I never thought I'd be here at thirty-four—and take a look; here I am. We don't all grow up with a Cinderella life. We experience the Cinderella syndrome—"Why am I not married; there's something wrong with me." "I'm not married, I haven't found my prince and life isn't happy." We talk about that. It's pretty funny. It's just like, "Oh god, I can't believe I'm thirty-four"—it's like, when did that happen? I think that song also says, "was I too picky? Did I wait too long?" [sic] ... And I guess this is all normal. Because we were brought up to believe, I was, in a Catholic home—you grow up, you get married, you have 2.5 children and live happy ever after, the end. And ooh, my life is so not there. So I guess it's pretty normal. We both can relate. She's twenty-eight, I think Janice, and she, ya know, it's like, "oh there's a cute boy, oh look at him." Eh, I'm not interested, I'm never looking, I'm never going out again. It's just so funny, it's just hilarious, it's just hilarious. And I think the media promotes—that there's something wrong with us if we're not in a relationship. And we all know that two half people don't make a whole relationship; there have to be two whole people and the more and more I learn ... the more I do that, the more I come to believe that there aren't a lot of healthy men out there. Like last night, this is hilarious, last night we were talking about it, somebody at the [horse] stable said, "Oh, have you met Michael?" And Michael is a new trainer—and Janice said, "No." And we were firing questions, "How old is he? What's he look like? Does he like to dance?" "What kind of—" Because Janice wants somebody that can dance and wears baseball caps.... So we were asking about—"Is he married? What's the matter with him, is he gay?" Because they're either married or gay or stuck on their mothers. "Hey, that's it, we'll love each other," and then eh—they're stuck on their mothers. It was hilarious. And the poor man doesn't have a chance. Not a chance. I'm like, "Is he pear shaped?" We were just bombarding this women with questions. And that whole song about being thirty something and not being married just cracks me up.... We can relate to her, I guess. (Patricia)

Identification and Appropriation

Patricia struggles with social assumptions that women *naturally* marry and have children. She even identifies it as the "Cinderella syndrome." Having a song that mirrors her real-life experience facilitates her seeing through this romance myth. Because of the song's relevance to her life, she comes away feeling less alone and is better able to cope with being over 30 and single in a culture that prescribes marriage for happiness. She and her friend Janice acquire a feeling of not being alone in this circumstance and feeling "okay" about being single.

Many women, including Jo, Terri and Patricia, identified with, turned to or appropriated music when their personal intimate relationships were not going well or even during the course of a breakup. Jo cites Melissa Etheridge's "Watching You" as a song that helped her deal with breakups. Again, similar to Patricia, she had a friend who related to the song as well. Jo even goes as far in her description of the moment as actually "sharing the pain with Melissa."

I think Melissa [Etheridge] is really cool and one of the lines that I keep thinking of is the one that has helped me through things—when you're coming out of relationships and someone says, "Oh, you'll get over it," and that's the last thing you want to hear because you don't want to get over it. You want it to go on forever. I remember driving my truck with a friend of mine, who was going through relationship stuff, we were both going through relationship stuff, and those lines from ["Watching You" about not wanting to love someone that you can't]. Those kinds of things. And sharing the pain with Melissa. (Jo)

Terri cites the Indigo Girls' "Love Will Come To You" as a song that she identified with and also suggested that the song helped her deal with her past troubled relationships with men and the yearning she felt still looking for that so-called perfect relationship often portrayed in Hollywood films.

When *Rites of Passage* came out, the song . . . "Love Will Come to You." That song came out, and it was at a time where I'd been out of a relationship for a little while, and I was just mourning my knight in shining armor. I turned twenty-five, did a married man, and, the line that "closing my eyes, wishing I'm fine, even though I'm not this time." And just knowing I'm not okay this time. I can't shrug it off. This hurts worse than being able to just go out and date somebody else. And just like letting go of that knight in shining armor, and just questioning. Those lyrics were awesome. (Terri)

In reference to relationships breaking up, Patricia spoke in detail about an emotionally wrought and poignant story. Patricia, who interestingly enough made reference to a Tracy Chapman song about battered women during the interview, was in a relationship with an abusive man but was able to escape the throws of his control. One day she got on a plane, leaving everything behind, and literally took off. As the plane pulled out of the runway, Patricia placed her headphones on her head and heard Sarah McLachlan sing, "Hold on, hold on to yourself, for this is gonna hurt like hell." Although the song is about a man dying of AIDS, Patricia appropriated this song to help her get through this traumatic time in her life. Again, many of the sentiments shared by Patricia in this extended excerpt resonate with many of the themes throughout this chapter and Chapter 3. Patricia, in her own words:

Sarah McLachlan's "Hold on, hold on to yourself, this is going to [sic] hurt like hell." That [song is] "Whoa!" [for me]. Really powerful for me. I was losing a relationship last November. A very abusive relationship and I literally ran away. Packed everything I owned, got on a plane and put on my headphones. And [when] we were backing out of the airport so we could get on the runway, that song came on. And I was going away from him and it was hurting, but it was the healthiest thing I could do at the time. The only thing I knew to do at the time. And it was just like, "Wow, she's there." And she was there for me, so I bonded with her. And I take things personally, both good and bad—and sometimes it sounds like they [female artists] are able to—like Sarah McLachlan is able to articulate my feelings better than I can. And sometimes the women I like and their music—they can more eloquently say what I'm feeling. Or help me become aware of what I'm feeling through their music. "Wow, this is why I'm so upset." I try to deny my feelings and pretend I'm not feeling them. "This is the best thing to do, this is the best thing to do, you have to do this. Just run, keep going." And that song just allowed me to stop and in the moment and say, "Okay, ya know what, this is hurting but I've got to do it anyway." Sarah is very, very calming to me. . . . [And] every time I've heard [that song] now, I go back there—there I am on that plane, going, "Wow, was I crazy. Wow, was that a tumultuous relationship or what. I can't believe I allowed this person to just absolutely control my life." And so, when I hear it, it's still painful because I go immediately right back into that [space]. . . . Thank god, I made it through, and here I am. (Patricia)

Identification and Appropriation

Despite the trauma of one of her recent relationships, and recognizing she did the right thing, Patricia still identifies with Paula Cole's "I Am So Ordinary" about the "want" to still be "his girl."

> [Paula Cole's] song "[I Am So] Ordinary." I think she [the female protagonist in the song] was a girlfriend of a man and he was taking a new girlfriend in the motorcycle seat. She sees them driving down the street—in the motorcycle seat that was meant for her.... [And] she's so ordinary. That's like, "Wow, that relates to me." ... I'm never gonna have another boyfriend. And it's just like, "Oh man, that sucks"—but she still loves him and wants to be there for him and she'll take whatever she can get. [It's] really, really poignant. (Patricia)

For all of the women, finding a song that mapped onto their own relationship experiences helps them to justify their feelings. In a society where romance novels, soap operas and "chick flicks" are devalued and dismissed, while detective novels, murder mysteries and actions films are valued, women are compelled to think their emotions are silly and unimportant—when in fact they are very real. Songs that ring true to women's experiences alter and affirm women's lives. Through female artists' music, women find they are not alone. When women talked about appropriating songs, talking about personal, intimate relationships was most common. But women also appropriated songs into their lives to cope with other life issues as well.

Fighting Depression

Several women talked about appropriating songs to cope with depression. There were several instances when women, including Julie, Paige, Sandi and Sue, talked about how they use music to pull themselves out of depression or to continue to wallow in it. Their experience with music here is not really about empowerment necessarily, as it is in other parts of the book, but more about having a musical companion when dealing with sorrow. Julie indicated that Sarah McLachlan's "Black" is a song that she turns to when she is depressed and wants to stay depressed. Julie listened to the song quite a bit the previous year when she was going through some personal changes. She played the song repetitively and committed the lyrics to memory.

When I'm really depressed [I listen to] Sarah McLachlan['s] "Black." [It's] off the *Solace* CD, track 8. I'm surprised it still plays. I had a really bad year last year, a really tough year—it was not fun. ["Black"] keeps me feeling depressed when I'm in the mood to feel depressed. I just—because the way she wrote it, the lyrics and the music that she uses and it's just—the lyrics are, "As the walls are closing in, and the colors fade to black, and my eyes are falling fast and deep into me, and if I cried me a river of all my confessions would I drown in my shallow regret." And it's just a real dark, black, awful depressing song. (Julie)

Paige, admitting that she suffers from depression, spoke about how she uses music to help deal with bouts and even describes this process as "therapeutic." Paige selects music that matches her mood and in turn aids her in owning her overwhelming sadness.

I have a real problem with depression. So, sometimes I will just want to be in my room, turn on the music and I'll just sit there for an hour, a couple hours, and just listen to music. And it's just one of those things where it either—sometimes it almost makes me feel kind of worse—but at the same turn it almost makes you feel better because it's just—it's that "identifying with" factor that will make you feel better. I really don't know how to pinpoint it, but you are in the mood, you have the music that you know creates the mood, you are in that mood. And your whole atmosphere, you can really experience what you are feeling, I mean fully.... It's just you and the music and just the whole situation itself is therapeutic. (Paige)

Sandi, who also suffers from occasional bouts of depression, talks about how Shawn Colvin's "Suicide Alley" to some extent diverted her thoughts away from depression. She even used the song as a way to reach out to her cousin. Colvin's song challenges Sandi to resist thoughts of ending her life.

There's a couple of songs of [Shawn Colvin's], on her most recent one that I like. I was really depressed [and] okay, I liked "Suicide Alley." ... I was just really depressed. And the song was like, "don't go down suicide alley." Okay, alright, good song. I also have a cousin who is really—we have like depression in my family. She's only like 18 or 17. So I made a tape for her and I put the song on the tape. (Sandi)

Similarly, Sue became depressed after a friend's recent suicide. To help her cope with this tragedy, she would take time to listen to

Everything But the Girl's "Missing." Although Sue recognizes her choice to listen to a song that brings about sadness is problematic, she nevertheless is compelled to listen and finds the experience cathartic.

There's another [Everything But the Girl] song that is kind of masochistic for me to listen to, called "Missing." You've probably heard it. But, anyway, it's like sort of about missing someone who's moved away and they've been gone for a long time, and realizes "they could be dead, you've always been one step ahead" and all this and it's really sad, but there's this jazzy beat. And I lost a really good friend [Robert] last December, a friend from undergrad. . . . I would come back and visit Robert and his wife and their baby and stuff and stay at their house and they got a divorce and he ended up declaring bankruptcy and he had had cancer before that and the cancer came back and he had no money and no insurance and he was working at the [a very small town] Public Library in [small town], Ohio, with one blinking yellow light in the whole town, making peanuts, maybe five bucks an hour and I guess the cancer came back and on the fifth of last June, he killed himself. And it was just a really, really hard time. I was really depressed. . . . I can't like get Robert out of my head because we had a good friendship and I would call him up and talk to him about my problems and stuff and he was always like my big brother and I never had a clue he was even contemplating it. I didn't know anything was wrong. I hadn't talked to him in three months before he did it and that bothers me too, and it wasn't that I didn't try. I called. But he didn't call me back. I wonder what was going on. But I hear this song and I think of him and it's kind of really sad, but it's kind of cathartic at the same time. I might even cry when I'm listening to it and then I feel better. And it's like my private time, nobody knows I cried. (Sue)

This Everything But the Girl song goads Sue to face the tragedy of her friend's suicide. The song is so personal for her that she shares the experience with no one, and in some ways the song becomes a companion to her experience.

Dealing with Past Abuse

Some women, including Jo and Sue, talked about appropriating music to help deal with issues of abuse. When dealing with her emotional self and in particular her childhood, Jo turned to Tori Amos. As previously detailed, Jo has a great deal of respect for Amos as an artist and for her politics. Here Jo grasps on to Amos's music to affirm that she has a voice that deserves to be heard. Jo finds hope and comfort in Amos's ability and courage to address issues many are uncomfortable to make public.

Right now . . . I'm working on me. That's a huge thing. I have things that I don't remember from my own childhood—and then there's Tori Amos. I turn her on a lot to try to get back in touch with stuff. And I don't even know what it is about her—I don't think that I was sexually abused, but it's the same kind of thing, it's being shut up, being shut down, not having a voice. When I'm saying to myself, which I think is important, "It's okay. Speak. You're allowed. Blah, blah, blah, blah," I turn her on. . . . I just think she helps trigger more thoughts and more—in a pretty way. In a way that you're calm with. Not in an upsetting way. I do that with her. (Jo)

Sue also deals with issues of abuse through music. In this extended excerpt, Sue cites a song of confrontational avant-garde performer Diamanda Galas's: "Do You Take This Man." Sue connects with and feels empowered by the song when reflecting on an emotionally abusive father. Sue is empowered through the rage of this song.

And I like this song [by Diamanda Galas]—because my Dad was totally emotionally abusive to me. Especially to my Mom and my sister. And the song is called, "Do You Take This Man?" And she goes through the vows and [you hear] "I do" and it's like somebody being forced, like they're being strangled when they say it. And pretty much they stop after a few quick questions and it's like [a gasp for air] instead of "I do." It's like they are being strangled and she keeps saying to her husband, "I'm very disappointed in you." She sounds really evil. And she's like, "Husband with this knife, I take you out of this world"[sic], and all this stuff and I'm like, "Ohhhhhhh . . . woooo," and it's scary and there's all this wailing and then the ending part is the best where she says like, "I have to get up off of my knees, I have some shopping to do, and I have to think about my reputation and chump [is] not my name." The way she says it is really cool and then she adds, "and I'm your best friend darling [sic], I always have been [sic] and I always will be." She's [saying] I'm the best friend you could ask for and you fuckin' dicked me over and I'm the best friend you'll ever have because nobody will let you do this to them again. It's kind of threatening, but in a slight sense that she has a touch of love for this person. And it's like a really powerful kind of song. . . . It's really cool. It's empowering and at the same time way over the top. It's further than I ever go. But it's way less than some men deserve. You know what I mean? And you almost get a fear response inside. Like almost a tightening of the chest. Like she's making me shake in my boots. At the same time, it's like, "Go, girl," and I can totally understand that feeling and you are totally right there with her. (Sue)

Sue actually has visceral responses to this song. Having had to deal with verbal abuse from her father, Sue takes great satisfaction in the song's protagonist standing up to a man who has treated her unfairly. Sue comes away with a greater sense of justice.

Coming Out

Some women, including Jo, Elisabeth and Sandi, shared stories about how lesbian or bisexual artists' music and/or the artists themselves helped them deal with their own sexuality. In some ways, high-profile celebrities' revelations about their sexuality provides closeted lesbians an opportunity to think twice about the difficulties and strain from not divulging their true identity. Despite gay political gains, telling family members and coworkers about one's sexual identity remains a risk for most women. Furthermore, gay positive music, images and celebrities challenge stereotypes and help to change the public's perception of gays. Just as Jo referred to the Indigo Girls' music helping her in the development of her own identity earlier in this chapter, Jo gets more specific and points to Melissa Etheridge's coming out as having a big effect on her. Jo also refers to feeling as though "she belonged" at a Melissa Etheridge concert. This harkens back to other themes as well as foreshadows a future, more specific discussion about concerts and community later in Chapter 4.

Melissa Etheridge probably had the biggest effect on me of all the female artists.... I actually dated men in my late teens, early twenties, and Melissa Etheridge, somehow listening to her music and my whole coming out happened during her whole thing [coming out] and I was like, "Whoa."... [A]bout the same time she came out with "Yes I Am"—it was about the same time I told my family.... I remember going to concerts and looking around the audience going, "Oh cool, neat, this is a group of people I can identify with and I felt I belonged with." And I think she—she was there and sort of helped me bridge the, helped me go through the [whole coming-out process]. (Jo)

Elisabeth also feels an affinity with Melissa Etheridge and her coming-out process. Elisabeth's discussion of memories is another instance that foreshadows a future theme in Chapter 3.

When I was coming out [Melissa Etheridge] was the music I was listening to. [It was] 1993–4, somewhere around in there, so it hasn't been that long. And when I was figuring myself out, when I was in the process of telling other people, when I was going through the process of getting divorced and the whole deal, that was the music I was listening to and I don't know if it's true for everybody, but certainly music brings out memories for different parts of your life. And those were actually real happy memories of going, "Oh, so this is what the deal was." (Elisabeth)

Sandi identifies herself as bisexual and is particularly attracted to the work of bisexual Ani DiFranco. She makes mention of Ani DiFranco's "In or Out" and how the song helped her feel justified in her sexual orientation despite pressure to identify one way or the other from the straight and lesbian communities.

There's one [Ani DiFranco song] in particular about being bisexual. There is like a lot of pressure to identify [either straight or gay]—you have to be one or the other. And I'm just [living my life], go to work and get through my day. So I'm not ready to handle the pressure of—I can either never date men again, or I have to start dating women right now! All of them. Ya know what I mean. It feels like [there's] that [pressure] and then it is like— "I don't really date anybody that much, so why don't I just take baby steps here." So that was kind of nice to hear. (Sandi)

Furthermore, Sandi, as a bisexual, and therefore a person who feels a sexual and emotional attraction toward women, also feels an appreciation of lesbian artists, their music and their courage to be out. She identifies with their predicaments as lesbians and is encouraged that k.d. lang and Melissa Etheridge continue to have success even though they are publicly out. Again, she mentions her cousin and contemplates what these possibilities might mean for her as well.

I would say for myself that I'm bisexual, but not very good at it because I always date men. But then I like being around something [that says], "it's okay, it's okay." "It's alright to like, just really be attracted to whoever you're really attracted to." Ya know? And it's the same thing. It's like, any song that talks about relationships in terms that seem real to me is going to be more interesting. And it seems that in a general sense that Indigo Girls or Tracy Chapman or I don't know if k.d. lang really counts—these artists are—"Yeah, yeah, I could—that's just like life." Alright, so that's just like life, you two are lesbian, everything's working out okay, okay that's good. Okay that's good. It's reaffirming in some way. That it's positive. That they're talking about themselves and they are like, "We're alive, I'm not going to kill myself, I'm going to live. It's like, "alright." And that the performers themselves—I mean like, everybody knows about k.d. lang and Melissa Etheridge [being gay]—and they're still selling like crazy. So that's like, "wow." It's a fairly new thing for women, at least performers to be openly lesbian or in lesbian relationships—not just lesbian. You can know who their partner is. And that's okay. And they still do very well. So it is kind of like, "Alright!" So you can have an open lifestyle, so it's just sort of like, okay, I don't know what is going to happen with my future or with anyone else's, but it's nice to know that if I want to send my cousin a tape with a bunch of songs on it I can have a song in there "we're a lesbian couple, and we're okay." And she might hear it and she might go, "Ew." Or she might go, "Hhmm. Sandi, I've been thinking about something." Ya know what I mean. It's just more accepting. It's just more like, "That's like life." (Sandi)

Other Transitions and Challenges

Many women, including Terri, Lynn, Jo and Julie, had particular and important stories about appropriating female artists' music in their life as a coping mechanism during times of transition and challenge. Many spoke about using female artists' music for comfort or support during difficult life experiences. Again, some of the sentiments contained within the whole of the stories harken back to themes already fleshed out, and others foreshadow themes yet to come.

There are a series of stories told in this section. Terri describes how she used particular songs by women to help her recognize her need to move away from a dependency on men for validation and to find strength from within. Lynn, who talked frequently about being comforted by female artists' music, relied quite specifically on female artists' music during a transitional moment of her young life as she moved toward independence. Jo shared stories about how she found support in the music of Ani DiFranco during her employment at a male-dominated factory. Julie shared stories about dealing with the conflicting religious faiths of her parents, how music by women helped her get through what she identifies as "the most tumultuous week of my life" and finally how music is something she can depend on in what she perceives as an otherwise forever-changing life. Julie and her appropriation of music is provided in length and in detail in this section—in part because of Julie's troubled life, her sincere and deep reliance on female artists' music and her willingness to share those experiences in depth. All different and particular stories—all the negotiation and appropriation of music by women.

Similar to an earlier comment shared by Terri about Tori Amos's "Silent All These Years," Terri talks again about how she gained strength from Liz Phair's "Fuck and Run" and Tracy Chapman's "Fast Car" when she was coming into her own after having unfavorable experiences with men prior to this period of personal evolution. Phair's "Fuck and Run" lyrics describe herself waking up in a man's arms again, a too-familiar place she thought she would never be again.

Liz Phair's "Fuck and Run" just kind of summarized my undergraduate experience with men. And maybe it's like the relationship stuff that I can't talk about, or that I don't. . . . [And] Tracy Chapman, "Fast Car." I still get goose bumps when I listen to that song . . . just [having a feeling of] wanting to belong. And it was just that point before, oh, how can I explain it. It's like when you make up your mind to stop letting life happen to you and to make some decisions to actually do something for yourself, instead of. . . . I don't know, for me it was kind of this awakening time, around that time. It took several years. But music marked my journey. . . . I got strength from female artists' songs. (Terri)

Lynn talked frequently about how female artists' music provided comfort for her. In one instance she reflected on some recent life changes she has gone through during the course of the year before this interview. She graduated from college, the job market wasn't quite what she thought it would be and she had to move back to her hometown. As she describes it, it was "a really humbling year for me." She had to deal with "issues of independence, what am I going to do, [and] where am I going to go." When dealing with these recent events and others, Lynn finds herself turning to female artists' music.

[I]f the people that are in my life right now can't—not that they can't be supportive—but there's times that you want to be by yourself, or you're seeking "answers from within." It's like—there's these women artists are here, but they're not physically here, and at certain times that's what I need. Like someone to—like feeling like somebody's there—but obviously they're not present right then and so—like that's the kind of comfort that I need or the kind of guidance in a way that I need. And so that strengthens that relation—that bond with that artist. [And] it's very important [to me]. I think especially right now—within the past year it's been a big comfort to me because I've been going through all of these changes. Not that it helps me get through—it's not like I wouldn't get through without them—but it gives me some perspective on things. "Everything's going to be alright." Like Amy and Emily [of the Indigo Girls] are here hanging out with me and they're just like, "Lynn, it's going to be alright." Ya know what I'm saying? So I think that it's really important to me to have them. (Lynn)

Jo worked for several years as the first female in her supervisory position at a male-dominated factory. Jo was very clear in crediting Ani DiFranco and her music for helping her get through what she viewed as challenging times. Jo refers specifically to Ani DiFranco's song "Blood in the Boardroom." Similar to Terri and Lynn, Jo draws comfort, strength and support from female artists and their music.

Ani [DiFranco] was really strong. She got me through that whole factory experience. Because like I said, I was the only female in the country at this place to have ever had this job and I had people waiting for me to fall on my butt all the time and if it wasn't for Ani—-she really helped me to get through that job.... No longer feeling alone—[and in the song] "Sitting in the Boardroom" by Ani DiFranco, [Ani] was the only female in [the boardroom] . . . [that was] my life at that point, and I love the song. . . . [Having Ani at that time] meant that I had a friend. I had someone who understood. I could not talk to anyone else about my position in this job with really feeling like anyone understood what the hell I was talking about. The women that I hired were not women in the position I was in. They were nice people, but they weren't sitting alone in the meeting rooms with all men and "Sitting in the Boardroom" helped me. I played it in my office all the time. She—it felt like somebody knew what I was going through. (Jo)

Furthermore, Ani [DiFranco]'s lyrics actually inspired Jo to take a more active role toward the advancement of women in the corporation. "I hired women. I hired women from everywhere. We had hardly any women in the factory, so I hired all these women and I was constantly sitting in my office listening to Ani [DiFranco], and if any of them came in, it was like, 'listen to this' " (Jo). DiFranco and her music had an impressive impact on Jo. DiFranco's "Blood in the Boardroom" offered strength to Jo when dealing with being the only female in meetings. More so, Jo was inspired by DiFranco and her music and was compelled to make a feminist difference in her workplace by hiring women.

Finally, 19-year-old Julie describes herself as having a very strong connection to female artists' music and in particular Sarah McLachlan. She was a flash of energy when talking about female artists and their music, even when the stories she told were heart wrenching. Similar to Terri, Lynn and Jo, Julie appropriates song lyrics to help her deal with a variety of issues in her life. Julie uses music to help herself get through difficult times and frequently describes female artists' music as one of the sole constants in her otherwise ever-changing life. In one instance, Julie shared a story about the difficulties she had in declaring a religious faith. With a Jewish mother and a Christian father, Julie uses music to deal with the pressure to commit to one faith or the other; in particular, she refers to Christian music crossover artist Amy Grant's "All I Ever Have to Be."

[I like] Amy Grant['s] "All I [Ever] Have to Be." . . . That song is amazing. I've always kind of battled with my religious faith. . . . I've got a Jewish mother and a Christian father and I've always depended—what kept me focused—and there is a God in my personal belief—is Amy Grant and her song "All I [Ever] Have to Be." [It] is basically about—no matter what happens in the world, no matter what I want to do, no matter what other people want me to do, no matter what I want to make of myself, all I have to be is what God created and put on this earth. And that's me and if I can do that then I'm okay. Whenever I feel like anything is going wrong, I just think of lyrics to that song . . . [and I realize all] I have to be is what God made me. (Julie)

Julie also talks about another very critical and difficult time in her life. At one point in her life, just a few years prior to the interview and at the age of 17, she found herself dealing with her parents' recent divorce, her mother's disclosure of her alcoholism and parting

Identification and Appropriation

from her first love. Julie refers to this time as "the most tumultuous week of my life." At this same time, Julie discovered the music of Sarah McLachlan and credits McLachlan for helping her get through it.

That whole summer, and particularly that week, really was a lot of growing up in a very short period of time. A lot had happened very recently in my family. A lot happened that week in my family.... [M]y parents had gotten divorced two years ago and I moved in with my Mom and I was kind of in the midst of dealing with that still. When I came back from church camp ... [my Mom told me she] was an alcoholic and—I didn't know that. [There was also a] guy that I met; his name's Scott. [He] was like my first love and that was kind of difficult because three weeks after I met him he left for boot camp—he was going into the Navy, and so I had to deal with that and just basically a lot going on with my family.... It was probably, if I could pinpoint like the most tumultuous week of my life, it would be that week, and it wasn't all bad, but it was just a lot happened and that happened to be the week that I discovered, for myself, Sarah McLachlan, her lyrics, and I could really relate to them and every song was different and every song meant something and every song kind of created a feeling of "I'm not the only one who feels like this." Because so much was going on. (Julie)

Throughout the course of the interview, Julie spoke several times about how music is a constant for her, and it's one of the few dependable and controllable elements in her constantly changing life.

[Considering] everything that's happened in my life, everything that's happened in my family, all the divorces and people moving out and people writing each other off and people are being alcoholic and people doing drugs, and people getting abortions and people getting married and people getting divorced again and people moving here and there and people screwing people over and people just going nuts—and there's always been my CD player or my tape player and music that I can put into it that I can listen to that fits it [my mood].... [It's something] I can always depend on.... [And it's great] just knowing there's a constant. Knowing that no matter how many things change through the days, through the week, through the months, through the year, in my family, in my friends, no matter how much changes, that song is there. I can put the tape in and cue it to the right spot and listen to that song when I want to hear that song. It's something that's constant. It's something that I can control, that I can focus on that will be there regardless of anything else, no matter what happens. Just having that constant is really important to me because so many things change—from minute to minute so many things change.... It can't get up and walk away. It's something that I can control that's always there. (Julie)

CONCLUSION

Female artists' music plays an important role in women's lives. Just as Tetzlaff (1994) contends, "Rock fans use their talk about music as a way to help develop and articulate ideas about what their social position is, and what it ought to be" (p. 112). These women clearly appropriate female artists' music to cope with transitional and challenging moments in their everyday lives and to feel a little less alone when dealing with them. Because of similar ideological positioning of the artists and the fans, the respondents identify with and are drawn to the text and in return are affirmed, validated and empowered as women. Because of the relevancy of the artists and their music to the women's lives, they make meaning of the text. Even if the meaning created and appropriated by the respondents is different than the songwriters' story intention, as in the case of Patricia's and Mary's stories related to McLachlan's "Hold On" and "Good Enough," respectively, music fans derive the greatest sense of satisfaction when they are actively involved in meaning making. This is similar to Fiske's (1988) writing about relevancy in relation to television. "These meanings are pleasurable when they are pertinent to the social allegiances of the viewer and when the viewer has been active in generating them. The pleasure is greatest and the attention given to the screen is greatest when the viewer is actively engaged in the production of socially pertinent meanings" (p. 247). Although perhaps different meanings than the artists intend, meaning making by the respondents makes the experience of engaging with music all the more valuable for the listener.

Especially considering the feminist or political nature of the artists and their music, this in turn serves to develop a strengthening consciousness in female listeners. Through this connectedness, as exemplified here, women are able to exert power and strength in their everyday lives or, at the very least, are better able to cope. This in turn continues the cyclical and interdependent process and relationship between the artists, the music and the female listeners, resulting in, or at the very least contributing to, the creation of discourse more representative of women's everyday lives. If rock music "cannot offer transcendence, it can at least promise a kind of salvation. If it does not define resistance, it does at least offer a kind of empowerment, allowing people to navigate through, and even to respond to, their lived context. It is a way of making it through the day" (Grossberg, 1994, p. 52).

I would like to close this chapter as I opened it by referencing journalist Brownsworth's (1995/1999) comments about Jill Sobule's "I Kissed a Girl": "One kiss doesn't necessarily make a girl a lesbian. But one positive song can certainly make her feel better about being queer" (p. 287). Although Brownsworth's comment is specific to queer-identified girls and women, the same can be said about women in general. Simply put, positive media representations of women can certainly facilitate women feeling better about being women, give them strength and encourage them to make positive changes in their lives.

SONG LYRICS

Tori Amos, "Precious Things"

So I ran faster
But it caught me here
Yes my loyalties turned
Like my ankle
In the seventh grade
Running after BILLY
Running after the rain

These precious things
Let them bleed, let them wash away
These precious things
Let them break, their hold over me

He said you're really an ugly girl
But I like the way you play
And I died
But I thanked him
Can you believe that sick
Holding on to his picture
Dressing up every day

I wanna smash the faces
Of those beautiful BOYS
Those Christian boys
So you can make me cum
That doesn't make you Jesus

These precious things
Let them bleed, let them wash away
These precious things
Let them break, their hold over me

I remember, yes
In my peach party dress
No one dared
No one cared to tell me
Where the pretty girls are
Those demigods
With their NINE-INCH nails
And little fascist panties
Tucked inside the heart of every nice girl

These precious things
Let them bleed, let them wash away
These precious things
Let them break, their hold over me

Tori Amos, "Silent All These Years"

Excuse me but
can I be you for a while
My DOG won't bite
if you sit real still
I got the anti-Christ
in the kitchen
yellin' at me again
Yeah I can hear that

Been saved again
by the garbage truck
I got something to say
you know but NOTHING comes
Yes I know what you think of me
you never shut up
Yeah I can hear that

But what if I'm a mermaid
In these jeans of his
with her name still on it
Hey but I don't care
Cause sometimes I said
sometimes I hear my voice
and it's been
HERE silent all these years

So you found a girl
who thinks really deep thoughts
What's so amazing
about really deep thoughts
Boy you best pray
that I bleed real soon
How's that thought for you

My scream got lost in a paper cup
You think there's a heaven
where some screams have gone
I got 25 bucks and a cracker
do you think it's enough
To get us there

But what if I'm a mermaid
In these jeans of his
with her name still on it
Hey but I don't care
Cause sometimes I said
sometimes I hear my voice and it's been
HERE silent all these

Years go by will I still be waiting
For somebody else to understand
Years go by if I'm stripped of my beauty
And the orange clouds raining in my head
Years go by will I choke on my tears
Till finally there is nothing left
One more casualty
You know we're too EASY easy easy

Well I love the way we communicate
Your eyes focus on my funny lip shape
Let's hear what you think of me now

but baby don't look up
The sky is falling

Your MOTHER shows up in a nasty dress
It's your turn now to stand where I stand
Everybody lookin' at you
here take hold of my hand
Yeah I can hear them

But what if I'm a mermaid
In these jeans of his
with her name still on it
Hey but I don't care
Cause sometimes I said
sometimes I hear my voice
I hear my voice
I hear my voice
And it's been HERE silent all these years
I've been here silent all these years
Silent all these
Silent all these years

Paula Cole, "I Am So Ordinary"

I nearly died I suicided softly
I saw her shadow through the cafe window
I watched you lean across the table
I watched you whisper in her ear

And she is your holy Mary
And I am so ordinary
And you can use me if you want to
I know you need me just like an old soft shoe

She looks like me but a bit prettier
She's a skater and a ballet dancer
I saw her on your motorcycle
In the seat I thought was meant for me

And when your mother came to Boston you disappeared
And then I saw you three together
I guess she makes the best impression
With her charming femininity . . .

Oh but I am the one you will call when alone
And I am the one who will give when she's gone

And so I give
So I give

I tell myself that love is truly giving
Somehow I justify this
Hoping you will understand me
Hoping you will love me back

And she is your holy Mary
And I am so ordinary
And she is your Queen Cleopatra
And I'm just your morning after
And she is your Star Spangled Banner
And I am just Frere Jaque
And you can lose me if you want to

And I am so ordinary

Shawn Colvin, "Suicide Alley"
By Shawn Colvin and John Leventhal

Wait for me by the banshee tree
Let me be your wailing companion
Pass 'em on by, don't look 'em in the eye
Suicide Alley is callin'
You thought you were dreaming
You could wake up dead
And you'll never know what's real
All this damage is runnin' loose in your head
And it really matters to me

Oh, no, baby don't go
Walkin' down Suicide Alley

Downtown baby it's a million to one
You might as well name your poison
And stand in line by the exit sign
Suicide Alley is waiting

You're a loose cannonball on a sinking ship
From the belly of the beast, shot from the hip
But you don't have to be going down the dark hall
You're not tied to the chair, you're not nailed to the wall

Oh, no, baby don't go
Walkin' down Suicide Alley

Sitting naked by the window in the middle of the night
I can see you wearing your halo
If only in the daybreak of the dirty street light
I know baby wasn't born to follow

You know I wasn't born I was spat out at a wall
And nobody even knew my name
The sun hatched me out, cradle and all
On the corner of First and Insane

For the souls of the departed and the renegades of love
You and me we gotta be all we dreamed of
In the ruins of mischief through the ravages of time
You got a place in this world of mine

Oh, no, baby don't go
Walkin' down Suicide Alley

Ani DiFranco, "blood in the boardroom"

sitting in the boardroom
the i'm so bored room
listening to the suits
talk about their world
they can make straight lines out of almost anything
except for the line of my upper lip when it curls
dressed in my best greasy skin and squinty eyes
i'm the only part of summer that made it inside
in the air-conditioned building decorated with a corporate flair
i wonder can these boys smell me bleeding through my underwear
there's men wearing the blood of the women they love
there's white wearing the blood of the brown
but every woman learns now to bleed from the moon
and we bleed to renew life every time it's cut down
i got my vertebrae all stacked up high as they can go
i but i still feel myself sliding from the earth that i know
so i excuse myself and leave the room
say my period came early but it's not a minute too soon
i go and find the only other woman on the floor
it's the secretary sitting at the desk by the door
i ask her if she's got a tampon i could use
she says oh honey, what a hassle for you sure i do you know i do
i say it ain't no hassle, no, it ain't no mess
right now it's the only power that i possess
these businessmen got the money

they got the instruments of death
but i can make life i can make breath
sitting in the boardroom
the i'm-so-bored room

listening to the suits talk about their world
i didn't really have much to say the whole time i was there
so i just left a big brown bloodstain on their white chair

Ani DiFranco, "in or out"

guess there's something wrong with me
guess i don't fit in
no one wants to touch it
no one knows where to begin
i've got more than one membership
to more than one club
and i owe my life
to the people that i love

he looks me up and down
like he knows what time it is
like he's got my number
like he thinks it's his
he says, call me, miss difranco,
if there's anything i can do
I say, it's mr. difranco to you

some days the line i walk
turns out to be straight
other days the line tends to deviate
i've got no criteria for sex or race
i just want to hear your voice
i just want to see your face

she looks me up and down
like she thinks that i'll mature
like she's got my number
like it belongs to her
she says, call me, ms. difranco
if there's anything i can do
i say, i've got spots
i've got stripes, too

their eyes are all asking
are you in or are you out

and i think, oh man
what is this about
tonight you can't put me
up on any shelf
because i came here alone
and i'm going to leave by myself

i just want to show you
the way that i feel
and when i get tired
you can take the wheel
to me what's more important
is the person that i bring
not just getting to the same restaurant
and eating the same thing

Everything But the Girl, "Missing"
By Ben Thorn and Tracey Watt

I step off the train
I'm walking down your street again and past your door
But you don't live there any more
It's years since you've been there
But now you've disappeard somewhere like outer space
You've found some better place
And I miss you—like the deserts miss the rain
And I miss you—like the deserts miss the rain
Could you be dead?
You always were two steps ahead of everyone
We'd walk behind while you would run
I look up at your house
And I can almost hear you shout down to me
Where I always used to be
And I miss you—like the deserts miss the rain
And I miss you—like the deserts miss the rain
Back on the train
I ask why did I come again?
Can I confess I've been hanging around your old address?
The years have proved to offer nothing since you moved
You're long gone
But I can't move on
And I miss you—like the deserts miss the rain
And I miss you—like the deserts miss the rain
And I miss you

I step off the train
I'm walking down your street again and past your door
But you don't live there any more
It's years since you've been there
But now you've disappeard somewhere like outer space
You've found some better place
And I miss you—like the deserts miss the rain
And I miss you—like the deserts miss the rain
And I miss you
And I miss you—like the deserts miss the rain
And I miss you—like the deserts miss the rain
The deserts miss the rain—like the deserts miss the rain
The deserts miss the rain
like the deserts miss the rain

Diamanda Galas, "Do You Take This Man"
By Diamanda Galas and John Paul Jones

I'm very disappointed in you
and I don't handle disappointment well
I'd like to say I could forgive you
But I can never forgive; just forget

Now it would take me ten long years to forget,
That's 12 months of the year
four weeks of the month
and seven days a week
Well that's a very tall order, I got to say—
I don't have that much time to FORGET
    That's a whole lot of hard and lonely time
When we could be together

Husband with this knife
I do you adore
I take you out of this world baby
with a lot of feeling
and with this feeling I do bestow upon you
all my worldly gifts

Honey wasn't it beautiful
the lovely time we spent together
It was SERENE
I will never forget you
Long as I live

"Do you take this man"

Husband, with this blade
I do you hold
I'll take what's mine
and let the future
keep the rest

Baby, I take you from this world
to my place
to a place of feeling
where I can love you
and we can be together

God I'm so grateful to be real with you baby
Lies are for a longer life
and I have got so *much* to say
      Shut up!!!
      Shut up!!!

Don't cry baby
I'm feeling better all the time—I don't
want to be angry, ok? I'm trying not
to do that, ok?

God I'm so disappointed in you!
Remember that drive
we talked about the wild thing
for 24 hours–7
while the dogs and the coyotes laughed
and the sun went up and down
and your rod went in and out
and the buzzards and the vultures *howled*:
      "Do you take this man?"

It was summer
It was hot
and you loved me so much
you said "Mama may I take your hand
May I please, mama?"
      BITCH! KEEP THOSE BUTTOCKS UP MOMITO!
Come on.
I'm all you need. Be sweet—seriously you know
I need to get in touch with you—
I need to get in touch with the real you

I'm very disappointed in you
I told you not to run off from me baby
There's nowhere for you to go
There's no one else you *need*
   you knew that

Now I have to get up off my knees
because I have some shopping to do
I have to think of my reputation
and chump is not my name
this hurts me *more* than you
so just think of the good times we had together
I'm your best friend baby
I really am, and I always will be, too.

Juliana Hatfield, "Nirvana"

I shut the windows and close the store.
I lay down on the bathroom floor.
Everyone I know is a bore.

I'm starting to think that everything stinks.
That I could really use a drink.
Then I got up and hit my head on the sink.
Father, father, father, father,
Do you call?
Father, father, father,
Should I end it all?

Now, here comes the song I love so much.
Makes me wanna go fuck shit up.
Now, I got nirvana in my head,
I'm so glad I'm not dead.

I slam my hand in the car door.
I scream 'till I could scream no more.
Bloody and mean and rotten to the core.
Father, father, father, father,
Do you call?
Satan, Satan, Satan,
Should I end it all?

You try to get off the ground.
But you always end up coming down.
When the sound comes around and goes in your ears.
You can do anything, you have no fears.

When that sound comes around and goes in my ears.
I can do anything I have no fears.

Now, here comes the song I love so much.
Makes me wanna go fuck shit up.
I got nirvana in my head.
I'm so glad I'm not dead.

Here comes the song, I love it so much.
Makes me wanna go fuck shit up.
Now, I got nirvana in my head.
I'm so glad I'm not dead.

Indigo Girls, "Love Will Come to You"
Words and Music: Emily Saliers

I guess I wasn't the best one to ask
Me myself with my face pressed up against love's glass
To see the shiny toy I've been hoping for
The one I never could afford
The wide world spins and spits turmoil and the nations toil
For peace
The pause of fear upon her chest
Only love can sooth that beast
And my words are paper tigers
No match for the predator of pain inside her

I said love will come to you
Hoping just because I spoke the words that they're true
If I offered up a crystal ball to look through
Where there's now one there will be two

I was born under the sign of cancer (Love will come to you)
Like brushing cloth I smooth the wrinkles for an answer (Love will
    come to you)
I'm always closing my eyes and wishing I'm fine
Even though I'm not this time

I said love will come to you
Hoping just because I spoke the words that they're true
If I offered up a crystal ball to look through
Where there's now one there will be two

Dodging your memories a field of knives
I'm always on the outside looking in on others' lives

I said love will come to you
Hoping just because I spoke the words that they're true
And if I've offered up a crystal ball to look through
Where there's now one there will be two

And I wish her insight to battle love's blindness
Strength from the milk of human kindness
Safe place for all the pieces that scatter
Learn to pretend there's more than love that matters

Sarah McLachlan, "Black"

As the walls are closing in
And the colors fade to black
And my eyes are falling fast and deep into me
And I follow the tracks that lead me down
And I never follow what's right
And they wonder sometimes when they see all the
Sadness and pain the truth brings to light

'Cause I can't see no reason
What is blind cannot see
'Cause I want what is pleasin'
All I take should be free
What I rob from the innocent ones
What I'd steal from the womb

If I cried me a river of all my confessions
Would I drown in my shallow regret
As the walls are closing in
And the colors fade to black
And the night is falling fast and deep into the sea
And in darkness all that I can see
The frightened and the weak
Are forced to cling to mistakes they know nothing of
At mercy are the meek

Sarah McLachlan, "Good Enough"

Hey your glass is empty,
it's a hell of a long way home,
Why don't you let me take you,
it's no good to go alone,
I never would have opened up
but you seemed so real to me,

After all the bullshit I've heard
it's refreshing not to see,
I don't have to pretend,
she doesn't expect it from me

So don't tell me I
haven't been good to you,
Don't tell me I
haven't been there for you
Just tell me why
nothing is good enough

Hey little girl would you like some candy,
your momma said that it's o.k.,
The door is open come on outside,
no I can't come out today,
It's not the wind that cracked your shoulder
and threw you to the ground,
Who's there that makes you so afraid
you're shaken to the bone,
You know I don't understand,
you deserve so much more than this

So don't tell me why
he's never been good to you,
Don't tell me why
he's never been there for you,
And I'll tell you that why
is simply not good enough,
So just let me try
and I will be good to you
Just let me try
and I will be there for you,
I'll show you why
you're so much more than good enough

Sarah McLachlan, "Hold On"

Hold on
Hold on to yourself
for this is gonna hurt like hell.

Hold on
Hold on to yourself.
You know that only time can tell

what is it in me that refuses to believe
this isn't easier than the real thing.

My love
you know that you're my best friend.
You know that I'd do anything for you
and my love
let nothing come between us
my love for you is strong and true.

Am I in heaven here or
am I . . .
At the crossroads I am standing.

So now you're sleeping peaceful
I lie awake and pray
that you'll be strong tomorrow
and will see another day
and we will praise it
and love the light that brings a smile
across your face.

Oh god
if you're out there won't you hear me.
I know we've never talked before

and oh god
the man I love is leaving
won't you take him when he comes to your door.

Am I in heaven here or
am I in hell
at the crossroads I am standing.

So now you're sleeping peaceful
I lie awake and pray
that you'll be strong tomorrow
and we will see another day
and we will praise it
and love the light that brings a smile
across your face

Hold on
hold on to yourself
for this is gonna hurt like hell.

Liz Phair, "Fuck and Run"

I woke up alarmed
I didn't know where I was at first
Just that I woke up in your arms
And almost immediately I felt sorry
'Cause I didn't think this would happen again
No matter what I could do or say
Just that I didn't think this would happen again
With or without my best intentions, and
Whatever happened to a boyfriend
The kind of guy who tries to win you over, and
Whatever happened to a boyfriend
The kind of guy who makes love cause he's in it
And I want a boyfriend

I want a boyfriend
I want a boyfriend
I want all that stupid old shit
Like letters and sodas
Like letters and sodas

You got up out of bed
You said you had a lot of work to do
But I heard the arrest in your head
And almost immediately I felt sorry
'Cause I didn't think this would happen again
No matter what I could do or say
Just that I didn't think this could happen again
With or without my best intentions, and

I want a boyfriend
I want a boyfriend
I want all that stupid old shit
Like letters and sodas

I can feel it in my bones
I'm gonna spend another year alone
It's fuck and run
Fuck and run
Even when I was 17
Fuck and run
Fuck and run
Even when I was 12

And I can feel it in my bones
I'm gonna spend my whole life alone

Fuck and run
Fuck and run
Even when I was 17
Fuck and run
Fuck and run
Even when I was 12

You almost felt bad
You said that I should call you up but
I knew much better than that
And almost immediately you felt sorry cause
'Cause you didn't think this would happen again
No matter what you could do or say
Just that you didn't think this could happen again
With or without your best intentions

And whatever happened to a girlfriend
The kind of chick who tries to win you over, and
Whatever happened to a girlfriend
The kind of chick who makes love cause she's in it and
You want a girlfriend
You want a girlfriend
You want all that boring old shit
Like letters and sodas
Letters and sodas
Letters and sodas
Letters and sodas

Pam Tillis, "All the Good Ones Are Gone"
By Dean Dillon/Bob McDill

She'll turn thirty-four this weekend
She'll go out with her girlfriends
They'll drink some margaritas, cut up and carry on
There'll be guys and there'll be come ons
She'll probably get hit on
But she thinks all the good ones are gone

She's got friends down at the office
And she can't help but notice
That when the day is over
How they all hurry home
Every day there's guys she works with
And even some she flirts with
But it seems like all the good ones are gone

And her mama called this mornin'
Said I'm worried about my baby
I wish you had a family of your own
She said mom it's not that easy
You make it sound so simple
But you can't take the first man that comes along

Once she had someone who loved her
Back when she was younger
Now she wonders if she held out
A little bit too long
Back then there were so many
Now there just aren't any
It seems like all the good ones are gone

And her mama called this mornin'
Said I'm worried about my baby
I wish you had a family of your own
She said mom it's not that easy
You make it sound so simple
But you can't take the first man that comes along

She'll turn thirty-four this weekend
She'll go out with her girlfriends
They'll drink some margaritas, cut up and carry on

Chapter 3

Finding Voice: Expression and Connection

Thirty-two-year-old Jo is feisty, energetic and passionate about the music she loves. She's taken up a new road in life recently, studying for her master's in English in the hopes of becoming a successful novelist. When growing up she was pressured by her father to be involved in and love music. As a booking agent her father had jazz bands playing in the living room before she could walk. The question for her and all of her siblings wasn't whether they would play an instrument but which one they would play. As a girl her choices were limited. The French horn and piano were acceptable, but the guitar was off limits. A regular part of childhood play with her dad was the Major-Minor Game. When a major note was played the children raced to be the first to stand; when a minor note was played the children sat down as fast as they could.

In junior high she "felt like an oddity and by the time she hit high school she was convinced of it." Other students listened to what she describes as lovesick-dependency music—she didn't understand its appeal. As she got older and the music of Ani DiFranco, Melissa Etheridge and Tori Amos came into her life, she found women she thought were just like her. "Finally," she thought to herself, "I'm not the only one—there's other women out there who are like me." At last she was less of an oddball. Though they are physically distant, their worldviews are cut from the same cloth. She talks dreamily of having a big house where Ani, Melissa, Tori and herself could all live. She is convinced female artists' music reminds her to act on her beliefs and speak her mind despite the social consequences. If forced to choose between blindness and deafness, she picks the latter—she can't imagine life without music.

As detailed in Chapters 1 and 2, the women interviewed for this project are discriminating and selective listeners and identify with and appropriate female artists and their music into their everyday lives. In addition, this study found that women find voice through female artists and their music. This chapter reveals the ways in which women use music as a communication tool—connecting to people and communicating with, through and in the presence of music. In some instances, women have actually used female artists to communicate and express their thoughts and feelings directly to loved ones. Music by women also provided listeners with an opportunity to connect or bond with others, through sharing music, experiences and concerts. Finally, many of the women associated particular songs with loved ones.

"IF MY SOUL COULD TALK": PERSONAL EXPRESSION

Many of the respondents talked about feeling as though female artists' music provided a voice for them. Frith (1997) argues that narrative, both lyrical and musical, is in part what draws individuals to particular pieces of music. Frith writes that a good performance relies on a "musician's ability to convince and persuade the listener that what they are saying matters.... [I]t puts into play an emotional effect, a collusion between the performer and an audience which is engaged rather than detached" (p. 117). The artists' narratives and what the listener sees as truth can act as a conduit for self-expression. Some women indicated that female artists were able to articulate emotions or feelings in a way they were unable to. Others actually appropriated female artists' lyrics and used them to communicate with others.

Of all the respondents, Terri was by far the one who would most often specifically mention the aspect of finding voice through female artists' music. In her own effort to express herself, Terri identifies very strongly with female artists. This is drawn out in the excerpts

Finding Voice: Expression and Connection 117

below with Terri citing two songs in particular, Tori Amos's "Hey Jupiter" and 10,000 Maniacs' "Verdi Cries."

> To me, it [a song] is more expressive than talking. I listen to some songs and I think to myself, "If my soul could talk, that's how it would sound." Or, "If it could speak, that's what it would sound like." I think it puts out there those things that I don't have words for. To me, it's a form of expression almost or I [express myself] vicariously through artists that I associate with. (Terri)

> [Tori Amos's] "Hey Jupiter." Oh! I cry every time I hear that song! It's about leaving a boyfriend, but it's not even that. It's when she's singing, she's not even using words. . . . And I'm just like, "Oh, yes!" If I could sing pain, that's how it would sound. Every time I hear it, it's almost gut-wrenching, that I can feel it in my gut, the feeling of it. (Terri)

> There's a [10,000 Maniacs] song, "Verdi Cries," it's the last song [on their *In My Tribe* album], and that's one of those songs that if I could sing my emotions they would sound like that. If I could sing this melancholy-ness or if I could speak what I'm feeling, that's how it would sound . . . [Earlier music I listened to] was really mellow at first, and it's probably because I was in therapy. . . . I didn't know how to speak my pain, so some of these songs did it for me. And I didn't know how to do it myself. (Terri)

Terri is not alone in indicating that female artists' music is a vehicle for personal expression. Julie, Jo, Sandi and Patricia also express similar sentiments. As detailed in Chapter 2, Julie feels a strong connection to Sarah McLachlan, feeling as though McLachlan's music has helped her through some difficult times since she was 15 years old. As Julie says, "[Sarah McLachlan's] lyrics are so incredible. . . . Her music is incredible . . . having somebody sing about it ["all the major things that have happened in my life"] and understand it and know what's going on and be able to vocalize how I feel the way she does [is great]" (Julie). Similarly, Jo finds female artists' music helpful to articulate thoughts that she is having difficulty expressing. "[Female artists' music] helps me express stuff. It really, really does. It means another way of saying something that maybe I couldn't articulate for whatever reason" (Jo). Sandi shares a similar remark: "Ani DiFranco has quite a few songs that are—ya know, you'll just sit there and you'll be like, 'Yeah, I had that exact situation, that's exactly what I wanted to say.' " Because of similar shared experiences of living as a girl and woman in a patriarchal world, female listeners' experiences were heightened when songs rang particularly true for them. Because of what they perceive as shared similar experiences, women solicit artists' songs as a vehicle of self-expression.

Beyond Terri's indication of female artists' music providing a voice for her, she also talked about feeling validated in her emotions (harkening back to a theme drawn out in Chapter 2) and how music helps her face issues that she tries to "keep in."

If I'm feeling really depressed or something, I'll put on really depressing music. . . . I need to listen to music that validates what I'm feeling. That articulates what I'm feeling, that spells it out for me. Because sometimes, you go through your life, and you try and keep it all in, and then music, for me, is a relief. (Terri)

Patricia also talks about how female artists help her to express her feelings. In addition to this similarity, Patricia's comment also echoes this latest comment of Terri's in another way. Patricia talks about how music helps her to unearth feelings that she otherwise tries to deny.

Sometimes it sounds like they are able to—like Sarah McLachlan is able to articulate my feelings better than I can. And sometimes the women I like and their music—they can more eloquently say what I'm feeling. Or help me become aware of what I'm feeling through their music. "Wow, this is why I'm so upset." (Patricia)

Along with female artists' music helping her to express herself, Jo cited some specific incidents of actually incorporating Ani DiFranco's lyrics into her everyday interactions with others. Jo described examples of using DiFranco's lyrics to help make her point writing papers for school and asserting herself at work.

Jo is a graduate student majoring in English with an emphasis in creative writing. An aspiring fiction writer herself, Jo was very keyed in on lyrics and found particular good use of Ani DiFranco's lyrics when dealing with life issues. In one of her creative writing courses, she would use Ani DiFranco's lyrics to help make her point. Sparked by discussions she's had with other graduate teaching assistants over concerns of how not to offend students in first-year composition classes, Jo referred to Ani DiFranco's "What If No One's Watching" song. She said of the incident:

We're [graduate school teaching assistants] always talking about . . . how do you go about not offending students. And I'm always—I just think of Ani saying "that no matter what I say I'm going to offend someone somewhere." That's not the specific lyrics—but the idea is that you're going to offend someone somewhere, so you might as well speak. (Jo)

In another instance, Jo used an Ani DiFranco poem to relate to and help make her point when writing a response paper to an article she read for a course. The article was about a woman who was working at a factory. Jo, having had just returned to school from working at a factory, "identif[ied] with this woman." When writing her response paper Jo cited the Ani DiFranco poem titled "The Slant." "['The Slant'] kind of defines the difference between the gender[s]. . . . [The poem] kind of gives you the feeling—like the difference between men and women and how it [gender behavior] is socialized into us." Jo refers to the lyrics:

"I am a work in progress"—which I think is really cool. . . . She's talking about getting stronger and I like that. "And dressed in the fabric of a world unfolding offering me intricate patterns of questions, rhythms that never come clean and strengths that you still haven't seen." I think that—that was a really neat woman thing. (Jo)

In another instance, Jo refers to another class discussion where students were contemplating the question, "Are we free?" Jo's spontaneous response was, "Yeah, within limits." Soon after that incident, Jo reconsidered what she meant by that and once again used an Ani DiFranco song, "Rush Hour," to help make her point in a paper on the same topic. She felt that people want to

turn their heads and say, "Yeah, we're free, yeah, the world's a nice place" and not really looking at things, and I somehow got off on a tangent in this paper quoting from her, a line from a song that says, "He said turn the TV off [sic], I've got problems of my own. I'm so sick of hearing about drugs, AIDS and people without homes." And I said, "I'd like to sympathize with that, but if you can't understand, then how can you act." . . . [I use Ani DiFranco's] words a lot because her words have to do with what's going on in the world right now. They're definitely thought provoking.

They definitely yell at people, "Wake up, open your eyes, what the hell's wrong with you, do something!" (Jo)

Jo not only used the words of Ani DiFranco as a catalyst in finding her voice at school, but she also used them to help her deal with her working conditions. As mentioned previously, Jo was the first female in the country to have a factory supervisory position at the company where she worked. When Jo first started working at the factory, she was young and naive and felt "lucky" to have the job. Moreover, Jo was remarkably underpaid as compared to men. Feeling very isolated at work, Jo used Ani DiFranco, her music and her lyrics to feel less alone. Again, Jo refers specifically to DiFranco's lyrics to help make her point.

I didn't know politics yet at the time and I luckily had a boss who liked me; luckily he probably let me get away with things he wouldn't have let other people get away with, but he was always trying to coach me on what was . . . the appropriate thing to say in some stupid issue we were faced with and I said, "I don't like my language watered down, I don't like my edges rounded off" [from Ani DiFranco's song "Make Me Stay"]. . . . But it was Ani, and I couldn't think of anything to say and that's what he was doing. He was shaping the way I spoke and I had had it. I worked for this place for five years and I didn't hold back and I said Ani things all the time. (Jo)

Ani DiFranco's songs have played key roles in Jo's development of self; they gave her courage to speak her mind and stand up to injustice. Ani DiFranco's work has had a compelling affect on Jo. This is transformative. These women appropriate music by women to find voice for themselves, whether they identify it as vicarious expression or actually incorporate the artists' lyrics into their everyday lives.

"LYRICS AS YOUR GREETING CARD": COMMUNICATING THROUGH MUSIC

Frith (1997) writes that the "use of music [is an] aesthetic process through which we discover ourselves by forging our relations to others" (p. 118). The first part of Frith's contention here was illustrated earlier when the women talked about identifying, appropriating and finding voice through music. In the remainder of this

Finding Voice: Expression and Connection

chapter, not only do the women share more nuances about their personal growth through music but also how they use music as a tool in relationship development or preservation. In fact, some of the women, including Lynn, Mary, Lisa and Jo, have actually talked about literally communicating through music. They use music as a device to reduce the awkwardness of sometimes-intimate communications. Whether trying to express something to someone, as in the case of Lynn and Mary, receiving a message from somebody, as in the case of Lisa, or communicating back and forth, as in the case of Jo. Women use music to help them express themselves to others.

Lynn is clear that she uses music to communicate feelings to others. She'll request that a significant other actually listen to a particular song.

It [female artists' music] is really important to me. Because for me, music, I can communicate feelings that I can't express—not that I can't express, but I can't find words for—through music. I'll be like, "Hey, will you listen to that song—ya know, this is the way." Not like, this is the way I feel about you—because it's not a cop-out necessarily—but they'll say it in such a way that it hits you and you're like, that's it. Ya know, and I couldn't have said that, but she said that. (Lynn)

Mary, who talked a great deal about her boyfriend, communicates her feelings through music for her boyfriend and referred to Jewel's "Angel Standing By" in particular. "[Jewel's] 'Angel Standing By'—I love that song. It's kind of a personal thing. Because my boyfriend and I are—have gotten really serious—and all of a sudden he started calling me his angel. So, I made a tape for him and that was the first song I put on. So, it's kind of mushy. He loved it. He cried" (Mary).

Lisa talks about receiving a tape from a friend. When she received it she knew immediately the music recorded on it was an explicit message for her to hear. Lisa even makes an interesting comparison to using music in this way similar to the way someone would exchange greeting cards.

[A friend of mine made a mix tape] and on it was a lot of Melissa [Etheridge]'s music and she said, "I've picked the songs, I've given you the tape," so then you know that there's a reason. So you don't want to listen to it as background noise. You want to listen to it as if that person's talking to you. . . . So I rolled the windows up [in the car] and turned on the air conditioning so I could listen to the music. . . . [Having that music helps facilitate communication] because sometimes the music can say things that you might find personally difficult to articulate. You can send lyrics back and forth and use that as your greeting card. (Lisa)

Jo also clearly indicates that she uses songs as a way to communicate with other people, particularly those she has an intimate relationship with. She even describes this practice as "talk[ing] through music," and similar to the other women, it's particularly helpful when she's finding it difficult to locate the words herself.

I have a tendency to hide in music, though. So if there's something I want to say to someone, like especially in romantic situations I've been known to—like they don't understand because I probably don't convey it, "this is my life and you should probably pay particular attention" instead of me saying it. Here's a song that'll do it for me. Kind of an underhanded way of going about exposing myself, I think, and I do that a lot with music. I do. Luckily, some people got it [but] some people don't. But the relationship I'm in now, it's a person who does the same thing. It's weird. We talk through music. When she can't think of anything to say she—it's lyrics from a song. And sometimes when she doesn't want to say—when I'm not supposed to know what she's thinking and she's singing around the house, well, okay, "What made you sing that?" And usually it's pretty clear. I think we turn on music; sometimes I turn on music just to relate something to someone else. (Jo)

Jo describes a more specific example:

[L]ately . . . I realize[d] that I'm so busy in my life sometimes that I'm not enjoying my life and there is this [Indigo Girls] song ["Get Out the Map"] on the newest one [CD]. They say something about "I wanna love you good and strong while our love is good and young." [And] I looked at my lover—I played that song . . . and I was like—because I realized "I haven't looked at you in weeks and I'm really sorry." So again I said it through a song. But I made it clear that I was saying it too. Like Jesus Christ, by the time I get un-busy, I probably will be 90. Our love wont' be good and young. (Jo)

BONDING, CONNECTING AND COMMUNITY

Music is not only a way for women to communicate with others; it's also a way for them to experience a unique connection with friends and family. Clearly, these women were drawn to these artists because the artists had relevancy to their lives and quenched the respondents' thirst for more diverse representative media symbols. These women found a voice through the music of female artists and used select music as a vehicle for them to communicate with friends, family, lovers and even workplace individuals. But music by women also provided listeners with an opportunity to relate to or bond with others, through the sharing of music, experiences and concerts, all of this contributing to a sense of connecting and building community among women.

Mattern (1998) used the phrase "acting-in-concert" as a metaphor for "community-based political actions through music." Mattern used it to describe how Chileans, Cajuns and American Indians "have used popular music as a means of defining and maintaining diverse communities as well as a way of promoting distinct forms of collective political action" (p. 4). Arguably, although perhaps not as politically organized or faced with as challenging circumstances, the women of this study used female music artists, knowingly or unknowingly, to create their own sense of community that emerged around and through the music of female artists.

Music can aid in the creation of a community or, at the very least, act as an operative in the manifestation of a sense of community. People who share similar interests, even though they may be physically separated, can develop a sense of connectivity based on these interests. The music and the artists posit themselves as representative of many women's lives, and because of this commonality among women throughout the makeup of all music listeners, some will be drawn to the artists and the stories of the music. Women are drawn to these artists and music because they feel an affinity toward the stories being told. In turn, women who feel as though the music speaks to them are likely to feel a sense of shared experiences with other women who are invested listeners of similar female artists. Furthermore, because of these shared interests, arguably the women who attend to these artists are also likely to be ideologically similarly focused, which contributes to a common sense of community. Simply put, this might also be referred to as being "in the know." Cavicchi (1998) refers to this in his work with Springsteen fans as a sort of separator between "real" Springsteen fans versus mere audience members at a Springsteen concert. The fans "in the know" are of a different class, level of dedication and knowledge about Springsteen.

Thornton (1995), drawing on French philosopher Pierre Bourdieu, refers to it as "subculture capital." And as one of my respondents commented, "It's about being in on the joke" (Sandi). The people around you, whether personal friends, a lover or other engaged women at a concert, "get" what this is about. "It" means something for you and for them. They understand the importance of the artists, the music and the message. And in part because of this connection, this sense of community, music becomes a vehicle for greater social good. "Music can increase the capacity or power of relatively marginalized people to choose and determine their own fate" (Mattern, 1998, p. 6).

The community discussed here is more fleeting than concrete and perhaps not as clustered or momentous as the music that evolved with and through major significant political movements such as the protests of the Vietnam conflict and the women's liberation movement of the 1960s and 1970s. Nevertheless, this more popularized sense or manifestation of feminism is important. Some of the same reasons that might be put forward to discredit it or declare the music less *authentic* (for example, the popularization of it and/or the garnering of a large audience) are precisely the same reasons that allow for this quasi-feminist or feminist message to attain a greater reach and have a significant cultural impact.

The music at the center of this book is a form of communication that allows for "people [to] develop the commonalities of community" (Mattern, 1998, p. 14). Music is not only a way for women to communicate with others; it's also a way for them to feel a connection with friends and family and to create a sense of community. Many women indicated that their conversations with others centered on new or particular songs or albums. However, there are many instances where their discussions and their experiences that surround music complement or go beyond this more superficial discussion. Women talked about how music provides an opportunity to bond with others and a way for them to connect with friends or family. Although essentially referring to the same experience, Elisabeth and Paige talk about it in terms of bonding, while Sandi, Deirdre, Jane and Julie talk about it in terms of connecting.

Elisabeth asserts that talking with friends about music, although simplistic, does indeed provide an opportunity for bonding. "[When I talk about Melissa Etheridge or the Indigo Girls with my friends] it's kind of a lesbian bonding. You know, we're all gay" (Elisabeth).

Similar to Elisabeth, although 21-year-old art therapy major Paige finds talk about female artists' music to be mostly about new artists or music, she does indicate that relating with friends about music does indeed provide an opportunity for her and her friends to bond.

[I talk about female artists' music with friends and] especially Jackie. I'll bring over CDs. "Oh listen to this. Listen to this. I found this new one. I think you might really like this song." Then there is one of my friends from high school that I see every once in a while and her and I have the same music taste and we'll be like, "Oh I really like this song." It's mostly just playing and being able to enjoy it together.... Having the same music taste, it can become a bond. (Paige)

Lynn and her friend Rebecca bond by both being fans of the Indigo Girls. They even go as far to map themselves onto the Indigo Girls' personalities and will play-act as the music duo for fun.

I live with Rebecca; she's been my really close friend since high school. She's a big Indigo Girls fan with me. The two of us always pretend that we're the Indigo Girls. And I've watched one of their videos . . . the two of us were like, "Yeah, we could do that! We could be the Indigo Girls." . . . [And] I think it's about Rebecca and I bonding. Because we enjoy spending time together—and, so I think that seeing ourselves as the Indigo Girls—I would be Emily and she would be Amy. And it kind of reflects our personalities in a way too. So, I think that's what it's about—it's about bonding through this music. (Lynn)

Similarly, Sandi talks about how discussions about music help her make a connection with one friend in particular, Marion.

Marion is a really good friend of mine [and] we talk about everything and she likes rap—and she doesn't really get into punk or hard core or anything, but if I played it [and even if] she would [say], "Oh, okay that's loud." She would [still] listen to it. We can talk about music. . . . We talk about rap. . . . I think it is a big connection. . . . And so that's just kind of nice [that] we can enjoy music together. (Sandi)

Similar to Sandi, Deirdre also talks about how music provides a connection. Deirdre also finds that talking with people about music can provide new insight into the meaning of a song.

Talking to people about that [certain songs or music] or how it touches our lives or connects with our lives . . . I think it's nice. I think it's a way of connecting with people and connecting more to the music, and it can give me an insight on it that I might not have thought of otherwise and vice versa. It's enjoyable—it's never not. It's something that's fun to talk about and music's important to me—so it's great to connect with other people and that's important too and learning things from each other. (Deirdre)

Similar to the other women, Jane indicates she finds music is a way to connect with a variety of people in her life.

Currently I am in a relationship that I feel that I am the stronger musical influence. I'm going out and finding things, and introducing; it's a way to connect with somebody personally. To get more intimate with them. Whether it's a partner or a lover or just a friend or a stranger. You can meet a person and sort of talk about music and before you know it, you've made a personal connection. That may be the avenue that allows that connection to happen that otherwise wouldn't have happened at all. (Jane)

Beyond friends or lovers, Julie finds that music can provide an avenue in which to further the intimacy of her relationship with both of her parents. "I talk to my mom about music. . . . She shares my excitement for live music. . . . We go to shows sometimes together. . . . We talk about live shows. We reminisce about live shows. We anticipate live shows that we are going to. . . . It's really cool" (Julie). Despite this noted connection she feels through music with her mother, Julie appears to have an even stronger connection to her father through music than her mother. As Julie describes it, this may be in part out of necessity. Julie has a strained relationship with her dad, and perhaps because of this tension, Julie finds that music provides her with one of the few avenues in which she is able to relate to her dad. Julie's comments also harken back to a theme drawn out earlier about women using music to communicate with others.

I talk to my dad about music constantly; he's always asking me who's coming out, who is new that I should be listening to. . . . My dad—it's just a connection that we've always had. A lot of stuff has happened between the two of us, lost contact and gotten contact back and a lot of crazy things have happened between us, but it's always a safe zone no matter what [has] happened. [Music is] always something we can talk about safely and it's the first thing that we ever connected with because I learned early that if you want to connect with Dad, you've got to get through to him through music. If you want to get to Dad, you have to get his headphones off his head. And I learned that that's a good way to connect with him, and I use musical analogies. If I can't find the right way to say something, I'll think of a song and like recite lyrics if I can't think of how to put something properly. That's how I am. I'll be like, "You know that song by 'blah, blah, blah.' " Kind of like that. It's just a connection that we've had. I mean, even a deeper connection than anything else we've had. (Julie)

THE CONCERT SCENE

The greatest sense of community is likely to arise when various women with shared experiences as women and intersecting ideologies gather for the experience of music performed live by the respondents' preferred artists. Live concerts provide an opportunity for the barriers of distance and recorded music to be broken down between a performer and her fans. The artists share their work with an audience usually all too eager to experience the music live. Difficult to describe, there is a combined energy between the performer and the audience that fills the venue. Most music listeners have experienced the intensity or energy of a live show at one time or another. However, the form this energy takes and the overall atmosphere can be markedly different at a female artist's rock concert, usually with a predominantly female audience in attendance, as opposed to a male artist's rock concert. Certainly, the genre of music, regardless of whether the performer or audience is predominantly one gender or another, also plays a contributory role in the concert energy. However, generally speaking, males interact and celebrate live music differently than women. Rock concerts that showcase male acts tend to be more aggressive, animated and physical. Men have largely been allowed to be active and engaged audience members, in turn allowing concerts to be a setting for "collective forms of male toughness, roughness and noisiness" (Frith & McRobbie, 1978/1990, p. 382).

Similar to what Lewis (1990) contends about the threat of "the street" in music videos, this sort of heightened, testosterone-influenced energy does not always make for a safe, let alone comfortable, atmosphere for women. As Rumsey and Little (1988) observed about the concert scene of rock/punk act the Clash:

[H]ad they [the girlfriends] not been under escort by their boyfriends, it is unlikely that the minority of women who did go to see the Clash would have been there at all. . . . [F]ear tends to detract from our [women's] feelings of excitement and exhilaration as we go to gigs wondering whether our friends will still be around at the end of the evening to get us home safely. (p. 242)

Woodstock 1999 is a quintessential example of wired male audience members, fueled by aggressive, testosterone-filled male rap-rock music with "lyrics freely describing raping, beating and dismembering women" (Kleiner, 1999, p. 59), turning a concert into a riotous, assaultive and violent disaster. Sadly, "forms of looting, disturbing the peace, and sexual assault are slowly becoming the norm at some concerts" (Kleiner, 1999, p. 59). Sheryl Crow, a performer at both Lilith and Woodstock 1999, was quick to make comparisons between the two events and regretted being a part of Woodstock.

Rock concerts with female headliners, which in turn usually attract a predominantly female audience, provide an altogether different atmosphere, one where women arguably feel more comfortable and less threatened. There tends to be more of a friendly camaraderie and more of a sense of community among the female participants. As Childerhose (1998) observed about the Lilith Fair, "[T]here is no menace here, no fear of violence or concern that someone might be crushed in a rush for the stage. Instead, there's a kind of gentle pulse, like the throb of a racing heartbeat on the inside of a wrist" (p. 7).

Artists have also recognized the benefits of female-oriented shows (see Childerhose, 1998). Bayton's work (1993, 1998) has focused on the careers of women musicians in which she noted that "[s]ome musicians said they felt safe at women's gigs because there were fewer fights, threats and less violence in general. Lesbians in particular found it safer to be 'out' at women's gigs than in a mixed context" (1993, p. 187). A concert with a female artist headlining, coupled with a predominantly or exclusively female audience, is a celebration of music that allows for the anticipation, excitement and fulfillment without a threatening atmosphere.

Concerts of female artists that are predominantly patronized by female fans provide a "safer space" for women to celebrate in their own cultural representation with women who are like them. Arguably and as discussed by the respondents, concerts are then prone to provide a heightened sense of camaraderie and community—whether within their immediate group of friends or the audiences as a whole.

Lisa finds concerts to be a pleasing shared experience. She experiences enjoyment in sharing the music with friends and introducing music to friends while at the same time supporting lesbian artists. Finally and similar to Sandi later, Lisa also takes notice and finds pleasure in the crowd singing along with the performer.

[I go to concerts] to have a social outing with friends doing something we'll enjoy.... It's [about] sharing the music.... [And it's fun b]ecause it's sharing something that has had an impact in my life and it's good supporting lesbians and exposing something to somebody new.... [And] when you get the whole lawn singing and everybody knows the words, you think wow, this is cool. (Lisa)

Sandi explains that concerts provide a real opportunity to connect with others. And similar to Lisa, Sandi also finds pleasure in the audience's initiative to sing along with the artists.

[Marion and I] went to the Indigo Girls concert. [And] everything's "get out the map" [from that Indigo Girls song]—"get out the map"—"get out the map"—he's "got the map"—she's "got the map." She doesn't "got the map." We don't even know the rest of the song. But it was really funny, at the concert—because everybody there was like—"Get out the map!" Everybody knows one line! It was "Get out the map! . . . And point your finger." . . . I think it is a big connection. . . . And so that's just kind of nice [that] we can enjoy music together. (Sandi)

Moreover, Sandi describes feeling a sense of community through concerts through the use of her analogy of being in on a joke.

[Female artists' music provides] a sense of community. Not only the actual community that I do have, the women that I know or the people that I know who are interested in that music, but also that feeling that if I went to a concert—there's some—it's that joke. Everybody there knows the joke—know what I mean? I think that is part of it. That it feels like, "We know." It's a little bit of an empowerment thing. (Sandi)

Thirty-one-year-old Elisabeth says, "[Being at that Melissa Etheridge concert was] kind of neat [because of] the camaraderie and [the people sitting next to us] were lesbian and that was kind of cool and that was fun." As a lesbian, Elisabeth lives most of her day as a (legally unrecognized) minority, closeted at the junior high school where she teaches and not accorded many basic human rights. At a Melissa Etheridge concert, Elisabeth finds herself as part of the majority, with more freedom to express herself genuinely.

Along with experiencing bonding, a shared experience or feeling a sense of community, many women also described an improved sort of comfort level or excitement at a concert that has a predominantly female audience. When discussing these various topics, many women, including Lynn, Julie and Sue, spoke specifically about the Lilith Fair. Lynn is truly excited about experiencing female artists' music live and makes mention of many of these themes:

[Concerts are] a shared experience too. It's this little bonding experience, I guess. . . . I love the feeling of being at a concert. I like being with all those people and they're so excited. I get really excited. At Lilith Fair I was beside myself. Oh! It's just so much! I love it. It's so much emotion and everybody gets caught up in it, I guess. At Indigo Girls—that's a great feeling of being at an Indigo Girls concert. Because there's a sense of a community. . . . [T]here's just a different feeling [at female artists' concerts]. There's [a feeling] I could exist without men forever—and that was the best feeling in the world. Ya know what I mean? Oh, gosh it's great! If you're somewhere where it's women focused and it's all women—you're just like—there could be a guy here and I do not care. Ya know what I mean? (Lynn)

Similar to Lynn, Sue also finds herself more comfortable at a female artist's concert with a predominantly female audience than she would in a predominantly male audience. Tellingly, it was at a concert of riot grrrl band Babes in Toyland.

I think, heaven forbid I sound cliché, but I like the positive female energy and not feeling threatened by anything [at concerts of female artists]. I've never been to a male concert where I didn't feel somehow threatened in whatever way, even mildly—that I didn't feel a little uncomfortable. . . . But women can rock out and have fun and you don't [feel threatened]. (Sue)

Finding Voice: Expression and Connection

With so little women-only space and so much of the dominant and popular culture's focus on men, women are overwhelmed by the sensation of attending a female artist's concert with predominantly female crowds. Fans are empowered by the strength of the artists and benefit from an incredible sense of belonging from the crowd.

Julie was particularly touched and energized by her Lilith Fair attendance. Not only did she feel assurance by being in a mostly female crowd, but she is even excited and impressed by the female artists' camaraderie. Again, Julie also refers to using music as a way to communicate with people. Finally, toward the end of this extended excerpt, Julie, so enthralled by music, and similar to an excerpt from Paige to follow, feels that music is not only a way to connect with other people but sort of a universal language that could make a significant difference in the world if more people were to attend to it.

[I went to the Lilith Fair] in [city in Ohio] with Lisa Loeb, Emmylou Harris, Indigo Girls, Jewel and Sarah McLachlan. That was an amazing show. Amazing, amazing. An entire day of euphoria. It was beautiful. . . . I definitely like going [to concerts]. Sometimes it's a real personal thing and sometimes I just want to be alone, but it's something that I like sharing with people because it's a really basic part of me, so I share it with the people who are really close to me. I went to Lilith Fair with my roommate and she's absolutely my best friend and sharing that experience with her was amazing; it was incredible. It was like there are these incredible women singing these beautiful songs on stage and I'm standing next to my best friend and it was just a great, incredible bonding experience for us. It's the way I can communicate with people—through music. . . . It was incredible. It was quite an experience. The female energy in that place was amazing. There were like five women to every man. It was just, women just being women and just doing what they wanted to do and hanging out and being cool and a lot of positive energy. When I've gone to concerts that are more male dominated, you feel like you have to kind of act mature and responsible, whereas at Lilith it was just like everybody was doing whatever they wanted to because this was just a festival just celebrating life basically. . . . It was really, really amazing to see all these people on the same stage. At one point Lisa Loeb, Emmylou Harris and both the Indigo Girls and Jewel and Sarah McLachlan and Emmylou Harris' two daughters and a couple of women that were singing on the side stages were all on stage and they all sang "Closer to Fine" of the Indigo Girls, and they all sang [Joni Mitchell's] "Big Yellow Taxi" and that was just absolutely phenomenal, that was incredible. To see them all, it was like all these women that I love. It was just great. It was just fabulous the way all of their voices were so different and each one of them, there's something about their voices that I love but to hear all of them blend together. It was just, "Wow." It was amazing. It was just so great.... [T]hese women should all be competing with each other, for profits, for attention, for media attention, for CD sales and they all just got together to sing a song and that's just great. It's the common strand for the whole world.... I mean Emmylou Harris sings country. Lisa Loeb sings kind of pop, and Indigo Girls are like folk, and I mean all of them together it just, you know if the whole world would just shut up and listen to a good song, then you know we can all get on stage together and sing and it would be great. (Julie)

Nineteen-year-old Julie's hopes that the world would be better if we just listened to music are simplistic. But music is an art form that transcends cultures and countries. Her Lilith Fair experience of witnessing more than 20,000 people singing, cooperating and participating in peace gives her hope for a better world through music. Paige learns a lesson too from the collective effort exemplified by Lilith Fair artists and fans. Paige contends that music certainly has some healing and energizing qualities.

I was just amazed at Lilith Fair. The whole entire crowd was singing. [Sarah McLachlan] came out and sang "Your love is better than ice cream." The entire crowd was singing, and I said, "You know what?" I said, "You wouldn't even notice if one person was out of tune." I mean, you wouldn't notice. I find that amazing.... If you have everybody together and if one person was singing out of tune but everyone was working together you wouldn't notice. If you have a whole bunch of people, helping—you know, the homeless or any volunteer work. If you have a huge [group working] to change something. If you have a lot of people doing it—if someone screws up, it is not going to be that big of a deal. Unless you have [only] one person doing all the work. (Paige)

MUSIC AS A "PHOTO ALBUM": MEMORIES AND REMINDERS

Music also triggers memories for many of these women. In fact, women not only associate music with memories of the past but will sometimes associate particular songs with certain friends or family members. For female music fans, music is the soundtrack of our lives. Songs provide women with tangible links to a myriad of past events in their lives. Happy and sad memories, time spent with family, friends and loved ones. Particular songs evolve into musical representations of different times in their lives. As suggested by married twenty-eight-year-old Sue below, in the same way the past emerges in detail through photo albums, songs can remind us of where we've been.

[Music is p]art of your root structure. Part of your history. And it's a part of your history that's a photo album that you can go back to and it brings up the same feelings, good or bad, just like it was yesterday. Or from an hour ago. It's like when you look through a photo album, sometimes it's really nice, sometimes it's masochistic. Sometimes it's like you had a really good time and it's long past and you'll never get that back and it kind of hurts. But you still do it. You look at those things sometimes and you feel good. But then there's times when it's like, "Oh yeah, that was last year at the party. Oh my God, she's so hilarious." And you'll call your friend up and say, "Oh, remember the time." Music is the same way to me. It's just like another medium; it's like an oral history in a sense, not literally. It's grounding. (Sue)

Terri, Patricia and Deirdre continue with an explanation of how music is tied to and triggers memories. They associate the course of their life with the music they were familiar with during periods of their lives. As Terri contends, "Oh! I live my life by songs. If you name a song, I can tell you what year, usually. Or what year it reminds me of in my life. I live my life according to songs that were popular or that I was [listening to]. . . . I mark my life according to music" (Terri).

Similarly, Patricia finds that memories of her life are very much tied to the music that she remembers.

When I'm sad, it's very difficult for me to listen to music because it triggers memories of different times and places. I often thought about putting together a story of my life just based upon the music that I grew up with and have them linked together. . . . I guess it's just that music triggers certain times and my brain immediately rewinds to that era and I'm in it all of a sudden. I don't know if that's a good thing; sometimes it's kind of sad. Sometimes it reminds me of sad times in my life, or just like, "Oh my god, I can't believe that they're playing this song," [you] step way back in time. (Patricia)

Deirdre even contends that memories are not only special when tied to music but even reinforced.

I think the [memories tied to music] are special. Also I think they stick with you more because there's something to accompany them. I think we forget about a lot of things, but I can hear a song and remember the memories associated with that. So I think they're special in that way—because they're what I retain and also they are special and fun. (Deidre)

Other women, Sue, Mary, Lynn and Julie included, talked about very specific ties between someone they know and a particular song. Sue's story about a song that reminds her of an old boyfriend also harkens back to an earlier theme drawn out, how women use music to cope with intimate relationships.

Everything But the Girl's ... "Politics Aside" reminds me of Tommy.... I went out with him for three years, and he totally stomped on my heart, he totally broke my heart.... He twisted my heart into knots. He was always playing games with me, and he was ten years older and I was young and naive and inexperienced and "Politics Aside," it was like [lyrics are] "crystal clear were my intentions but you didn't want to know, when there's no point in staying, you just go." And that's how it got to be, because after undergrad I stayed on seven months after undergrad thinking something was going to come of it with Tommy and I. Guess it was like, there's no point, I'm going. Good bye. And I mean, literally, like that, I was gone. I mean, it was one night I decided, "Okay, I've had enough.... Okay, I'm going home tonight." So that reminds me of him. (Sue)

Sue also had two examples of certain songs that remind her of two friends in particular.

I listen to Everything But the Girl all the time. On the album *Idlewild* there's a song on there that totally reminds me of Donna. "Blue Moon Rose." About a girlfriend that comes over [and we hang out in the kitchen and she makes me feel better] and something like that, because Donna's always saying, "Oh don't sweat it, come on." "You got any money? C'mon, let's go shopping." But I always have to smile when I hear that song because I think of Donna; it totally reminds me of her.... There's another one that reminds me of Sharon on there because we always have our talks about—because we still want to have our own kitchen book and the song is called "Apron Strings." . . . It kind of reminds me of all the conversations we've had about what we want to do with our lives. And she really wants to have a child some day and there's connections there. I don't think I've told either of them that I think of them when I hear these songs. It just kind of makes me smile. (Sue)

Mary, in addition to the songs that she feels reflect her relationship with her boyfriend, also finds the life of her parents and even that of a friend's parents reflected in Paula Cole's "Where Have All the Cowboys Gone." Mary identifies with the disparity in the delegation of responsibilities per each gender in the relationship portrayed in this song. She eventually concedes the song is also reminiscent of her own family life.

[Paula Cole's] "Where Have All the Cowboys Gone" reminds me of my other best friend because what [Paula Cole is] singing about in there is kind of reflective of my best friend's life at home. Not a good situation. I guess I would have to say it does reflect my whole life too. I guess that's kind of why I like that song. In the song [the female protagonist] talks about how her husband will go out or will just sit and drink while she runs the house. And that's my life, that's my parents. My Dad will come in, watch TV, drink and do all that, while my Mom runs the household. She works two jobs—while he won't even sign up to work overtime. So, that song kind of does mean a lot. (Mary)

Lynn talks about how different songs remind her of a lot of different people throughout her life. In fact, complementing Deirdre's earlier comments, Lynn also feels that music provides memories with some staying power.

The Indigo Girls have been two women that I can apply to almost every relationship in my life. There's certain artists that it's like—"Oh, this reminds of" whoever the past person was—[songs] seem to move along with me—I can relate, "Like, okay, I feel this way about this person." And of course there's when you're in intimate moments with somebody—those are the ones that stick out the most. If you're talking with somebody or they're going through a rough time and there's a CD on. . . . [For example,] 10,000 Maniacs. "These Are Days." I love that song. It reminds me of a really good friend of mine in college because we would play it—almost every time we would get ready to go out or—it reminded us of the spring and the summer and things like that. So, that's one example. [And] just recently a friend of mine came to visit and we listened to [Sarah McLachlan's 1993] "Fumbling towards Ecstasy" continuously. So that'll remind me of her, right now. And even if things don't work out with her—or things go bad, I'll always have that. That moment or those moments. There's Madonna songs that remind me of my friends too. So, it's just interesting because songs remind you of moments and those moments are never going to go away. Ya know what I mean? That person could totally change or that relationship with that person can completely change; but if you think about that song, it'll bring back those positive memories in most cases. (Lynn)

Julie appropriates Sarah McLachlan's song "Adia" and is reminded of her mother.

[I like] "Adia" by Sarah. I've decided I want to name my second daughter Adia. That song always reminds me of my mom. I feel like it's supposed to be like a mother talking to her daughter, but I feel more like it's me talking to my mom . . . basically saying, I know I haven't exactly done what you want me to do, but what I've done is because of the way I thought I had to do things to show you that I love you. So that reminds me of my mom. (Julie)

Julie describes a really poignant story about a shared experience between her and her mom. Julie's story about a Linda Ronstadt song reminding her of her mom also reinforces the earlier theme of connecting with people through music.

Anything by Linda Ronstadt from *What's New?* reminds me of my mom. She loves that album. We used to listen to it during dinner all the time, and during *What's New*—at the very end there's this one note that Linda Ronstadt can hold forever and then the orchestra comes back in and there used to be a skip there on the album and I knew exactly where it was and mom knew exactly where it was and we would listen to it during dinner and that song would come on and that part would come on and my mom would calmly put her fork down, get up from the table, wait for it to skip, and put it on the next song and sit back down. And now I have the CD and the CD doesn't skip and I need to find a way to make it skip because it's just not that fun without that skip in it. I think it's hilarious. I brought it [the CD] home—and I surprised my mom—because her turntable doesn't work and we haven't listened to that album in years and I had gone out and bought the CD and I had surprised her with it and we were listening to it and she was sitting in my room, we were kind of reminiscing when I was younger and everything and that song was on and at the end of the song we both just looked at each other and I said, "I know, I can't find a way to make it skip." She's like, "It's not right, it's just not right—it doesn't skip." So that always reminds me of my mom. (Julie)

Music is the soundtrack to invested female music fans' lives—female artists' shared stories about their life experiences as women in a patriarchal world. The artists' stories resonated with female listeners in very particular ways. Each respondent can compile a series of songs that are representative of their life history. As the songs play, the memories, the people, the good and the bad surface in very real ways. The pain or happiness feels just as real and the distant memory feels like yesterday.

CONCLUSION

These women's ability to use female artists' music as a communication tool clearly provides a vehicle for women to express and assert themselves. They were more able to experience emotions that might have otherwise been kept in and were able to more clearly articulate their feelings or thoughts to others. Through this expression they were able to free themselves of social constraints that might have urged them to remain silent. Furthermore, their ability to find expression through female artists is only enhanced when coupled with women's shared experiences with other women. Similar to what Mattern (1998) argued:

The music opened social and public spaces for the communicative interaction that are necessary for the sharing of meaning and the creation of commonalities of identity and orientation. In addition to music, these interactions included everyday conversation, affective interplay and expression and dance—social practices that defined spaces in which youth and others could identify each other as members of a group with shared characteristics. (p. 16)

These women experience their own personal vicarious expression through female artists' music; and other women's similar appreciation, utilization and/or acceptance of such experience strengthens and heightens the entire process. These moments are now not only one individual's validated personal experience; collectively they engage in a feminist discourse—one that alters their lives.

SONG LYRICS

Tori Amos, "Hey Jupiter"

no one's picking up the phone
guess it's me and me
and this little masochist
she's ready to confess
all the things that I never thought
that she could feel and

hey Jupiter
nothing's been the same
so are you gay
are you blue
thought we both could use a friend
to run to
and I thought you'd see with me
you wouldn't have to be something new

sometimes I breathe you in
and I know you know
and sometimes you take a swim
found your writing on my wall
if my heart's soaking wet
boy your boots can leave a mess

hey Jupiter
nothings been the same
so are you gay
are you blue
thought we both could use a friend
to run to
and I thought I wouldn't have to keep
with you
hiding

thought I knew myself so well
all the dolls I had
took my leather off the shelf
your apocalypse was fab
for a girl who couldn't choose between
the shower or the bath

and I thought I wouldn't have to be
with you
a magazine

no one's picking up the phone
guess it's clear he's gone
and this little masochist
is lifting up her dress
guess I thought I could never feel
the things I feel
hey Jupiter

Paula Cole, "Where Have All the Cowboys Gone"

Oh you get me ready in your 56 Chevy
Why don't we go sit down in the shade
Take shelter on my front porch
The dandy lion sun scorching,
Like a glass of cold lemonade
I will do laundry if you pay all the bills

CHORUS:
Where is my John Wayne
Where is my prairie son
Where is my happy ending
Where have all the cowboys gone

Why don't you stay the evening
Kick back and watch the TV
And I'll fix a little something to eat
Oh I know your back hurts from working on the tractor
How do you take your coffee my sweet
I will raise the children if you pay all the bills

I am wearing my new dress tonight
But you don't even notice me
Say our goodbyes

We finally sold the Chevy
When we had another baby
And you took that job in Tennessee
You made friends at the farm
And you joined them at the bar
Almost every single day of the week

I will wash the dishes while you go have a beer
Where is my John Wayne
Where is my prairie son
Where is my happy ending
Where have all the cowboys gone
Where is my Marlboro Man
Where is his shiny gun
Where is my lonely ranger
Where have all the cowboys gone
Yippee Aw, Yippee Yea

Ani DiFranco, "make me stay"

i'm going to turn
and walk away
you wait till i
am far along
then run and come
and catch my arm
and say you'd die
if i were gone
i want to hear you
call my name
it's too easy just to
say it soft
i don't like my language
watered down
i don't like my edges
rounded off

i can't always wait
for your circumstance
to improve
love is loose
it shifts each time you move
go ahead put my
back against the wall
give it all up
or don't give it to me
at all
you never know
this could be
our last night
so step back

step back into the light
so i can see
your silhouette
i'm not done looking yet

save the profile
for the camera
give me your eye to eye
i know all your secrets
and you know
all of mine
mostly i don't go
for the soft focus
and the fantasy
i need something real
i can think
and say and see so

i'm going to turn
and walk away
you wait till i
am far along
then run and come
and catch my arm
and say you'd die
if i were gone
yes, i'm going to turn
and walk away
you can watch me go
or make me stay

Ani DiFranco, "rush hour"

rush hour
and the day's dawning
the rain came and pushed me under the awning
the puddles grew and threw themselves at me
with every passing car
i'm shielding my guitar
there were some things that i
did not tell him
there were certain things he did not need to know
there were some days that i
did not love him

he did not understand me
and i don't know why i didn't go
he said change the channel
i've got problems of my own
i'm so sick of hearing about drugs and aids
and people without homes
and i said well, i'd like to sympathize with that
but if you don't understand then
how can you act
i expected summer to be there in the morning
i awoke to the alarm
but she was out of arm's reach
sneaking out on silent thighs
that were spent and sore
from the hot nights that came before
he said i looked for you
and i don't know why
i said i was wearing black
so you could see me against the sky
take your big leather boots
and your buckles and your chains
put them on a downtown train
i expected he would be there in the morning
i awoke to the alarm
he was still in arm's reach
but his body was just a disguise
his mind had wandered off long ago
i could tell by his eyes
love isn't over when the sheets are stained
in my head there remains
so much left to be said
make me laugh, make me cry, enrage me
but just don't try to disengage me

Ani DiFranco, "the slant"

the slant
a building settling
around me my
figure female
framed crookedly
in the threshold
of the room

door scraping floor
boards with every opening
carving a rough history
of bedroom scenes
the plot
hard to follow
the text
obscured
in the folds of sheets
slowly gathering the stains
of seasons
spent lying there
red and brown
like leaves fallen
the colors
of an eternal cycle
fading with the
wash cycle
and the rinse cycle
again an un-
familiar smell
like my name misspelled
or misspoken
a cycle broken

the sound
of them strong
stalking talking
about their prey
like the way
hammer meets nail
pounding
they say
pounding
out the rhythms
of attraction
like a woman
was a drum
like a body
was a weapon
like there was something
more they wanted
than the journey
like it was owed

to them
steel toed they walk
and i'm wondering why
this fear of men
maybe it's 'cuz i'm hungry
and like a baby
i'm dependent on them
to feed me
i am a work in progress
dressed in the fabric
of a world unfolding
offering me intricate
patterns of questions
rhythms that never
come clean
and strengths
that you still
haven't seen

Ani DiFranco, "what if no one's watching"

if my life were a movie
there would be a sunset
and the camera would pan away
but the sky is just a little sister
tagging along behind the buildings
trying to imitate their gray
the little boys are breaking bottles
against the sidewalk
the big boys, too
the girls are hanging out at the candy store
pumping quarters into the phone
'cause they don't want to go home

and i think,
what if no one's watching
what if when we're dead, we are just dead
what if it's just us down here
what if god ain't looking down
what if he's looking up instead

if my life were a movie
i would light a cigarette

and the smoke would curl around my face
everything i do would be interesting
i'd play the good guy
in every scene
but i always feel i have to
take a stand
and there's always someone on hand
to hate me for standing there
i always feel i have to open my mouth
and every time i do
i offend someone
somewhere

but what
what if no one's watching
what if when we're dead, we are just dead
what if there's no time to lose
what if there's things we gotta do
things that need to be said

you know i can't apologize
for everything i know
i mean you don't have to agree with me
but once you get me going
you better just let me go
we have to be able to criticize
what we love
say what we have to say
'cause if you're not trying to make something better
then as far as i can tell
you are just in the way

i mean what
what if no one's watching
what if when we're dead
we are just dead
what if it's just us down here
what if god is just an idea
someone put in your head

i mean what
what if no one's watching
what if no one's watching . . .

Everything But the Girl, "Politics Aside"
Lyrics and music by Ben Watt

you always loved the sad songs
like you loved it when i lost
so i don't tell you when i'm happy
because it only makes you cross.

and i thought as i was leaving
and it strikes me every time
politics aside
we always
i thought we always got on fine.

crystal clear were my intentions
but you didn't want to know,
when there's no point in staying,
you just go.

and i'll be driving through provincial towns
and places sweetly named
and i'll be looking for a centre,
for a sense of life contained.

but then i'm out the other side
and through suburban avenues
and i realise it never was there.
well, that's how i feel about you.

crystal clear were my intentions,
but you didn't want to know,
when there's no point in staying,
you just go.

Indigo Girls, "Get Out the Map"
Words by Emily Saliers

I'm gonna clear my head
I'm gonna drink that sun

The saddest sight my eyes can see
Is that big ball of orange sinking slyly down the trees
Sitting in a broken circle while you rest upon my knee
This perfect moment will soon be leaving me

Suzanne calls from Boston the coffee's hot the corn is high
And that same sun that warms your heart will suck that good earth dry
With everything its opposite enough to keep you cryin'
Or keep this ol' world spinning with a twinkle in its eye

Get out the map, get out the map and lay your finger anywhere down
We'll leave the figurin' to those we pass on the way out of town
Don't drink the water there seems to be something ailing everyone
I'm gonna clear my head
I'm gonna drink that sun
I'm gonna love you good and strong while our love is good and young

Joni left for South Africa a few years ago
And then Beth she took a job all the way over on the west coast
And me I'm still trying to live half a life on the road
Seems I'm heavier by the year (heavier by the year) and heavier by the load (heavier by the load)

Why do we hurtle ourselves through every inch of time and space
I must say around some corner I can sense a resting place
With every lesson learned a line upon your beautiful face
We'll amuse ourselves one day with these memories we'll trace

Get out the map, get out the map and lay your finger anywhere down
We'll leave the figurin' to those who pass on the way out of town
Don't drink the water there seems to be something ailing everyone
I'm gonna clear my head (I'm gonna clear my head)
I'm gonna drink that sun (I'm gonna drink that sun)
I'm gonna love you good and strong while our love is good and young
I'm gonna clear my head
I'm gonna drink that sun
I'm gonna love you good and strong while our love is good and young

Chapter 4

The Industry, Society and Self

As a little girl Patricia was amazed and impressed by her baby-sitter's ability to remember the words to Nancy Sinatra's "These Boots Are Made for Walkin' " and Roberta Flack's "Killing Me Softly with His Song." "How did she do that?" Patricia thought to herself. "That's awesome!" And she quickly figured it out. Patricia was part of a mostly amateur country duo with one of her best friends. Patricia wrote the lyrics and her friend the music. Patricia's dad used to record them on a reel-to-reel tape machine with the dreams of making it all the way to country music's most revered stage, the Grand Ole Opry. Her aspiring country dreams didn't last long. She became a self-conscious teenager, like most of us, and when she went to high school, it became apparent to her that country music wasn't "cool" anymore, and she turned to other activities—one that included boys.

She never did follow that Grand Ole Opry yearning—but she still daydreams about it. When she attends concerts today she'll imagine herself in the position of the artists on the stage and wonder what it must feel like to sing to such a large adoring crowd. She's onto a new dream now. At 34 years old, soft-spoken yet strong Patricia has a new goal. She just sold her condominium, moved back in with her parents, and bought 20 acres of land in the country to build a retreat center to help men and women during times of transition. To prepare herself she is pursuing a master's in clinical counseling. Though she never gives returning to music much serious thought, she does continue to play piano and guitar.

Patricia explains a very close relationship with music. Music really affects her moods. If she's feeling sad, she can't listen to a sad song, and when she's stuck in rush-hour traffic, she can't listen to fast-paced music. She's had some difficult and unhealthy relationships. Patricia also revealed her tendency to put a lot of self-worth into how others perceive her. For strength, she compares herself to female music artists she respects—including Sarah McLachlan, Sheryl Crow, Paula Cole and Jewel. She senses a certain kinship with them because, like her, they weren't married yet either! She joked, "Maybe they have all wised up or something!"

This final chapter of detailed excerpts from the respondents focuses on women's recognition of the music industry's reasons for allowing female artists access and their arguments that female artists' presence is important for society in general and in their own lives.

"GIVE ME A FUCKING BREAK": WOMEN ARE NOT DUPES OF MUSIC INDUSTRY IDEOLOGY

Since the advent of rock and roll in the 1950s, women have been involved as ardent fans, but the music industry and press never did grant them credence as connoisseurs of music. Young girls and women's visceral responses to music were considered silly and lacking of an understanding or appreciation of music. Garratt (1984), a teenage fan of the Bay City Rollers pop group, noted that "[m]ost of us scream ourselves silly at a concert at least once, although many refuse to admit it later, because like a lot of female experience, our teen infatuations have been trivialized, dismissed, and so silenced" (p. 140). When a group's predominant fan base was made up of women, the group was considered bland, a sellout, and the music dismissed.

This is evidenced during the emergence of the so-called British invasion. As Frith and McRobbie (1978/1990) argued in their germinal work, the pop sound of the early Beatles music resulted in the perception of the Beatles as a girl's band, while the rock sound of the Rolling Stones led to the Stones' status as a boy's band. In turn, this resulted in the early Beatles' work being categorized into the less credible (perhaps even "feminized") category of "teeny-bop" (Frith & McRobbie, 1978/1990).¹ The rock versus pop distinction is well established. Martin (1995) wrote, "Music that had been popular with young women has been typically defined as not art but 'superficial sentiment,' not rock and roll, but 'mere entertainment' and 'teenybopper' fare" (p. 69). Similarly, Reynolds and Press (1995) wrote about the commonly held perceptions of rock and pop. Rock is "the correct response (male connoisseurship, discerning and discriminating) as opposed to [pop as] degraded feminine fan-worship (superficial, hysterical, idolatrous, at once fickly and blindly loyal)" (p. 5). Today, this is perpetuated with the commonly, artistically dismissed boy groups—'N Sync, Backstreet Boys and 98 Degrees—with their female fan base in tow.

Mainstream and male derogatory labeling shifts when the artist is an outspoken female rocker with an assertive stance and feminist-themed lyrics. Feminist-inclined rockers and their fans are commonly labeled with adjectives such as "embittered," "fuming" or "man haters." Women's musical contributions judged by patriarchal standards perpetuate the marginalization and dismissal of their work. Despite the industry's shortsightedness when evaluating women as artists or fans, the quest for profit is the major industry motivator, and if sales increase, mainstream music labels regardless economically support artists.

Although not music industry insiders, the respondents were very aware that the music industry does not value women as credible music listeners or performers but instead sees them as "angry," "bitter" or "silly" women. These women made it clear that female artists did not garner the respect from the industry they rightfully deserved; the industry only allowed female artists access to the stage because of the potential for profits and by no means in the interest of being egalitarian. These women were clearly not dupes of the music industry.

Jo indicated that the industry holds incorrect assumptions about female artists and expressed being annoyed when female artists have to defend their feminist sensibilities, while male artists don't have to defend their biases and privilege within patriarchy.

[The industry] probably thinks they [female artists] are a pain in the ass and outspoken and bitter. I think they think they're silly and I think they don't take them seriously. . . . I think that rather than seeing [that] a lot of the women are speaking out against the way society is, are not doing so because they're [viewed as] man haters, which a lot of them are perceived as. (Jo)

Jo then goes on to talk about McLachlan's and other Lilith Fair performers' fielding of questions from the media accusing the fair of being man-hating because of its female-only lineup. Jo keys right into the fact that accusations of women-hating were never leveled at the organizers and participants of the multiple all-male music festival lineups such as Lollapalooza and HORDE.

They [female artists] are all making sure that they reminded the world that they were not man haters. It is irritating that they had to say anything about it; you know, they certainly aren't saying anything about them [male artists and industry insiders] not being women-haters . . . so that pisses me off. If they [the music industry] would just listen [to the music], maybe they would open up their minds, but instead, I think they just write them off as silly. (Jo)

Lynn, a fan of Sarah McLachlan's musical talents and the staging of Lilith Fair, is very aware of the critiques leveled at the fair and McLachlan by the mainstream media. Lynn also recognizes that female artists still have to struggle.

I think the Lilith Fair was great. . . . I appreciate the idea, I really like the idea of the whole fair. . . . [And] it's interesting to see the media's response to this because they're like "Dyke Fair." And the "We're bashing men fair." It really pisses me off that Sarah . . . has to defend it in a way. Because, give me a fucking break. People don't see [that] before this, it was all men in these little fairs, ya know? And not to say that I didn't go to some of the fairs, but in the discussion of those music fairs, they weren't like, "Well ya know, this is women hating, and na, na, na, na, na." And now because she has this idea to have—"Hey, these women haven't been included and I think it is important that people notice that there are women artists out there"—that all of a sudden it's some big like—"Oh gosh, we hate men." That really aggravates me. The mainstream media just pisses me off. . . . It's sooo aggravating, because they're just not treated as fairly, I don't think. And they have to push, they have to work so much harder—to get into the lime light. . . . What they have to do to get there really aggravates me. (Lynn)

Similar to Jo, Paige refers to the industry's negative, "angry feminist" stereotype that she finds some of her favorite artists accused of.

I know some of the stereotypes that come through are, you know, like Liz Phair, Alanis Morissette, Paula Cole, you know, is the angry hard core—even Ani DiFranco—angry, hard core, feminist woman who is just angry at the world and that's all they sing about. And I think that's very shortsighted. And sort of disserving. . . . And I just, it's one of those stereotypes. . . . It's just a simple overview, 'cause they don't see the music as the same way as other people—as I do. (Paige)

Vivian echoes these same sentiments. She reflects that these assumptions are most unfortunate because certainly there is something for both men and women to gain from feminist social critiques found in a variety of female artists' music.

I think that they view female artists almost like angry grrrl women who are steaming about and wanting the condemnation of men. Which is false, generally. I think that that is unfortunate the establishment feels that way because in some girl rock-music, there are these wonderful little educational pieces that men and women need to hear, to better communicate with one another and themselves. (Vivian)

Vivian turns her critique toward the industry's view of female fans. Vivian suggests that these sweeping assumptions are terribly unfortunate and suggests it would be better to heed the musical and lyrical expressions of these artists and resist the stereotypes.

I think that the establishment views those female fans . . . of Tori [Amos] and Ani [DiFranco] as highly obsessive, boy-haters, odd balls from high school who never had dates to the prom. . . . [I think the establishment views female fans] of boy rock as girls who just wanna be groupies. I think there are a lot of people in the establishment who would be wise enough not to fall into such narrow-minded sentiments towards female fans. Again, I think that it is unfortunate that people would feel that way about female fans, because there is this terrible stereotyping going on, when we need the real picture. (Vivian)

Even the younger participants such as Julie and Mary, both 19, just beyond the so-called teenyboppers age, were quick to notice society's injustices. Their responses are witness to the fact that feminist sensibilities are still alive in the youth of today despite common beliefs to the contrary. Julie is very clear in recognizing discrimination against women. "I think a lot of times women are underestimated just because they are women, and I think the music industry is just another situation where that happens" (Julie). Mary spoke more specifically. She talked about being annoyed by obvious patriarchal bias in a radio DJ's comment and music critics' reviews of Sarah McLachlan's *Surfacing* album and Jewel's song "Foolish Games." Mary even goes as far as to compare a male critic's album review of McLachlan's *Surfacing* as compared to a female reviewer's remarks.

They're [male DJs] always making fun of Sarah McLachlan. They're always making fun of [Jewel's] "Foolish Games." Because they're [the songs] so emotional. . . . I don't think the male producers, or whatever, can handle it, because they are so emotional. And I read a review of *Surfacing* by a male, and he just totally knocked it. He said it was "emotional, sobby"—and almost not worth listening to. I read a female review—and it just got an incredible review. And there was a big difference. (Mary)

Although many of the respondents were happy and excited that female artists garnered mainstream attention in the mid-1990s, many were aware of the industry's reasons for acceptance and were quick to recognize the limitations of this new presence. Jo knows female artists are given opportunity because of the potential for profit: "Money. They're [female fans and artists] money. . . . I see it as a capitalist society and they are trying to make money." Forty-two-year-old business professional in industrial purchasing, Jane made similar observations to the respondents' comments cited above—from transposing how women are viewed in society more generally to the music industry's profit motivation.

I think it [women in music are viewed] the same as women in society. They tend to be ignored, not taken seriously, not given opportunities. I think the ones [female artists] who have made it have made it because the market has been made by women, not necessarily the people that market them, which is the establishment, which tends to be more male dominated—the critics, the producers. The industry realized that records were selling and somebody was buying them and they better get behind them. . . . When the numbers change, they have to change, but I don't think they do it unless the numbers change. . . . I think all they really care about is that they are buying their records. Female artists are starting to become popular. They might be going out to find more [female artists], but it's not to promote those artists because they think they're good, but promote those artists because they will increase their profit. (Jane)

These women knew about the music industry's motivations for including female artists in the lineup. Sadly, the industry is primarily, if not exclusively, motivated by profit. But this drive is only partly responsible for what music makes it to the airwaves. There are other complicated obstacles that make women's climbing of the charts all the more treacherous. One of the primary parts of the equation for success is promotion, and this precedes audience awareness and interest. Labels choose the artists that get contracts and ones that get heavy promotion. Radio stations choose who gets played and how often. These aspects impose on who gets "popular" and, in turn, heard. The majority of these industry insider selections are made by people who hold faulty beliefs about women both as fans and as artists. Keep in mind, it wasn't that long ago that the very broad belief that women couldn't *rock* existed—in fact, for many it still does. This mind-set clouded and continues to cloud views of female artists and fans. Remember, Sarah McLachlan was in part motivated to launch Lilith Fair because of the widely held assumptions that audiences wouldn't go to see two women on the same stage. Beliefs that some might characterize as archaic are very much alive today. Therefore, before female artists even have the opportunity to prove themselves with high sales and profit, they must overcome ignorant mind-sets still alive in the industry. There's still a long way to go.

Although discussion focusing on the plight of female artists in the music industry was not a regular part of the interview protocol, women were cognizant and articulate when discussing the lack of encouragement and support for women and female artists in music. And although all recognized the increased mainstream exposure female artists garnered in the mid- to late 1990s, some of the women were quick (and rightfully so) to comment that although this was an improvement, it did not mean the obstacles faced by women have been removed nor that women have achieved the level of acceptance bestowed on male artists.

Some of the women, including Jo and Lynn, recognize that there is a marked improvement in the mainstream acceptance of female artists, but they are quick to indicate that it is not that female artists didn't exist before. As Lynn asserts, "I don't think that [female artists] were not there—I just think they weren't recognized by like the mainstream media. . . . [And] I think that sucks. But I think—I think I'm lucky to have found these women [now]" (Lynn).

Similar to Lynn, Jo was excited about this new presence of female artists while at the same time asserting that female artists existed prior to this time and questions why their access was limited in the first place.

I love this whole thing. I mean, I remember growing up and when I was in high school there didn't seem like there was any real, there wasn't this huge bunch of women out there to listen to. What was there? Foreigner and Journey? I mean—now it's like all these women seem to be popping up. And I think it's a good thing, a good sign and I hope it keeps happening. And I think they all seem to be part of this whole movement. . . . [W]omen seem to be coming out with all this other half which didn't used to exist which is really good. . . . I think that [this kind of female artists' music did] exist. I think maybe it wasn't being allowed to reach the level that it's reached. I don't know exactly. I don't know enough about it to know exactly what the politics of it are, but I am sure that it existed before. (Jo)

Some of the women were not only reflective of women's past and present roles in the music industry but recognize the problems that persist. Radical feminist Deirdre acknowledged the improvements made but simultaneously argued that there is still a long way to go. Further, she also clearly recognized that there is a lack of diversity and female instrumentalists in the music industry more generally, but in reference to the first year of Lilith Fair in particular. She clearly identifies what she sees as an imbalance between males and females on the stage and behind the scenes.

Just being at Lilith Fair and seeing all these very skinny white women performing. Okay, like where's the difference [diversity]? . . . And women artists are still the exception. So while I'm hearing there's this big women's revolution of music, I think it is mostly crap. Okay, so you're playing them one-hundred percent more, but that means I'm hearing them three times an hour instead of one. . . . I was gonna compile them [the local newspaper's reviews] just to show how often they review women. And it's not often. . . . [It has to do with] patriarchy in society and its male reviewers and male DJs primarily and male producers. . . . I think they have traditional views of what women in music means. . . . [They see it as] women fronted bands. I mean, that's another thing in terms of this women's revolution; at Lilith Fair [in 1997 in Detroit] I didn't see women playing bass or drums. I saw them singing. I wanna see women doing all these instruments—because I know they do, and I know they're out there. . . . Male fans have way more to choose from—in male performers and male concerts—and I think producers and promoters are all primarily male. And some of the women who get air play . . . [they] look a certain way and dress a certain way and sound a certain way. Really Melissa Etheridge is the anomaly—we're not seeing a ton of Melissa Etheridges out there. (Deirdre)

Jill, a singer/songwriter who herself performs on occasion, indicated that always seeing men perform while the women watched was one of the reasons why she took up the guitar. Jill is very reflective about the lack of women as instrumentalists and rock performers through the course of Western music history.

I think men are encouraged to do so many more things than women. We are taught from the time we are very young not to get out there and rough around and play hard. [We are taught] to do the things that are quiet, soft and gentle. And being a musician [or] being a performer . . . is not very encouraged. I mean, when I took the guitar classes on campus—I took 2 different guitar classes—and the first one—in the beginning one, there were probably 15 students—3 of who were women. And then when I went on to the intermediate level, I was the only woman. I just don't think that women are really encouraged to participate in activities like that. (Jill)

Terri categorizes female artists and the music industry with quite a bit of insight.

Well, currently, female music is "in" and I think that the music establishment is treating this popularity as a "fad," which is wrong because women-driven music has always been present but obscured by a patriarchal music industry which often pigeonholes female artists into traditional gender roles—either the virgin or the whore. . . . I like female artists who fuck with those conceptualizations of what it means to be "female." I like female artists who are more political than the love song singing chicks, which is where the music industry (as a whole) want to place female artists. I think that women artists should have more artistic control over their work and the industry should leave them the fuck alone. The music industry wants to make money and keep producing Top 40 crap. (Terri)

SOCIAL IMPORTANCE

Many of the women were clear to indicate that the mainstream acceptance of female artists at this level is socially important and beneficial. Some of the women talked about the value of artists as role models for themselves and/or young people. Some also indicated that just as they have, young people could locate strength and the encouragement to speak out through female artists' music. These women share a general consensus that female artists' increased acceptance into mainstream popularity improves society's view of women and provides valuable role models. Both Jo and Jill are clear about the pleasure involved in seeing these female artists reach this level of popularity.

Jo: I'm glad that they're out there—that they are reaching other people. And I would hope that they have, I would think they have an impact on other people. I wish I'd grown up with them. . . . [S]ome people need to hear this stuff to know that they are not the only ones thinking it.

Jill: It's just so amazing that these women are so out there—with what they're doing for all the world to see.

Julie, Lisa, Sue and Paige all refer to the positive role models these artists provide for young women. Nineteen-year-old Julie finds that these artists, typically seen as strong women, act as role models not only for herself but for young girls as well.

Sarah [McLachlan] portrays herself with a certain amount of maturity and Jewel carries herself like an adult woman. . . . I look up to my female music idols as role models, but there are younger girls who do it more so and I would like to think that they would be looking up to people more like Sarah or Jewel or the Indigo Girls, or somebody who is a strong woman. (Julie)

Lisa, recognizing the limited number of role models during her youth, appreciates the part that female artists play as role models. Lisa is glad to see girls and young women today have successful career women to look up to as compared to what was more typical during her childhood: scantily clad women customarily seen sprawled across a sports car.

[I like to see women succeed because] I relate to that. I just think we're always looking for role models. At this point in my life, I'm forty years old now and I don't know that a musician would necessarily be a role model anymore as opposed to somebody I would respect. I wouldn't aspire to be like that, but when I was growing up, there weren't a whole lot of women who were successful. [There were] actresses and what else? There just weren't women in business. They weren't putting women on the moon. And this was a way for women to achieve professional credibility, not necessarily by wearing bikinis and laying all over cars. (Lisa)

Sue points to one instance in particular where an artist set what Sue identifies as a positive example. Sue applauded Fiona Apple's acceptance speech at the 1997 MTV Video Awards. Sue lauded Apple's efforts to dissuade young girls from trying to emulate the purported and manufactured images of rock stars.

Fiona Apple was on [the] MTV [Video Awards]. I was so proud of her. I was like, "Oh my God." ... [When she accepted her award] she got up there and she said something like, "The people I have to thank, they know who they are, and I'll thank them later in person, but this is my time. And my platform." And she quoted Maya Angelou—[it] went something to the effect that "you have to use the time you have wisely and get something" and said, "This world is bullshit." And they bleeped her. And she's telling young girls not to emulate them. "Don't be like me; don't be like these other people. This is crap." She literally said, "Be yourself." Oh, yeah, well, good for you! You know. Maybe somebody's going to listen to her. (Sue)

Paige feels that musicians, as well as athletes, act as role models. Paige views the mainstream acceptance of female artists as an opportunity for greater acceptance of women in other positions of power. Furthermore, Paige not only views female artists as positive role models but sees their success as another step in combating stereotypes and therefore making her life path an easier one to tread.

[Female artists have] become strong. They are successful. And I think that helps. Music people or musicians are put on a pedestal—not heros, but they—you got your athletes, you got your musicians. Those are the two big groups that people really are like, "Oh, I really admire these people."

And a lot of times it's superficial. It's just because it's America. And for women to be so popular is just great on its own because people never realized that they kind of take it unconsciously that, "Oh if they can be this, then they—" Kind of have a new admiration for women and know that they can do these things. [And that's] extremely important because I am a woman. I mean, plain and simple, I am a woman. And for women to be able to do things I think is important—I would have an opportunity or an easier time obtaining my goals than it would be in the past. And I don't have to combat falsehoods. (Paige)

Similar to Julie, Lisa, Sue and Paige, Jo, who earlier described very strong ties to the music of Tori Amos, Ani DiFranco and Melissa Etheridge, contends that she is a benefactor of female artists' music and further that female artists' music also has the potential to reach out to young people. Jo refers specifically to Amos's "Silent All These Years" as a vehicle for encouraging young people to speak out.

Tori Amos's lyrics are incredible. . . . There's this one song, "Silent All These Years," which I love . . . and the words, they're incredible. The whole idea of having a voice and just being silent and I think that's kind of neat, because I think for young people, especially listening to her, I think she would help them to get to realize their own inner voice. So it's good for young people. I think she could have a great effect on young people. (Jo)

Elaborating on this issue, Jo is very clear in her assertion that female artists' music makes a difference for the individual and therefore society. Jo again refers to Tori Amos and Ani DiFranco's attitude and song "I'm No Heroine." In "I'm No Heroine," DiFranco asserts her voice but acknowledges she does not hold real establishment power; it is men who have designed uncomfortable women's shoes like high heels, assembled the right-angled buildings we occupy and then benefit from profit.

I think it makes a difference. . . . [W]e are socialized to not want to stand out on our own, and [individuals] are more apt to say what they're thinking when they know that other people think the same thing. I think it will, it can make a difference in the way things go in the world—if we have some young girl who, say, has been abused by her father since she was five or something and hears Tori Amos say, "Hey, this is wrong; I'm not putting up with it" or "I'm telling somebody," or people like Ani DiFranco say,

"I don't care if you are offended by what I say. I'm going to say it." Or "these shoes were invented by men." Like she says, "These angles aren't my angles." I think all of that makes a difference. It makes people start thinking, "Yeah!" And maybe there's something they can do about it too. Like I said it made me want to. I think it helped me to become as ambitious as I've become. I think it makes a huge difference. (Jo)

Jo, Jill, Julie, Lisa, Sue, Paige and Patricia all talked about how the mainstream acceptance of female artists' music serves to help individual youths to derive strength. One other area that these artists' mainstream presence makes a difference is through inspiring females to get involved in music. Deirdre talks about this in general, but both Jill and Vivian tell of their own personal experiences of being inspired by a female artist to play an instrument.

Deirdre clearly recognizes the benefits of female performers' ability to gain visibility. She talks specifically about rocker Melissa Etheridge.

Melissa Etheridge . . . [is] this great rocker . . . somebody you can turn up loud and somebody that's great to see. I love to see women doing that—because it's been such a male dominated thing for so long. . . . In some ways it's like any career field where women have had to struggle. And it's doing something that has been considered unfeminine. And it's paving the way in some way. And there are people, there were women before her that paved that way too. Chrissie Hynde—all those other women. But she's like doing it, I don't know, louder or something. So, just showing that's possible, which I think shows other women that it's possible, and even if it's not just for rock'n'roll it's for whatever—it can be inspiring. (Deirdre)

Jill, a singer/songwriter and sometime live performer, clearly credits female artists for inspiring her not only musically but also in terms of maintaining autonomy over her music and career. Jill finds this particularly appealing and important because, similar to Deirdre, she recognizes that women have been denied access to this sort of career. Both Deirdre's and Jill's comments harken back to the themes drawn out earlier that female artists' presence culturally makes a difference.

I find so much inspiration from them [female artists], from listening to their stuff. [And] well everything is about the guys all the time. All the history we learn is about men and all the people in power are men. I know I am being sweeping here . . . but across the board, it's all about men in our society—and above that it's all about white men. . . . And being able to hear women on the radio and being able to buy their music is so important to me because that's a little part of the female culture that can get out there. Where people will listen. Maybe they won't get it, but at least it will be out there for them to hear. . . . I am glad that there are women that have come before me. Because it makes it easier to be a female musician. . . . But I am glad that we are getting more exposure and that women are getting out there more—and that [it's] more accepted and desirable to be a female musician. (Jill)

Again, Jill is not only musically inspired but draws confidence from the Indigo Girls' and Ani DiFranco's independence and control of their careers.

I think they [Indigo Girls and Ani DiFranco] are really strong women and they don't let the media dictate what they are doing. It's just kind of like their thing. . . . I like that they just do what they want to do. [It's appealing because] I don't like anybody telling me what I should do with my music. It's mine! It started with me, it started in my head, it started on my guitar, with my voice. And so I think that's appealing that they just do their thing—and happen to be very successful at it. [And] even if they weren't, I think that's what they would still be doing. Ani DiFranco is my idol. Oh my God, I love her. And [it's the] same kind of thing [as with the Indigo Girls]. She's got her own recording enterprise now. I think that's inspiring too. (Jill)

Vivian spoke about two different instances when she felt inspired by female artists to take up an instrument. Her first recollection was taking notice of two females (Janice Marie Johnson and Hazel Payne) holding guitars on one of her mother's A Taste of Honey album covers. She describes the moment as an awakening declaring that if those women could play guitar, she might be able to as well. Similar to Deirdre and Jill, Vivian is also aware that music, and playing instruments, was not an arena where women were readily accepted.

My mom . . . would play a song [from a] group called A Taste of Honey and the album cover is two women and one had the guitar and one had the bass. . . . I think that had an influence on me too like, "Oh, she's playing a guitar and she's playing a bass and they sound cool." . . . I think that was significant because to see something different from the norm, just like an all guy band. It was really cool because it seems like I had some kind of awakening. "Well if that girl can play guitar, then maybe I could too." It was empowering, I guess, to see two women have the band. And I guess they were the centerpiece of the band too because they were the only people that were on the cover. So that kind of gave me like a new perspective in music, I guess. Because they were playing funky music too. So that has some kind of a power edge to it.... Because you don't really get that I don't think from society—where I was looking at the time. That women could actually play guitar and have it sound good—and make it. (Vivian)

The other influence that Vivian described was when she was first introduced to the music of Tracy Chapman. Feeling like a misfit as a child, Vivian recalls how hearing Tracy Chapman for the first time inspired her to learn to play guitar.

I think Tracy Chapman has inspired me to play because when I was younger in high school, I felt like I kind of was a misfit. And my friend from high school, he made a copy of both of her albums, and I just totally saturated myself in them. I thought they were really powerful because they were political and they also dealt with a lot of emotional things and spirituality. And so I just decided that I wanted to play the guitar. (Vivian)

INDIVIDUAL IMPORTANCE

These women have clearly expressed a unique connection with female artists and their music and contend that female artists' music makes a difference for society at large. In consideration of what has emerged, an appropriate and heartening way to end the respondent section of this book is to allow all 15 respondents to express—in their own words and without interruption—the importance of female artists' music to each of them individually.

The excerpts below are primarily in response to either one or two questions: "What does female artists' music mean in your life?" and "What if you could no longer listen to female artists' music?" Although each excerpt stands on its own, many of them harken back to some of the earlier themes fleshed out throughout the last three chapters and also support the notion that female artists' music means a great deal to invested female listeners.

I think my life would be different without [female artists' music]. I can't imagine it not existing. It's important to me and it's like a background music or it's always there. . . . I think it [female artists' music] has affected how I look at my life—the same way women authors do. . . . I think [female artists' music] opened up new possibilities. I think it still does. There are things that I'll hear in a lyric or primarily lyrics but that's tied into the music. . . . It's all connected. That it will affect how I look at something, or show me a different way to look at it. Or cause me to remember something that I had forgotten about. And for me in particular doing a [music by women] radio show. If there wasn't women's music, I wouldn't be doing a women's music show. And feeling like that has that ripples on the water effect. There are people who are listening to this. . . . So I feel like it's making me make a difference to other people too. It's introducing them to musicians they otherwise would not have heard. And making a difference in their life. . . . I don't like to imagine [not being able to listen to women's music]. Old hand maids tale kind of world. I think there'd be music that I'd listen to, but it would be a huge hole. I can't imagine. . . . I'd be missing a lot. I don't think life would be as enjoyable on some level. There'd be something huge lacking. (Deirdre)

[Female artists' music] means a lot. It's definitely, part of it just connects with the idea of my feeling good about myself. That's a lot of what it means. It's also a way I connect with [my lover] June, with my friends. It's also something that makes me feel good to listen to. . . . I really think there is a spirit about music. Even if I didn't know a whole lot, I could tell at least if I liked them [female music artists] or not because you could tell by what they say and what they write about in their music. And that kind of stuff is really important to me because it makes you feel good to hear it, so I think that it's just an important part of my life. . . . [If it was eliminated] that would be quite distressing because certainly male artists certainly do not provoke the same sensations or the same emotions and then they do not give me the same satisfaction in any way, so certainly, definitely, it would be quite a void. I would be very unhappy. . . . And there's definitely a political agenda for me, too. About patronizing women and listening to women and that's definitely part of it. (Elisabeth)

[If I couldn't listen to female artists' music anymore] I would be really disappointed. . . . In my life right now, it would just be something that was missing, was lacking, because I am so women identified. . . . In my life right now, it is so wrapped up with who I am; it's women's music, it's women authors. I even like women contractors to work on my house and I like to support women in business, so I think for me that's pretty important. (Jane)

[It] would break my heart [if I could no longer listen to female artists' music]. Oh, god that would break my heart. . . . Oh, that would be harsh, that would be sad . . . [because] I just can never really get inspired by male musicians. . . . I find so much inspiration from them, from listening to their stuff. . . . And being able to hear women on the radio and being able to buy their music is so important to me because that's a little part of the female culture that can get out there. (Jill)

[Having this music is] wonderful. It means there are like-minded people that I can listen to that I can relate to. It means a ton to me. I cannot imagine not having them around. I find things in [my] journals that are later said in different ways in music, in their songs and I can say, "Oh, cool." . . . I think that it means a lot to me. It means there are other people out there who think like I think. . . . And if they weren't allowed to be making the records and getting on the radio, I wouldn't even know they are out there. I would feel more of a freak than I normally do. . . . [And female artists' music means] connection. It means [I] don't feel so alone in the world. . . . I've walked around my whole life feeling rather alone, so I really need to listen to these people. . . . [Without female artists' music] I'd be miserable. I'd be absolutely miserable. . . . [T]o be without music, I would be very unhappy. I would be a very depressed individual. . . . I would feel definitely alone and . . . I wouldn't have that connection and I would probably be feeling rather lonely and not very happy. . . . It would not be a good life. (Jo)

[Female artists' music means] continuity and dependability [to me]. [It's] something that is constant. Basically, something that is just always there and something that I can relate to and I can turn to, no matter what is going on. . . . [And if they didn't exist] I'd go nuts. I'd sing the songs to myself. I'd go insane just because they are my favorites. And I would hate to have to deal with not being able to hear them. (Julie)

[Female artists' music is important to me because] I spend about sixteen hours a day working at a frantic pace, mostly with men. And taking close to no time out for personal [things], hardly even time for lunch. And it's kind of a release. I feel like I'm connecting with somebody. . . . [And if I couldn't listen to them anymore] I would think the world was unfair. . . . [But] I would probably find similar releases through male music. [However, it wouldn't serve the same purpose], they've never had a [menstrual] period. . . . So I would feel a sense of loss. (Lisa)

I think [not being able to listen to female artists] would suck. I don't even want to think about [it]. There's still a lot of male artists that I appreciate and that I like. So it wouldn't be—it would blow. I would still have that, but it wouldn't mean the same thing. (Lynn)

I guess [female artists' music] plays a big role in my life because I do listen to female [artists'] music all the time. And I guess it's a way for me to relax. If I get really stressed out it's a relaxing part of my life. It makes me think; it makes me sit down and think. To just think about things in my life. I'll put on one of my Sarah [McLachlan] CDs or Jewel or whatever and I'm just gone. Everything else doesn't matter.... [And if I didn't have it to listen to anymore] I would be lost. I could not survive. I need to have some kind of female music in my life. I think it would be hard to listen to music if I couldn't turn on the radio or turn on the CD player and have Sarah or Jewel or whoever. They've become such a big part of my life, their music, their lyrics, that I think it would be hard for me to relax or to think. (Mary)

[Female artists' music] probably means several things [to me]. The identification and that I can sing along. It gives me enjoyment. It gives me all these feelings that helps me create the mood that I want to create. And also women artists especially now ... they've become strong.... I mean, plain and simple, I am a woman. And for women to be able to do things I think [are] important ... I would have—an opportunity or an easier time obtaining my goals than [maybe I would have] in the past. And I don't have to combat falsehoods.... There's nothing like music. You can't compare it—you can't have anything else. [Music is] a big part of my life and if it wasn't a part of my life, there would be something missing.... [To go through a day] without music—I couldn't imagine. [It] would be hard.... Of all the things that I enjoy in life, it's definitely close to the top. There's my art, music, my family, my friends. You know my family and friends honestly I think are most important, but if you kind of had to rate it—it would definitely fall in the top 10. (Paige)

I think [music is] very powerful. I think it can be therapeutic and I also think it can trigger some real devastating memories and emotions, depending on where I am at that time. Some songs are very nurturing, I feel very comfortable and [it's] refreshing to hear [them], or they're funny or you remember funny or stupid things you were doing at the time. I think that music is a very, very powerful tool in psychological states.... I really think it can shape a person's piece of mind or mood.... [And if I could no longer listen to female artists] I'd be sad. It would be sad. It would be hard to do. I can't imagine.... [It] would be awful. I think we would miss out on a lot. I would personally miss out on a lot. I'd miss that bonding, I'd miss that relatedness.... [For me, in my everyday life] it would be isolating. I would feel isolated or disconnected or removed—not participative, not as important.... I think it would make me feel more suppressed. (Patricia)

[If I could no longer listen to female artists] I would get very uppity. Who the hell is telling me who I could listen to! But see, if they said I could never listen to male artists—I would get a little uppity. But I would probably get a little more uppity about the female artists. . . . I think it would be less interesting music. . . . It's not even necessarily that I like their music more—it's just that I appreciate that they have to fight harder. . . . It would be limiting. (Sandi)

[If I could no longer listen to female artists] I probably wouldn't listen to music at all anymore. In fact, that's kind of how I am when I'm at work. I listen to a lot of electronic music—because it doesn't really have vocals. It's not really political or challenging. And I think that's what I'd resort to. It would definitely have a dulling effect. It would take a little spirit out of you. (Sue)

Chick music means a great deal in my life and I can't imagine life without it. As I said, often the music parallels or evokes feelings in me that would otherwise be buried. Female music is very cathartic. . . . [And] I would feel really bummed if I couldn't listen to the music. After my [temporarily debilitating] accident, [my boyfriend] had all my CDs. And at my mom's house [recovering], I had four CDs that he had forgot to take with him. And they were New Order, one of the Cranberries, an REM, and some other dude. Oh, it was like an instrumental. I was going crazy, because I couldn't hear what I wanted to hear. And when I went to his house . . . all I did was stick Indigo Girls, all of my CDs, in my—because he had my stereo, too—I put them all in the turnstile, and, when we got to his house, the first time I got to go there, I said, "Okay, put in *Rites of Passage* now!" And I just sat there and just cried, listening to the music, because I, well, maybe because it was that choice was taken away from me, and so were a lot of other choices in my life at that point. But it just felt so good to listen to something that I identified with. Because I couldn't listen to anything. My mom listens to classical, or Frank Sinatra or MTV; you don't get to choose what you listen to. It's awful, not being able to listen to it. And at [my boyfriend's] I had this whole list of music I wanted to listen to that I hadn't heard in so long. 10,000 Maniacs, all the stuff that really means something to me, the Cranberries, even P.J. Harvey, that I hadn't heard in a long time. . . . It's awful, it's really awful, not being able to listen to that music. And like I said, I use it as a form of expression, like vicarious expression. (Terri)

[If I could no longer listen to female artists' music] I would probably cry, or feel like my arm was ripped off or something like that. Not that I would—because I wouldn't feel like totally annihilated—but I would know that something significant was missing—if that was the case. (Vivian)

NOTE

1. Although Frith and McRobbie (1978/1990) contend that there was a contrast between the musical styles of the early Beatles and the Rolling Stones, they concede that the contrast was not maintained. The Beatles began to fuse "a rough R&B beat with yearning vocal harmonies derived from black and white romantic pop; the resulting music articulated simultaneously the conventions of feminine and masculine sexuality" (p. 383). In turn, the Beatles' work began to gain greater critical acclaim.

SONG LYRICS

Tori Amos, "Silent All These Years"

Excuse me but
can I be you for a while
My DOG won't bite
if you sit real still
I got the anti-Christ
in the kitchen
yellin' at me again
Yeah I can hear that

Been saved again
by the garbage truck
I got something to say
you know but NOTHING comes
Yes I know what you think of me
you never shut up
Yeah I can hear that

But what if I'm a mermaid
In these jeans of his
with her name still on it
Hey but I don't care
Cause sometimes I said
sometimes I hear my voice
and it's been
HERE silent all these years

So you found a girl
who thinks really deep thoughts
What's so amazing
about really deep thoughts

Boy you best pray
that I bleed real soon
How's that thought for you

My scream got lost in a paper cup
You think there's a heaven
where some screams have gone
I got 25 bucks and a cracker
do you think it's enough
To get us there

But what if I'm a mermaid
In these jeans of his
with her name still on it
Hey but I don't care
Cause sometimes I said
sometimes I hear my voice and it's been
HERE silent all these

Years go by will I still be waiting
For somebody else to understand
Years go by if I'm stripped of my beauty
And the orange clouds raining in my head
Years go by will I choke on my tears
Till finally there is nothing left
One more casualty
You know we're too EASY easy easy

Well I love the way we communicate
Your eyes focus on my funny lip shape
Let's hear what you think of me now
but baby don't look up
The sky is falling

Your MOTHER shows up in a nasty dress
It's your turn now to stand where I stand
Everybody lookin' at you
here take hold of my hand
Yeah I can hear them

But what if I'm a mermaid
In these jeans of his
with her name still on it
Hey but I don't care

Cause sometimes I said
sometimes I hear my voice
I hear my voice
I hear my voice
And it's been HERE silent all these years
I've been here silent all these years
Silent all these
Silent all these years

Ani DiFranco, "i'm no heroine"

you think i wouldn't have him
unless i could have him by the balls
you think i just dish it out
you don't think i take it at all
you think i am stronger
you think i walk taller than the rest
you think i'm usually wearing the pants
just 'cause i rarely wear a dress
well . . .

when you look at me
you see my purpose you see my pride
you think i just saddle up my anger
and ride and ride and ride
you think i stand so firm
you think i sit so high on my trusty steed
let me tell you
i'm usually face down on the ground
when there's a stampede

i'm no heroine
least not last time i checked
i'm too easy to roll over
i'm too easy to wreck
i just write about what i
should have done
i sing what i wish i could say
and I hope somewhere
some woman hears my music
and it helps her through her day

some guy designed
these shoes i use to walk around
some big man's business

turns a profit every time
i lay my money down
some guy designed this room
i'm standing in
another one built it
with his own tools
who says i like right angles
these are not my laws
these are not my rules

i'm no heroine
i still answer to the other half
of the race
i don't fool myself like i fool you
i don't have the power
we just don't run this place

Chapter 5

Conclusions

As stated from the start, this book set out as a venue for women's often dismissed voices to be heard about rock music (including pop/rock, singer-songwriters, and folk rock). My hope is that we all have a better understanding of women's relationship with female music artists who embody a political and/or feminist sensibility. The music and the artists described by the listeners clearly played an important role in their everyday lives, and their "use" of music manifested itself in a variety of ways. First, this chapter summarizes the women's responses in terms of interpellation and articulation. Second, it considers its contributions to feminist media studies.

INTERPELLATION: ATTRACTION THROUGH AFFINITY

These women expressed that their attraction to these artists was in large part due to their sense of affinity toward them. The respondents were interpellated (hailed) (Bobo, 1988) by the text—the artists and their music—because of the relevancy (Fiske, 1988) to their lives. Because of a shared, similar ideological positioning, which was manifest in the artists and their work, these women embraced and engaged in the text. This is detailed in the women's explanations for their preferences for female artists over male artists and their indication of well-marked preferences for particular, favored female artists. The respondents were clearly interested in female artists with substantive, meaningful and creative lyrics. They also described a greater appreciation for female artists who maintain a significant level of involvement in the production of their art. These women also described a preference for quality sound—identifying and being attracted to artists who are skilled as musicians and vocal artists. They favored artists who produced work from a political perspective and worked in an effort to affect change and were clearly interested in female artists who maintain control and autonomy in their attitude, art and career decisions.

They recognized, appropriated and were attracted to female artists through primarily the singular commonality of being a woman and the female artists' ability to provide a perspective in their music unique to female experiences. These women expressed experiencing a certain affinity with and identifying with female artists, and this resonated the most when respondents spoke of lyrics. Women also found a particular attraction to the female voice as opposed to the male voice—whether to sing along with, or to be comforted by, some women found female vocal qualities more pleasing to the ear. The respondents also felt that female artists were better able to capture the nuances of relationships, emotions and feelings. Some of the women found that their interest in music by women paralleled their interest in feminism, and lesbians in particular found distinct pleasure in listening to woman-identified music. Finally, women expressed an appreciation of these artists' abilities and their courage to succeed in a male-dominated industry. They recognized the artists' political efforts, and some respondents even chose to consciously support female artists as a part of their own political activism.

ARTICULATION: TRANSFORMING CULTURE?

Women clearly have a strong connection to female artists' music. All of the women described moments of engagement with the text that in turn had implications in their lives. These are moments of articulation, and this is where this study makes its unique contribution: These women are engaged in the practice of articulation and are in effect taking part in cultural transformation. Arguably, these moments of articulation contribute to the development of a more feminist-minded media fare and an increasingly informed public and in turn contribute to the efforts for a more egalitarian culture.

More specifically, these moments and processes of articulation are evidenced in the inductively emergent themes as follows. These women declared that female artists and their music helped them to feel validated, justified and empowered and allowed them to achieve a sense of affirmation. Some of the women even explained that the development of their personal identity was tied in with particular artists or songs. Some of the women also described the appropriation of female artists' music into their everyday lives as a coping mechanism. The women described stories revolving around transitions and challenges in their lives, including personal intimate relationships, fighting depression, working through past abuse and dealing with their sexual orientation.

Furthermore, these women described finding voice through female artists and their music. The women indicated that female artists were able to articulate emotions or feelings in a way they were unable to. In some instances, women actually used female artists to communicate with others and to express their thoughts and feelings to others. Music by women also provided listeners with an opportunity to connect or bond with family and friends. Women felt that concerts provided an arena for bonding, sharing experiences with others and finding a sense of community. Many of the respondents also tied life experiences to music and/or associated particular songs with loved ones. The women were also very aware of the industry's dismissive views about female fans and the industry's profit-motivated reasons for allowing women access. Despite the industry's economically motivated reasons, they were eager to point out that the mainstream acceptance of female artists was indeed socially important. Finally, these women were clear in indicating that female artists' music played an important role in their lives.

In sum, the role of music by women in women's lives is one of political, social and cultural significance. These findings suggest that contrary to some of the contentions made in academic and popular press, women are discriminating music listeners. When making comparisons between female artists, these women placed value on talent (as a songwriter, singer, musician and performer), authenticity, autonomy and artists who create from a political perspective and work toward effecting change. Overwhelmingly, because of the commonality in the experience of living as a woman, individual respondents described an astute affinity with female artists. Having largely been symbolically annihilated (Tuchman, 1978) in popular music in the past, these women are drawn to a musical representation of their varied female experiences. These respondents, as invested listeners, shared social allegiances with these feminist and/or politically minded female artists. These artists, consciously and unconsciously, created and provided their own, and that of the listeners, symbolic representation. Female audiences, starved for a more realistic and diverse representation, supported these female artists.

Through interpellation (Bobo, 1988), these women are hailed by the text and are drawn into the text through a sense of relevancy (Fiske, 1988) of the text to their lives. Musical artists and audiences, at least in a performative sense, have a reciprocal relationship, for without one, the other would not exist; and both define themselves through the other. Women who feel an allegiance with other women will tend to listen to music from that perspective. Although each and every woman's life experiences are varied and multiple, there are some commonalities in the experience of living as a women in a patriarchal society. Arguably, artists' life experience influences their songwriting and performance style. In turn, a female artist's music is bound to ring true for, be relevant to, other women's lives.

Furthermore, these artists and their music play a distinct role in women's negotiation of their daily lives. This is noted in particular in women's appropriation of female artists' music for coping. The repeated stories of women's appropriation of female artists' music suggests the level of importance that female artists' music means in women's lives. These respondents recognized similarities in their female experiences in the work of female artists and in turn used the music of these female artists to cope with life. As Bobo (1988) contended about female African American authors and their female African American readers, these women are empowered through the music and in turn—especially through sharing music and concerts—empower their social group. Both the artists and the listeners recognize and celebrate their own existence.

In turn, there is power in this representation (Gross, 1989). Through representation and in particular the mainstream acceptance of this representation, women's lives are recognized and validated. In turn, individual women locate a sense of personal empowerment. More so and especially when considering the feminist and political nature of these artists and that they maintain a marked level of control over their work, are comparatively talented and are politically and feminist minded, this music serves a greater purpose of informing and teaching the larger public. This is power through representation in search of transformation. These artists not only serve the purpose of empowering enlightened and invested listeners, but they affect people who are not feminist or politically minded. In fact, Mary's story about becoming feminist identified through the Lilith Fair serves this point. These artists effect change. In this instance, it is more than representation—it is an important political representation: a political representation for women to identify with and develop their own identity from.

Most important, this results in transformation through articulation. The *transformation* may not be wide reaching, radical or revolutionary, but instead slow and determined and beginning with the individual, but it is change nonetheless. Cultural critic Stuart Hall posits that

> the theory of articulation asks how an ideology discovers its subject rather than how the subject thinks the necessary and inevitable thoughts which belong to it; it enables us to think how an ideology empowers people, enabling them to begin to make some sense of intelligibility of their historical situation, without reducing those forms of intelligibility to their socio-economic or class location or social position. (Hall as cited in Grossberg, 1996, p. 142)

The collective political discourse, some of which is based on personal experiences, of these individual female artists has acted as a catalyst for social change. Whether intentional or not, the artists, music and audience contribute to the development and perpetuation of feminist-minded discourse. The mere existence and level of mainstream acceptance of this feminist and political discourse within a patriarchal industry alone exemplifies the political and cultural transformation that took place. In fact, respondents themselves have indicated that these artists and their music are transformative. Some reflected on their own childhood and teen years, identifying what they saw as a lack of female role models, and suggested that the mainstream acceptance of these artists helped to alleviate this absence for young girls and women. Although not demolished, past "naturalized" gender roles have been disrupted through these artists' musicianship and performances. Young women and girls now have role models and access to a cultural symbolic system that had been previously denied them. Young females' involvement in rock music no longer appears flagrantly outside of the "norm." In turn, they are more easily able to take part in this cultural practice—a cultural practice that can potentially provide a vehicle for more women's stories to be told. Clearly, music listening is far more than mere idle entertainment.

The political and feminist nature of this music, the artists and fans challenge the status quo. The engagement of these performers, the music and the audience creates an ideological interdiscourse that works in opposition to, contests and contradicts the dominant ideology. Through the support of the audience, these artists have attained a marked level of success and in turn a significant amount of exposure. This mainstream exposure and acceptance of this feminist and politically minded cultural product are evidence of cultural transformation. As Pratt (1990) posits, music can indeed be "a means of effecting change in society" (p. 143).[1] Moreover, by economically supporting female artists with a political and/or feminist sensibility, these listeners in effect reject—and act in resistance to—male artists and less credible female artists. As Lewis (1990) contends, "Involvement in cultural arenas such as popular music can change the life conditions of those participants who use their participation as a means of resisting oppressive social conditions" (p. 150). Clearly this music forwards feminist issues and causes.

Some might still argue that the success of artists and fan reaction as described here still does not constitute real, significant political change, and frankly, especially considering the recent dramatic downturn female rock artists with a political and/or feminist sensibility have taken in the last couple of years, I've struggled with this quite a bit myself. An argument could be made that women's engagement with the type of artists discussed here is not transformative because many of the artists still operate and produce their work within a patriarchal and capitalist structure—the male-dominated, profit-seeking music industry. For example, Riordan (2001) makes a good point in her comparison of the DIY (do-it-yourself) politics of the riot grrrls to the commodification of the Spice Girls' "girl power"—suggesting that the riot grrrl movement acts in opposition to the dominant patriarchal and capitalist structures, while the Spice Girls act in concert with the same constructs and therefore do no good in changing sociopolitical structures that continue to oppress women. Riordan writes about "girl power," "Collective transformations cannot occur if individuals only work to make themselves feel better" (p. 284). It is a convincing argument. If music is only used to make one's self "feel better," a revolution will not occur in a timely fashion, and considering women's oppressed and subordinated place in the world, we do need change now. However, I also believe that using music by female artists to make one's self "feel better"—or justified, validated or empowered—facilitates an *evolution* of change. It's not dramatic or quick, but it is progressive change nonetheless. If I as an activist, feminist and educator take pride in my teaching because it changes students' worldviews, and even if on occasion it is only one student per course, it is still worthwhile. The same can be said about female rock music artists. Women's engagement with female music artists with a political and/or feminist sensibility is transformative. And although the artists work within a patriarchal and capitalist industry, the music and the political interests and causes of the artists challenge the status quo and seek to effect change. Perhaps many of the artists mentioned make some concessions in working within industry constraints and not strictly independently, but they also have the potential to reach a larger audience—which directly affects the number of people who might meaningfully engage with the feminist or political text.

For example, in fall 2000 I taught a "Women and Rock" course at Butler University. One unit of the course focused on riot grrrls. Although I agree that riot grrrls more often provide better, stronger examples in their efforts to effect change more so than some of the artists mentioned by the respondents, and although I commend and support them, it is also true their reach is limited. Almost none of the students had heard of riot grrrls—therefore allowing little opportunity for them to engage in the cultural resistance of the music and politics.

Furthermore, although most of the artists mentioned in this book are not riot grrrls, it is also important to remember that most are also not "pop" stars in the vein of the Spice Girls, Britney Spears or Christina Aguilera. Most of the artists mentioned by the respondents fall somewhere in between these divergent styles. Although operating within a decidedly patriarchal and capitalist system, through their music and political actions, the female artists most frequently mentioned by the respondents in this book do act in resistance to this dominant paradigm. In particular, it is hard to see anything but the best of politics manifested in the work of Indigo Girl Amy Ray and Ani DiFranco. Therefore, I contend there is undoubtedly value in their presence and women's engagement with them; at the very least, the transformation manifests itself at the individual level but arguably also at the cultural level. It is transformation. Similar to how I feel about my successes in the classroom and as respondent Deirdre talked about her "Womyn and Music" radio show at a local university station, "It is that ripple in the water effect." It does make a difference; the respondents said as much when they detailed the personal and social importance these artists have.

CONTRIBUTIONS TO FEMINIST MEDIA STUDIES AND RECEPTION ANALYSIS

This study complements many of the theoretical assumptions made by the collective of feminist media studies and reception analyses. However, it is important to first point out that when considering the nature of the text for this study (feminist and/or politically minded artists and their music), as compared to the text of a majority of feminist media audience studies (romance novels, soap operas), mapping out the differences based on this textual difference is futile to explicate. The women in this interpretive audience study were ideologically similar to the text under consideration, whereas most feminist audience studies of the past examined negotiated or oppositional readings with an ideologically contrasting text-reader relationship. For instance, noting that Seiter et al. (1996) found that female soap opera viewers criticized the text, and my respondents did not, or that the women in Bobo's (1988) study relayed oppositional readings of a text (*The Color Purple*) thought to be unflattering to African Americans, and my respondents did not relay oppositional readings, is pointless. Most of the past audience studies sought out women's negotiation of a primarily patriarchally constructed and nonfeminist media fare, whereas this study focused on women's reaction to feminist and/or politically minded artists and music. Therefore, this conclusion focuses solely on similarities between the findings of this study and past audience studies. Moreover, because the text-reader relationship is so different, the similarities are all the more striking and significant.

This music-focused audience study supports many of the contentions made by feminist audience studies and reception analyses. Similar findings include contentions that women contemplatively engage with media and that media fare plays a role in interpersonal relationships and provides a vehicle for women to talk about their own lives. Women also develop an emotional involvement and identify with some media texts. Finally, women use media fare as instruments of survival, to fight against gender inequality and feel empowered. This section details each of these.

The most overwhelming and sweeping similarity that runs across most feminist audience studies is the assertion that women do indeed incorporate media into their everyday lives (Ang, 1985; Hobson, 1989; Lewis, 1990; Radway, 1984; Seiter et al., 1996). This music-focused interpretive audience study's findings were no different in this respect. The women in this study were invested in, related to and talked about female artists' music. Women's relationship with media can be an important aspect of their daily lives.

Hobson (1989, 1990) contended that watching soap operas contributed to the interpersonal relationships of women. The same can be said of the women in this music-focused interpretive audience study. Similar to Hobson's observation about soap opera viewers, these respondents indicated that they shared music with friends and used music to communicate with others. They spoke of actual moments of bonding with other women through the music of these female artists. Furthermore, many of the women even indicated experiencing a sense of community at the concerts of female artists. Both this study and Hobson's work suggest that women extend the actual moment of media engagement beyond the individual moment and into the interpersonal realm.

Relatedly, Hobson (1989, 1990) also contended that soap operas provided a vehicle for women to think and talk about their own lives. The findings in this music-focused audience study support this contention as well. Many of the respondents talked about how they identified with or related to the experiences detailed in songs and mapped their interpretations of particular songs onto their own lives. Women use media fare to reflect on their lives and seek out representation within media. Frequently, women parlay these moments of recognition into reflections about their own lives. Likewise, oftentimes these same moments of identification can be carried over into talk about their lives and the music within the context of interpersonal relationships with women.

This study also supports past contentions made about women's emotional involvement with media fare and identifying with soap opera characters. Hobson (1989, 1990) contended that women felt an emotional involvement with soap operas, and Seiter et al. (1996) found that women felt connected to soap opera characters. Both of these findings are supported by similar findings by Ang (1985). Ang found that female viewers of *Dallas* identified with characters and their emotional predicaments and even found them realistic. This was in contrast to earlier notions that this genre of programming was for mere fantasy or escape. Ang described this as an "emotional reading." Again, although the text in this study is markedly different to the text under examination in these studies, certainly the findings of this interpretive audience study support this contention. Women can feel an emotional involvement and connection with media fare. Similarly, where Seiter et al. (1996) and Ang indicate reader identification with characters, the respondents in *They're Playing Our Songs* indicated a similar connection to female music artists. The women in this study felt very connected to the musical performers. This is most notable in the respondents' frequent reference to the artists by their first names, suggesting a level of perceived intimacy. Women also connected with artists by identifying deeply with the artists' self-written songs. The respondents were likely to feel a sense of identification because of a perceived shared experience.

Radway (1984) contended that women's incorporation of romance novels into their everyday lives was in part to reconcile their feminist notions with their continued existence and familial oppression in a patriarchal system. Radway contended that women negotiated the text of romance novels to make do with their social situations. Furthermore, Radway suggested that because the readers were attentive to romance novels and perhaps neglecting motherly/wifely/household duties, the act of reading itself could be interpreted as a site of resistance. Interestingly, although very different forms of text, these same sort of contentions are reinforced by the findings of this study. Although the text under consideration in this study was primarily feminist minded, the female music listeners still experience their everyday lives within a patriarchal system. Arguably, these women's stories about appropriating music to cope with their everyday lives, in part, are an effort by them to negotiate their social situation. This is of particular note when considering the stories that tell of intimate and/or romantic relationships or dysfunctional or troubled family lives or friendships. This study's findings coupled with Radway's contentions suggest that women can use media fare as an instrument of survival within a patriarchal system. They make the text "work" for them. Furthermore, although the text in Radway's 1984 study is different from the text under consideration in this study, the suggestion that women can act in resistance while engaging with either text runs through both studies. Clearly, considering the feminist and/or political nature of the music and artists under consideration in this study, this act of resistance is more obvious. And in fact, some have even criticized Radway's suggestion that the act of reading romance novels can function as a site of resistance (see Van Zoonen, 1994). Nonetheless, these contentions go to prove that engagement with media fare by women can be moments of political action. Moreover, once again considering the feminist and political nature of the artists and music, this study demonstrates that one can find pleasure through the political. Women's engagement of these political- and/or feminist-minded artists is a pleasurable political act.

Lewis (1990) found that "gender experience became the common point of reference" (p. 150) between Madonna, Cyndi Lauper and their respective fans. Similarly, Bradby (1993) suggested that lesbians (and one bisexual woman) were not only interested in but also debated and hypothesized about singers' sexual identity, looking to make a connection through that shared attribute. The findings in this study support these contentions. The women in this study quite clearly identified an affinity with female artists that was primarily based on sharing similar experiences as women. Furthermore, Lewis (1990) found that identifying with these artists (Madonna, Cyndi Lauper) enabled fans "to formulate their own response to the experience of gender inequality" (p. 150). Certainly, the women in this study clearly felt empowered by, and better able to negotiate their daily lives through, female artists' music—daily lives that persist within a patriarchal society where gender inequality is experienced. Radway's (1984) and Lewis's (1990) contentions—along with this study's findings—suggest that media engagements have the potential to become moments of political action. Relatedly, this study also clearly supports Bobo's (1988) contention that representation in media fare authenticates and empowers the lives of those formerly symbolically annihilated. The experience detailed by the women in this music-focused interpretive audience study bears this out. The women regularly spoke in favorable terms about feeling validated and affirmed through the music of female artists.

This study makes a respectable contribution to the field of feminist audience studies and reception analyses, precisely because the nature of the text under consideration in this study differs so much from past audience studies suggests a running theme in women's relationship with media. Media fare can play a role in positively enhancing women's relationships with other women, strengthening women's own views of themselves and their lives and empowering and validating female experience.

DIRECTIONS FOR FUTURE RESEARCH

Although this study provides insight into unchartered territory regarding women's relationship with female artists' music, this area of study remains largely unexplored. As Johnson (1986) posits, there are several moments of meaning making—and reception is only one phase of this cyclical process. To understand the nature of music, the artists, the listeners and the industry a variety of approaches from a variety of perspectives are warranted. Obviously this study and the conclusions drawn would benefit greatly from a critical textual and political economy analysis of the production process. Although there have been studies that have focused on feminist lyrics, a comprehensive textual analysis of performance, dress, music videos and the music itself (as opposed to only lyrics) while also including lyrics is lacking. All of these factors contribute to moments of experiencing music, and all are a part of the text.

Furthermore, a detailed analysis of the creative and production process and the music industry deserves further study. Examination of the creative process—from song origination to cutting the CD—also warrants more attention. Songwriting and producing an album constitute a unique creative process, a process that, especially when compared to the authoring and production of other media forms, such as television or film production, can maintain a marked level of individualism. Documenting, critiquing and evaluating this process provides a better understanding of the text and these particular moments of meaning making. The promotion process also deserves serious analysis. Which artists are promoted and which aren't is of critical importance. Millions of records are produced a year, yet only a small fraction end up on radio playlists. This process is one of timing, bias and financial backing. An analysis of this process would help to explain why certain music is allowed access, while other music remains in the dark. Research of this nature could serve to explore and in turn expose bias toward genre, gender, color and sexual orientation.

Relatedly, considering the patriarchal structure and sexist tendencies of the music industry, the unique struggle of female artists warrants particular attention. Not only is it important to expose the overall discriminating nature of record promotion; it is also important to recognize and document what could arguably be a hostile work environment. These sort of practices in the production and promotion process could prove to be a factor in silencing women. This sort of activity needs to be exposed. In turn, the same can be said about the silencing of people of color and lesbian/gays.

Furthermore and as stated earlier, many of the women who were allowed access to the stage in the 1990s were thin, white, able-bodied and *attractive*. This is a condition not only of self and cultural segregation but also of institutionalized racism and discrimination based on body ability and appearance. This is untenable. As a result, research is warranted on music's racialization and why, as well as on additional genres. Although there has been this demise of the popularity of female rock artists (as described here) on the charts, fortunately there has almost simultaneously been a rise in the success of decidedly strong female artists with a mix of rhythm and blues, hip-hop and soul. Many of these artists who provide pro-women and pro-black musical and lyrical representations, which started with Macy Gray, Eryka Badu and Lauryn Hill in the latter 1990s, continued with Alicia Keys, Jill Scott and India.Arie, in 2001. Not only is an exploration of women drawn to these artists needed but also an exploration of women's experiences with other genres as well. What is female teenagers' or young women's attraction to pop stars (Spice Girls, Britney Spears, Christina Aguilera) utilizing the more traditional female role in pop (as defined by Stewart, 1995)? Women's attraction to more established pop stars in the vein of Whitney Houston, Mariah Carey and Celine Dion is also worthy of note. The possible research directions are seemingly endless.

Any accurate and thorough review of a topic of this nature—and as suggested here—would require the expertise and cooperation of scholars from a broad range of disciplines and perspectives—including musicologists, ethnographers, ethnomusicologists, feminists, political economists and communication, popular culture, critical and semiotic scholars. Recorded music is an incredibly affecting and pervasive medium and form of communication—a medium that deserves serious analysis.

NOTE

1. For arguments about music and its transformative capacity, see Douglas (1993, 1994), Gottlieb and Wald (1994), Lewis (1990), Martin (1995), Pratt (1990) and Rose (1994).

Appendix A

Participant Profiles

These are brief individual profiles of each respondent at the time the interviews were conducted. In addition to the demographic information, five of each respondent's favorite artists are listed, whether indicated on the filtering questionnaire or during the course of the interview. It should be noted that most women talked about and indicated far more than just the few listed after their name. The profiles are included to provide some context to better understand the women's responses. Pseudonyms are used to maintain the respondents' anonymity. The names and profiles are listed in alphabetical order.

Deirdre is a 32-year-old Caucasian lesbian who works at a battered women's center and in child care. She identifies herself as a radical lesbian feminist and is politically active. She has a B.A. in journalism and does a weekly "women's music" show on a local university radio station. Some of her favorite artists include Cheryl Wheeler, Nanci Griffith, Indigo Girls, Tracy Chapman and Dar Williams.

Elisabeth is a 31-year-old Caucasian lesbian and is a junior high school teacher. She is currently working on her master's degree in French. She plays an instrument and sings in a gay choir. Some of her favorite artists include Melissa Etheridge, Indigo Girls, k.d. lang, Tracy Chapman and Sarah McLachlan.

Jane is a 42-year-old Caucasian lesbian and works in purchasing at a Fortune 500 company. She has a B.A. in business. She played the French horn in the past. Some of her favorite artists include Catie Curtis, Michelle Shocked, Angelique Kidjo, Tracy Chapman and Indigo Girls.

Jill is a 24-year-old Caucasian who disclosed some uncertainty about her sexual orientation. When asked on the questionnaire, she wrote, "I'm not sure, heterosexual or bi?" Jill just completed her B.A. in women's studies and is a member of a feminist student organization. Jill plays the trumpet, piano and guitar. She performs live at small clubs and indicates that when she took up the guitar she "was definitely consciously doing it because there were not any women playing guitar." Some of her favorite artists include Ani DiFranco, Indigo Girls, Jewel, Tori Amos and Alanis Morissette.

Jo is a 32-year-old Caucasian lesbian who, after working several years in a supervisory position in a factory with a predominantly male workforce, is working on her master's degree in English with a focus in creative writing. Music was a big part of her family life. "It wasn't a question of . . . whether or not we were going to play, it was what instrument were you going to play." A family game was even built around music, called the Major-Minor Game. "We would stand up when he [our Father] would play a major chord on the piano and sit down when he played a minor [chord]." When Jo reflects on her involvement with music as a child, she now thinks "it was little over-kill . . . we never had a chance to decide if we were going to be really into it." In spite of this, Jo's interest in music continues. Some of her favorite artists include Tori Amos, Ani DiFranco, Melissa Etheridge, Tracy Chapman and Annie Lennox.

Julie is a 19-year-old Caucasian heterosexual who is a third-year college student majoring in communications. Julie took flute lessons as a young girl and describes her father as a "huge music buff." Music was always on in the house when she was growing up. Julie says that "no matter how much money we had for food or anything, the money always went to music first. We had the crappiest TV in the world, but we had an incredible stereo." Some of her favorite artists include Sarah McLachlan, Jewel, Indigo Girls, Shania Twain and Madonna.

Lisa is a 40-year-old Caucasian bisexual who works as a business process consultant. She has an M.B.A. She played flute for eight years. She describes her family as "not very musical." Some of her favorite artists include Indigo Girls, Melissa Etheridge, Fleetwood Mac, the Supremes, and Tracy Chapman.

Appendix A: Participant Profiles 189

Lynn is a 22-year-old Caucasian lesbian who is working on her master's degree in counseling. She says that her "parents weren't really big into music." Some of her favorite artists include Sarah McLachlan, Indigo Girls, Janis Joplin, Ani DiFranco and Sarah Vaughan.

Mary is a 19-year-old Caucasian heterosexual who is a sophomore majoring in elementary education. She says, "Everyone in my family is musical." Some of her favorite artists include Sarah McLachlan, Deana Carter, Jewel, Celine Dion and LeAnn Rimes.

Paige is a 21-year-old Caucasian heterosexual and is a junior in college majoring in art therapy. Her dad "has a music collection from A to Z." Some of her favorite artists include the Cranberries, Fiona Apple, Sarah McLachlan, Jewel and Ani DiFranco.

Patricia is a 34-year-old Caucasian heterosexual who is currently working on her master's degree in clinical counseling. She is organizing a motivational seminar to help women in transition. She recently sold her condo and purchased 20 acres to build a retreat center for men and women. She was an aspiring country singer/songwriter during her childhood and early adolescence and still plays the piano and guitar on occasion. Some of her favorite artists include Paula Cole, Sheryl Crow, Sarah McLachlan, Alanis Morissette and Melissa Etheridge.

Sandi is a 23-year-old Caucasian bisexual who is a senior majoring in English with a writing emphasis. Her father listened to jazz, and her mother listened to Motown and blues. Some of her favorite artists include Salt 'n Pepa, Ani DiFranco, Sarah Vaughan, Nanci Griffith and Indigo Girls.

Sue is a 28-year-old Caucasian heterosexual with an M.A. in multicultural studies currently working in computer database entering. She took 12 years of piano lessons. Some of her favorite artists include Everything But the Girl, Cocteau Twins, Dead Can Dance, Babes in Toyland and Joan Jett.

Terri is a 29-year-old Caucasian heterosexual working on her Ph.D. in communications. Voice was her first major as an undergraduate. Some of her favorite female artists include Tori Amos, Indigo Girls, Ani DiFranco, Sarah McLachlan and Michelle Shocked.

Vivian is a 21-year-old African American heterosexual and is a senior majoring in communications. "Music has always been highly regarded with my Mom." Vivian plays guitar and piano and does a radio show at a university radio station. Some of her favorite artists include P.J. Harvey, Tracy Chapman, Lois, Cassandra Wilson and Tori Amos.

Appendix B

List of Artists Appealing to Respondents

Abba
Adams, Oleta
Amos, Tori
Anderson, Laurie
Andrews, Julie
Apple, Fiona
Armatrading, Joan
Babes in Toyland
Baker, Anita
Benatar, Pat
Bishop, Heather
Blige, Mary J.
Block, Rory
Blondie
Braxton, Toni
The Breeders
Brickell, Edie
Bush, Kate
Cadell, Meryn
Carpenter, Karen
Carpenter, Mary Chapin
The Carpenters
Carter, Deana
Chapman, Tracy
The Chenille Sisters
Cherry, Neneh

Clooney, Rosemary
The Cocteau Twins
Cole, Natalie
Cole, Paula
Colvin, Shawn
Cowboy Junkies
The Cranberries
Crow, Sheryl
Curtis, Catie
Da Brat
Dead Can Dance
Deelite
DiFranco, Ani
Dion, Celine
Dobkin, Alix
Doubting Thomas
Enya
Estefan, Gloria
Etheridge, Melissa
The Eurythmics
Everything But the Girl
Ferrick, Melissa
Ferron
Fitzgerald, Ella
Flack, Roberta
Fleetwood Mac

Appendix B: List of Artists Appealing to Respondents

Fordham, Julia
Franklin, Aretha
The Fugees
Fure, Tret
Galas, Diamanda
Gibson, Debbie
Gordon, Kim
Grant, Amy
Griffith, Nanci
Hall, Kristen
Harris, Emmylou
Harvey, P.J.
Hatfield, Juliana
Hawkins, Sophie B.
Hill, Lauryn (of the Fugees)
Hill, Ubaka
Hole
Holiday, Billie
Horne, Lena
Houston, Whitney
Hunter, Lisa
Hynde, Chrissie (of the Pretenders)
Indigo Girls
James, Etta
Jaw Box
Jett, Joan
Jewel
Johnson, Janice Marie
Johnson Reagon, Bernice (of Sweet Honey in the Rock)
Jones, Rickie Lee
Joplin, Janis
Katrina and the Waves
Kidjo, Angelique
King, Carole
Knight, Gladys
L7
lang, k.d.
Latifah, Queen
Lauper, Cyndi
Lennox, Annie (of the Eurythmics)
Loeb, Lisa
Lois
Love, Courtney (of Hole)
Love, Laura
Luscious Jackson
Lush
MacColl, Kirsty
Madonna
Malone, Michelle
Manchester, Melissa
Manhattan Transfer
Mann, Amy
McCalla, Deidre
McLachlan, Sarah
Merchant, Natalie
Midler, Bette
Mitchell, Joni
Moore, Abra
Morissette, Alanis
NdegéOcello, Me'Shell
Near, Holly
Newton-John, Olivia
Nicks, Stevie
No Doubt (with Gwen Stefani)
O'Connor, Sinead
O'Riordan, Dolores (of the Cranberries)
Osborne, Joan
Osmond, Marie
Parton, Dolly
Payne, Hazel
Peter, Paul and Mary
Phair, Liz
Poe
The Pretenders
Raitt, Bonnie
Ray, Amy
Reagon, Toshi
Reddy, Helen
Rimes, LeAnn
Ronstadt, Linda
Ross, Diana
Ruby and Cloverfish
Sade
Sadia

Appendix B: List of Artists Appealing to Respondents

Sainte-Marie, Buffy
Salt 'n Pepa
Shocked, Michelle
Siberry, Jane
Sinatra, Nancy
Sister Seven
Sister Sledge
Sleater-Kinney
Smashing Pumpkins
Smith, Bessie
Smith, Patti
The Spice Girls
Squirrel Nut Zippers
The Story
Sundays
The Supremes
Sweet Honey in the Rock
A Taste of Honey
Team Dresch
10,000 Maniacs
Throwing Muses (with Kristin Hersh)
Tiffany
Tillis, Pam
Turner, Tina
Twain, Shania
Two Guys and a Girl
Two Nice Girls
Vaughan, Sarah
Vega, Suzanne
Warwick, Dionne
Wheeler, Cheryl
Wheeler, Erica
Williams, Dar
Williams, Victoria
Williamson, Cris
Wilson, Cassandra
Yearwood, Trisha

Select Discography

Amos, Tori. (1991). *Little earthquakes*. New York: Atlantic Records.
Amos, Tori. (1996). *Boys for Pele*. New York: Atlantic Records.
Anderson, Laurie. (1989). *Strange angels*. New York: Warner Brothers.
Apple, Fiona. (1996). *Tidal*. New York: Sony Music.
Babes in Toyland. (1992). *Fontanelle*. New York: Warner Brothers.
Brooke, Jonatha. (2001). *Steady pull*. Malibu, CA: Bad Dog Records.
Bush, Kate. (1998). *Sensual world*. New York: Columbia Records.
Chapman, Tracy. (1988). *Tracy Chapman*. New York: Elektra.
Chenille Sisters. (1988). *At home with the Chenille Sisters*. St. Paul, MN: Red House Records.
Childs, Toni. (1988). *Union*. New York: A&M Records.
Cole, Paula. (1994). *Harbinger*. New York: Warner Brothers.
Cole, Paula. (1996). *This fire*. New York: Warner Brothers.
Colvin, Shawn. (1989). *Steady on*. New York: Sony Music.
Colvin, Shawn. (1996). *Few small repairs*. New York: Sony Music.
Crow, Sheryl. (1996). *Sheryl Crow*. New York: A&M Records.
DiFranco, Ani. (1990). *Ani DiFranco*. Buffalo, NY: Righteous Babe Records.
DiFranco, Ani. (1992). *Imperfectly*. Buffalo, NY: Righteous Babe Records.
DiFranco, Ani. (1993). *Puddle dive*. Buffalo, NY: Righteous Babe Records.
DiFranco, Ani. (1995). *Not a pretty girl*. Buffalo, NY: Righteous Babe Records.
DiFranco, Ani. (1999). *To the teeth*. Buffalo, NY: Righteous Babe Records.
Etheridge, Melissa. (1988). *Melissa Etheridge*. New York: Island Records.
Etheridge, Melissa. (1993). *Yes I am*. New York: Island Records.
Etheridge, Melissa. (1999). *Breakdown*. New York: Island Records.

Everything But the Girl. (1988). *Idlewild*. New York: Atlantic Records.
Everything But the Girl. (1991). *Worldwide*. New York: Atlantic Records.
Everything But the Girl. (1994). *Amplified heart*. New York: Atlantic Records.
Ferrick, Melissa. (1997). *Melissa Ferrick plus 1*. Boulder, CO: What Are Records.
Franklin, Aretha. (1998). *Rose is still a rose*. New York: Arista Records.
Galas, Diamanda. (1994). *Sporting life*. London: Mute Records.
Grant, Amy. (1980). *Never alone*. Nashville, TN: RCA Records.
Griffith, Nanci. (1991). *Late night grande hotel*. New York: MCA Records.
Harris, Emmylou. (1995). *Wrecking ball*. New York: Elektra.
Harvey, P.J. (1993). *Rid of me*. New York: Island Records.
Hatfield, Juliana. (1992). *Hey babe*. Carrboro, NC: Mammoth Records.
Hill, Lauryn. (1998). *The miseducation of Lauryn Hill*. New York: Columbia Records.
Hole. (1994). *Live through this*. Santa Monica, CA: Geffen Records.
Indigo Girls. (1992). *Rites of passage*. New York: Epic Records.
Indigo Girls. (1997). *Shaming of the sun*. New York: Sony Music.
Jewel. (1995). *Pieces of you*. New York: Atlantic Records.
Joplin, Janis. (1978). *Pearl/cheap thrills*. New York: Columbia Records.
King, Carole. (1971). *Tapestry*. New York: Epic Records.
lang, k.d. (1989). *Absolute torch and twang*. New York: Warner Brothers.
Lennox, Annie. (1992). *Diva*. New York: Arista Records.
Lois. (1996). *Infinity plus*. Olympia, WA: K Records.
L7. (1992). *Bricks are heavy*. New York: Warner Brothers.
Madonna. (1998). *Ray of light*. New York: Warner Brothers.
McLachlan, Sarah. (1991). *Solace*. New York: Arista Records.
McLachlan, Sarah. (1993). *Fumbling towards ecstasy*. New York: Arista Records.
McLachlan, Sarah. (1997). *Surfacing*. New York: Arista Records.
Morissette, Alanis. (1995). *Jagged little pill*. New York: Maverick Records.
NdegéOcello, Me'Shell. (1996). *Peace beyond passion*. New York: Warner Brothers.
O'Connor, Sinead. (1987). *Lion and the cobra*. Los Angeles, CA: Chrysalis.
Phair, Liz. (1993). *Exile in guyville*. Los Angeles, CA: Capitol Records.
Queen Latifah. (1993). *Black reign*. Los Angeles, CA: Motown Records.
Raitt, Bonnie. (1991). *Luck of the draw*. Los Angeles, CA: Capitol Records.
Ray, Amy. (2001). *Stag*. Decatur, GA: Daemon Records.
Reddy, Helen. (1975). *Greatest hits*. Los Angeles, CA: Capitol Records.
Ronstadt, Linda. (1983). *What's new?* New York: Elektra.
Sainte-Marie, Buffy. (1970). *Illuminations*. New York: Vanguard Records.
Salt 'n Pepa. (1986). *Hot, cool and vicious*. New York: Mercury Records.

Shocked, Michelle. (1988). *Short sharp shocked*. New York: Mercury Records.
Shocked, Michelle. (1992). *Arkansas traveler*. New York: Polygram Records.
Shocked, Michelle. (2002). *Deep natural*. Los Angeles, CA: Mighty Sound.
Sister Sledge. (1995). *We are family*. Los Angeles, CA: Rhino Records.
Sleater-Kinney. (1996). *Call the doctor*. Olympia, WA: Chainsaw Records.
Sobule, Jill. (1995). *Jill Sobule*. New York: Atlantic Records.
Sweet Honey in the Rock. (1992). *In This Land*. New York: Warner Brothers.
10,000 Maniacs. (1987). *In my tribe*. New York: Elektra.
Tikaram, Tanita. (1988). *Ancient heart*. New York: Warner Brothers.
Tillis, Pam. (1997). *Greatest hits*. New York: Arista Records.
Vaughn, Sarah. (2002). *Interlude 1944–1947*. Kowloon Bay, Hong Kong: Naxos.
Vega, Suzanne. (1987). *Solitude standing*. New York: A&M Records.
Vega, Suzanne. (1992). *99.9F*. New York: A&M Records.
Williams, Dar. (1996). *Mortal city*. New York: Razor & Tie Entertainment.
Williamson, Cris. (1975). *Changer and the changed*. Oakland, CA: Olivia Records.

References

Anderman, J. (2000, December 3). Shut up three years ago, women raised their voices at Lilith Fair and elsewhere in pop music. The *Boston Globe*. Retrieved May 31, 2001, from Lexis-Nexis.

Ang, I. (1985). *Watching Dallas*. London: Methuen.

Atkinson, T. (1997, March 20). Pop music flips for sounds of female artists. *Star Tribune*. Retrieved May 31, 2001, from Lexis-Nexis.

Auslander, P. (1998). Seeing is believing: Live performance and the discourse of authenticity in rock culture. *Literature and Psychology: A Journal of Psychoanalytic and Cultural Criticism, 44*, 1–26.

Bayton, M. (1992). Out on the margins: Feminism and the study of popular music. *Women: A Cultural Review, 3*, 51–59.

Bayton, M. (1993). Feminist musical practice: Problems and contradictions. In T. Bennet, S. Frith, L. Grossberg, J. Shepherd & G. Turner (Eds.), *Rock and popular music: Politics, policies, institutions* (pp. 177–192). New York: Routledge.

Bayton, M. (1998). *Frock rock: Women performing popular music*. New York: Oxford University Press.

Berry, V.T. (1994). Feminine or masculine: The conflicting nature of female images in rap music. In S.C. Cook & J.S. Tsou (Eds.), *Cecilia reclaimed: Feminist perspectives on gender and music* (pp. 183–201). Urbana: University of Illinois Press.

Bobo, J. (1988). *The Color Purple*: Black women as cultural readers. In E.D. Pribram (Ed.), *Female spectators: Looking at film and television* (pp. 90–109). London: Verso.

Bradby, B. (1990). Do-talk and don't-talk: The division of the subject in girl-group music. In S. Frith & A. Goodwin (Eds.), *On record: Rock, pop, and the written word* (pp. 341–368). New York: Pantheon Books.

Bradby, B. (1993). Lesbians and popular music: Does it matter who is singing? In G. Griffin (Ed.), *Outwrite: Lesbianism and popular culture* (pp. 148–171). Boulder, CO: Pluto Press.

Bradby, B. (1994). Freedom, feeling and dancing: Madonna's songs traverse girls' talk. In S. Mills (Ed.), *Gendering the reader* (pp. 67–95). New York: Harvester Wheatsheaf.

Brownsworth, V. (1999). Pop tunes can comfort teens unsure of their sexuality. In L. Gross & J.D. Woods (Eds.), *The Columbia reader on lesbians and gay men in media, society, and politics* (pp. 286–287). New York: Columbia University Press. (Reprinted from *Philadelphia Daily News*, July 25, 1995)

Burns, L. & Lafrance, M. (2002). *Disruptive divas: Feminism, identity & popular music*. New York: Routledge.

Butruille, S.G. & Taylor, A. (1987). Women in American popular song. In L.P. Stewart & S. Ting-Toomey (Eds.), *Communication, gender and sex roles in diverse interaction contexts* (pp. 179–188). Norwood, NJ: Ablex.

Cavicchi, D. (1998). *Tramps like us: Music and meaning among Springsteen fans*. New York: Oxford University Press.

Childerhose, B. (1998). *From Lilith to Lilith Fair: The authorized story*. New York: St. Martin's Griffin.

Cohen, J.R. (1991). The "relevance" of cultural identity in audiences' interpretations of mass media. *Critical Studies in Mass Communication, 8*, 442–454.

Cooper, S. (Ed.). (1996). *Girls! Girls! Girls! Essays on women and music*. New York: New York University Press.

Cooper, V.W. (1985). Women in popular music: A quantitative analysis of feminine images over time. *Sex Roles, 13*, 499–506.

Cooper, V.W. (1992). Lyrical sexism in popular music: A quantitative examination. In K.J. Bindas (Ed.), *America's musical pulse: Popular music in twentieth-century society* (pp. 229–238). London: Praeger.

DeSantis, C.A. (2001, May 1). Shawn Colvin: A whole new her. *ROCKRGRL, 39*, 23–26.

DeVoe, J. (2000, November). Women in rock. Guest lecture for "Women and Rock" course. Butler University, Indianapolis.

Dibben, N. (1999). Representations of femininity in popular music. *Popular Music, 18*, 331–355.

DiFranco, A. (1997). Ani DiFranco's open letter to *Ms*. magazine. Retrieved August 25, 2002, from http://folkandbluesnews.com/anidifranco.htm.

Douglas, S.J. (1993). Will you love me tomorrow? Changing discourses about female sexuality in the mass media, 1960–1968. In W.S. Solomon & R.W. McChesney (Eds.), *Ruthless criticism: New perspectives in U.S. communication history* (pp. 349–374). Minneapolis: University of Minnesota Press.

Douglas, S.J. (1994). *Where the girls are: Growing up female with the mass media.* New York: Random House.

Douglas, S.J. (1997, August 25). Girls 'n' Spice: All things nice? *Nation, 265,* 6. Retrieved May 29, 2001, from Academic Search Elite.

Driscoll, C. (1999). Girl culture, revenge and global capitalism: Cybergirls, Riot Grrls, Spice Girls. *Australian Feminist Studies, 14,* 173–195.

Faludi, S. (1991). *Backlash: The undeclared war against women.* New York: Crown Books.

Fiske, J. (1988). Critical response: Meaningful moments. *Critical Studies in Mass Communication, 5,* 246–250.

Forman, M. (1994). "Movin' closer to an independent funk": Black feminist theory, standpoint, and women in rap. *Women's Studies, 23,* 35–55.

Frith, S. (1990). Afterthoughts. In S. Frith & A. Goodwin (Eds.), *On record: Rock, pop, and the written word* (pp. 417–424). New York: Pantheon Books. (Reprinted from *New Statesman,* August 23, 1985)

Frith, S. (1996). *Performing rites: On the value of popular music.* Cambridge, MA: Harvard University Press.

Frith, S. (1997). Music and identity. In S. Hall and P. Du Gay (Eds.), *Questions of Cultural identity* (pp. 108–127). London: Sage Publications.

Frith, S. & McRobbie, A. (1990). Rock and sexuality. In S. Frith & A. Goodwin (Eds.), *On record: Rock, pop, and the written word* (pp. 371–389). New York: Pantheon Books. (Reprinted from *Screen Education,* 29, 1978)

Gaar, G.G. (1992). *She's a rebel: The history of women in rock & roll.* Seattle, WA: Seal Press.

Garratt, S. (1984). All of us love all of you. In S. Steward & S. Garratt (Eds.), *Signed, sealed, and delivered: The true life stories of women in pop* (pp. 138–150). Boston: South End Press.

Gaunt, K.D. (1995). African American women between hopscotch and hip-hop: "Must be the music (that's turnin' me on)." In A.N. Valdiva (Ed.), *Feminism, multiculturalism, and the media: Global diversities* (pp. 277–308). Thousand Oaks, CA: Sage Publications.

Gilgoff, D. (2001, April 30). Rewriting women and rock. *U.S. News & World Report, 130,* 17. Retrieved June 12, 2001, from Academic Search Elite.

Gottlieb, J. & Wald, G. (1994). Smells like teen spirit: Riot grrls, revolution and women in independent rock. In A. Ross & T. Rose (Eds.), *Mi-*

crophone fiends: Youth music and youth culture (pp. 250–274). London: Routledge.

Gross, L. (1989). Out of the mainstream: Sexual minorities and the mass media. In E. Seiter, H. Borchers, G. Kreutzner & E. Warth (Eds.), *Remote control: Television, audiences, and cultural power* (pp. 130–149). London: Routledge.

Grossberg, L. (1994). Is anybody listening? Does anybody care? On talking about "The State of Rock." In A. Ross & T. Rose (Eds.), *Microphone fiends: Youth music and youth culture* (pp. 41–58). London: Routledge.

Grossberg, L. (1996). On postmodernism and articulation: An interview with Stuart Hall. In D. Morley & K. Chen (Eds.), *Stuart Hall: Critical dialogues in cultural studies* (pp. 131–150). London: Routledge.

Guzman, I. (2001, March 8). She's a defender of Shocked values. *Daily News*. Retrieved March 10, 2001, from http://www.nydailynews.com.

Hinckley, D. (1996, November 26). Radio's hit formula: Girls, girls, girls. *Daily News*. Retrieved May 31, 2001, from Lexis-Nexis.

Hirshey, G. (2001). *We gotta get out of this place: The true, tough story of women in rock.* New York: Atlantic Monthly Press.

Hobson, D. (1989). Soap operas at work. In E. Seiter, H. Borchers, G. Kreutzner & E. Warth (Eds.), *Remote control: Television, audiences and cultural power* (pp. 150–167). London: Routledge.

Hobson, D. (1990). Women, audiences and the workplace. In M.E. Brown (Ed.), *Television and women's culture: The politics of the popular* (pp. 61–74). London: Sage Publications.

Hobson, D. (1996). Housewives and the mass media. In H. Baehr & A. Gray (Eds.), *Turning it on: A reader in women and media* (pp. 111–117). New York: St. Martin's Press.

Hollows, J. (2000). *Feminism, femininity and popular culture.* New York: Manchester University Press.

hooks, b. (2000). *Feminism is for everybody: Passionate politics.* Cambridge, MA: South End Press.

Howard, L. & Cerio, G. (1994, March 28). Roll over, Suzanne Vega. *Newsweek, 123,* 13.

Johnson, R. (1986). The story so far: And further transformations? In D. Punter (Ed.), *Introduction to contemporary cultural studies* (pp. 277–313). New York: Longman.

Jones, S. (1992). *Rock formation: Music, technology and mass communication.* Newbury Park, CA: Sage Publications.

Kearney, M.C. (1997). The missing links: Riot grrrl—feminism—lesbian culture. In S. Whiteley (Ed.), *Sexing the groove* (pp. 207–229). London: Routledge.

Kleiner, C. (1999, September 6). When "ready to rock" becomes ready to riot. *U.S. News & World Report, 127,* 9, 59.

Kolawole, H. (1996). Sisters take the rap . . . but talk back. In S. Cooper (Ed.), *Girls! Girls! Girls! Essays on women and music* (pp. 8–21). New York: New York University Press.

Leonard, M. (1997). "Rebel girl, you are the queen of my world": Feminism, "subculture" and grrrl power. In S. Whiteley (Ed.), *Sexing the groove* (pp. 230–256). London: Routledge.

Lewis, L.A. (1990). *Gender politics and MTV: Voicing differences.* Philadelphia, PA: Temple University Press.

Lewis, L.A. (1993). Being discovered: The emergence of female address on MTV. In S. Frith, A. Goodwin & L. Grossberg (Eds.), *Sound and vision: The music video reader* (pp. 129–152). London: Routledge.

Lewis, L.A. (1995). Form and female authorship in music video. In G. Dines & J.M. Humez (Eds.), *Gender, race and class in media: A text reader* (pp. 499–507). Thousand Oaks, CA: Sage Publications.

Longhurst, B. (1995). *Popular music and society.* Cambridge: Polity Press.

Lont, C.M. (1993). Feminist critique of mass communication research. In S. Perlmutter Bowen & N. Wyatt (Eds.), *Transforming visions: Feminist critiques in communication studies* (pp. 231–248). Cresskill, NJ: Hampton Press.

Martin, C.R. (1995). The naturalized gender order of rock and roll. *Journal of Communication Inquiry, 19,* 1, 53–74.

Mattern, M. (1998). *Acting in concert: Music, community, and political action.* New Brunswick, NJ: Rutgers University Press.

McClary, S. (1991). *Feminine endings: Music, gender, and sexuality.* Minneapolis: University of Minnesota Press.

McClary, S. (1994). Same as it ever was. In A. Ross & T. Rose (Eds.), *Microphone fiends: Youth music and youth culture* (pp. 29–40). New York: Routledge.

McDonnell, E. & Powers, A. (Eds.). (1995). *Rock she wrote: Women write about rock, pop, and rap.* New York: Delta.

Meade, M. (1972). The degradation of women. In R.S. Denisoff & R.A. Peterson (Eds.), *The sounds of social change: Studies in popular culture* (pp. 173–178). Chicago: Rand McNally.

Modleski, T. (1996). The rhythms of reception: Daytime television and women's work. In H. Baehr & A. Gray (Eds.), *Turning it on: A reader in women and media* (pp. 104–110). London: Arnold.

Morris, B.J. (1999). *Eden built by Eves: The culture of women's music festivals.* New York: Alyson Books.

O'Brien, L. (1995). *She bop: The definitive history of women in rock, pop and soul.* New York: Penguin Books.

O'Dair, B. (1997). *Trouble girls: The Rolling Stone book of women in rock.* New York: Random House.

Parmar, P. (Director and Producer). (1998). *Righteous babes* [Videotape]. (Available from Women Make Movies, 462 Broadway Suite 500, New York, NY WS 10013)

Pattie, D. (1999). 4 Real: Authenticity, performance and rock music. *Enculturation, 2.* Retrieved July 28, 2003, from http://enculturation.gmu.edu/2_2/pattie.html.

Pendle, K. (Ed.). (1991). *Women and music: A history.* Indianapolis: Indiana University Press.

Pesselnick, J. & Caulfield, K. (2000, December 16). Where have all the cowgirls gone? *Billboard, 112,* 51. Retrieved May 29, 2001, from Academic Search Elite.

Potter, M. (1998, August 1). Women's work WTN wades into huge territory with series on female voices, but question remains: Aren't we past the point of lumping music by gender? *The Toronto Star.* Retrieved April 25, 1999, from Lexis-Nexis.

Powers, A. (1994, October 9). When women venture forth. *New York Times.* Retrieved May 29, 2001, from Academic Search Elite.

Pratt, R. (1990). *Rhythm and resistance: Explorations in the political uses of popular music.* New York: Praeger.

Radway, J.A. (1984). *Reading the romance: Women, patriarchy, and popular literature.* Chapel Hill: University of North Carolina Press.

Raphael, A. (1995). *Grrrls: Viva rock divas.* New York: St. Martin's Griffin.

Reynolds, S. & Press, J. (1995). *The sex revolts: Gender, rebellion, and rock 'n' roll.* Cambridge, MA: Harvard University Press.

Riordan, E. (2001). Commodified agents and empowered girls: Consuming and producing feminism. *Journal of Communication Inquiry, 25,* 279–297.

Roberts, R. (1996). Independence day: Feminist country music videos. *Popular Music and Society, 20,* 135–154.

Rose, T. (1994). *Black noise: Rap music and black culture in contemporary America.* London: Wesleyan University Press.

Rumsey, G. & Little, H. (1988). Women and pop: A series of lost encounters. In A. McRobbie (Ed.), *Zoot suits and second hand dresses: An anthology of fashion and music* (pp. 239–244). Boston: Unwin Hyman.

Seiter, E., Borchers, H., Kreutzner, G. & Warth, E. (1996). Don't treat us like we're so stupid and naive: Towards an ethnography of soap opera viewers. In E. Seiter, H. Borchers, G. Kreutzner & E. Warth (Eds.), *Remote control: Television, audiences, and cultural power* (pp. 223–247). London: Routledge.

Shuster, F. (1995, October 26). Young women rockers free to express all their emotions. *Star Tribune*. Retrieved May 31, 2001, from Lexis-Nexis.

Sloat, L.J. (1998). Incubus: Male songwriters' portrayal of women's sexuality in pop metal music. In J.S. Epstein (Ed.), *Youth culture: Identity in a postmodern world* (pp. 286–301). Malden, MA: Blackwell.

Stewart, A.D. (1995). "You're not rid of me": Riot grrrl bands and new roles and old roles in the work of female performers. In C.M. Lont (Ed.), *Women and media: Content, careers and criticism* (pp. 359–371). Belmont, CA: Wadsworth.

Straw, W. (1997). Sizing up record collections: Gender and connoisseurship in rock music culture. In S. Whiteley (Ed.), *Sexing the groove: Popular music and gender*. New York: Routledge.

Tayler, L. (1998, July 12). They said it couldn't be done. *Newsday*. Retrieved May 31, 2001, from Lexis-Nexis.

Tetzlaff, D. (1994). Music for meaning: Reading the discourse of authenticity in rock. *Journal of Communication Inquiry, 18*, 95–117.

Thornton, S. (1995). *Club cultures: Music, media and subcultural capital*. Hanover, NH: University Press of New England.

Tuchman, G. (1978). Introduction: The symbolic annihilation of women by the mass media. In G. Tuchman, A. Kaplan Daniels & J. Benet (Eds.), *Hearth and home: Images of women in the mass media* (pp. 3–38). New York: Oxford University Press.

Udovitch, M. (1994, October 6). Mothers of invention. *Rolling Stone*, 692. Retrieved May 29, 2001, from Academic Search Elite.

Udovitch, M. (2001, July 5). How do you mend a broken heart? *Rolling Stone*, 872. Retrieved July 10, 2001, from http://www.rollingstone.com.

Van Zoonen, L. (1994). *Feminist media studies*. London: Sage Publications.

Vaziri, A. (1999). Q & A with Sarah McLachlan. *The San Francisco Chronicle*, 38. Retrieved May 31, 2001, from Lexis-Nexis.

Wald, G. (1998). Just a girl? Rock music, feminism, and the cultural construction of female youth. *Signs: Journal of Women in Culture and Society, 23*, 585–610.

Wall Street Journal. (1997, June 11). Women's music tour handpicks its backers. *The Tampa Tribune*. Retrieved May 31, 2001, from Lexis-Nexis.

Whiteley, S. (1997). *Sexing the groove: Popular music and gender*. London: Routledge.

Whiteley, S. (2000). *Women and popular music: Sexuality, identity and subjectivity*. London: Routledge.

Zach, P. (1996, February 16). Rock music changes tune: It's a man's world no more. *The Straits Times*, (Singapore). Retrieved May 31, 2001, from Lexis-Nexis.

Index

Abortion, 7, 50, 62
Abuse, 87–89
"Adia" (McLachlan), 136
Affinity, 173–176. *See also* Attraction
Affirmation, 69–97. *See also* Abuse; Coming out; Coping through appropriation; Depression; Relationships; Transitions and challenges
Aguilera, Christina, 12, 13, 179, 185
"All I Ever Have to Be" (as performed by Amy Grant), 94
"All the Good Ones Are Gone" (as performed by Pam Tillis), 81, 113–114
Amos, Tori: affirming, 74, 75; appropriation of, 80, 87, 88, 92; "Father Lucifer" lyrics, 59–60; favorite of, 24, 115, 153; feminist sensibility, 2, 7, 51; Grammy nominations, 11; "Hey Jupiter" lyrics, 138–139; musical abilities, 43, 44, 45; "Precious Things" lyrics, 97–98; as producer, 10; professional autonomy, 56; releases and touring, 13; "Silent All These Years" lyrics, 98–100, 168–170; social importance, 160; substantive lyrics, 36, 37, 39; as used for expression, 117; why included in study, 19 n.5
Anderson, Laurie, 50; "Beautiful Red Dress" lyrics, 60–62
Anderson, Lynn, 23
Ang, Ien, 181, 182
Angels, The, 4
"Angel Standing By" (Jewel), 121
"Angry feminist" stereotype, 151–158
Apple, Fiona, 8, 45, 71, 159
Appropriation of female artists' music, 69–97. *See also* Abuse; Coming out; Coping through appropriation; Depression; Relationships; Transitions and challenges
"Apron Strings" (Everything But the Girl), 135

Arie, India., 20, 185
Armatrading, Joan, 5
Articulation, 173–177
Attraction: to authorship, 39–40; to female over male artists, 27–32; to feminism/women's issues, 49–52; to lesbian/gay/bisexual issues, 52–54; to music, vocal skills and musicianship, 40–46; to political activism, 46–49; to professional autonomy, 54–57; to substantive lyrics, 34–39
Authenticity, 3, 32–33, 39, 58, 175
Authorship, 39–40
Autonomy, 39, 54–58, 75, 161, 174, 175
Autour De Lucie, 8

Babes in Toyland, 41, 56, 130
Backstreet Boys, The, 12, 151
Bad Dog Records, 10
Badu, Erykah, 8, 185
Baez, Joan, 5, 6
Barbero, Lori, 56
Bay City Rollers, The, 150
Bayton, Mavis, 15, 17, 128
Beatles, The, 150
"Beautiful Red Dress" (Anderson), 50, 60–62
"Behind the Wall" (Chapman), 50
Benatar, Pat, 6
"Big Yellow Taxi" (Mitchell), 132
Bisexuality, 14–15, 52–54, 89–90, 183
Bitch and Animal, 10
"Black" (McLachlan), 85–86, 109–110
"Blood in the Boardroom" (DiFranco), 93–94, 102–103
"Blue Moon Rose" (Everything But the Girl), 134
Bobo, Jacqueline, 173, 176, 180, 183

Bonding through music, 122–127
Bradby, Barbara, 14–15, 27, 30, 183
Brill Building, 3, 5
Brooke, Jonatha, 10, 42
Bush, Kate, 74
Butchies, The, 13

Captain Swing (Shocked), 41
Carey, Mariah, 42, 185
Carpenter, Mary Chapin, 8
Carter, Deana, 71
Cave, Nick, 3
Chapman, Tracy: as affirming, 74; appropriation of, 84, 91, 92; feminist/political sensibility, 2, 46–47, 50; Grammy Award, 11; importance of, 163; preference for, 29; as producer, 10
Chenille Sisters, 42
Cherry, Neneh, 8
Christian, Meg, 4
"Christians and the Pagans" (Williams), 48
Cole, Paula: as affirming, 74; appropriation of, 85; favorite of, 150; Grammy nomination, 11; "I Am So Ordinary" lyrics, 100–101; as producer, 10; professional autonomy, 56; as reminder, 135; as stereotyped, 153; "Where Have All the Cowboys Gone" lyrics, 139–140
Colvin, Shawn, 11, 57, 86; "Suicide Alley" lyrics, 101–102
Coming out, 89–91
Communicating through music, 120–122
Community through music, creating, 122–127
Concerts, 127–132
Connecting through music, 122–127

Coping through appropriation, 79–81, 91–96, 175–176
Cranberries, The, 167, 189
Crow, Sheryl, 11, 13, 74, 128, 150
Cultural transformation, 18, 174–178

Daemon Records, 10
Depression, 85–87
DeVoe, Jennie, 13
DiFranco, Ani: as affirming, 72–74, 76, 78; appropriation of, 90, 91, 93; as author, 39; "Blood in the Boardroom" lyrics, 102–103; favorite of, 24, 115; feminist/political sensibility, 2, 7, 47, 50, 51, 179; Grammy nomination, 11; "I'm No Heroine" lyrics, 1, 20–21, 170–171; "In or Out" lyrics, 103–104; "Lost Woman Song" lyrics, 62–63; "Make Me Stay" lyrics, 140–141; "The Million You Never Made" lyrics, 63–65; musical abilities, 43; professional autonomy, 55; Righteous Babe Records, 7, 10; "Rush Hour" lyrics, 141–142; "The Slant" lyrics, 142–144; social importance, 160, 162; as stereotyped, 153; substantive lyrics, 35–37, 39; touring and releases, 13; "What If No One's Watching" lyrics, 144–145; as used for expression, 117, 118, 120; why included in study, 19 n.5
Dion, Celine, 185
DIY (do-it-yourself) politics. *See* Riot grrrl bands
Domestic violence, 7, 9
Douglas, Susan, 4, 15, 20, 70
"Down 'N' Outer" (Griffith), 48, 65

"Do You Take This Man" (Galas and Jones), 88, 105–107
Drag (lang), 71
Dylan, Bob, 33

Elliott, Missy, 8, 10
Eminem, 3, 12
Empowerment: through attitude and lyrics, 37, 47, 51, 55, 73; through music, 72–97, 175–177; in the 1960s and 1970s, 4–5
Etheridge, Melissa: as affirming, 72, 74; appropriation of, 80, 83, 89, 90, 91; bonding through, 124; communicating through, 121; concerts, 130; as an exception, 157; fan support, 13; favorite of, 115; feminist/political sensibility, 2, 7, 51; influences, 6; lesbian activism, 53–54; musical abilities, 44; as producer, 10; social importance of, 160, 161; why included in study, 19 n.5
Everything But the Girl, 87, 134; "Missing" lyrics, 104–105; "Politics Aside" lyrics, 146
Expression through music, 116–120

"Father Lucifer" (Amos), 37, 59–60
Female singing voice, 27
Feminism: attraction to, 49–52; backlash, 58; challenging the status quo, 178; exemplar feminist artists, 7–8, 19 n.5; importance of, 124; Lilith Fair debate, 7–10; second wave, 4
Feminist and/or political sensibility, 2, 7–8, 16–17, 24–25, 58, 79
Feminist media studies, 173, 180
Feminization of rock music, 4, 151

Ferrick, Melissa, 10
Fighting depression. *See* Depression
Flack, Roberta, 149
Folk music, 4–6, 33, 70
"Foolish Games" (Jewel), 154
Foreigner, 156
Frith, Simon 6, 19 n.4, 71, 116, 120, 127, 150
Frith, Simon and Angela McRobbie, 19 n.4, 127, 150
"Fuck and Run" (Phair), 92
"Fumbling towards Ecstasy" (McLachlan), 45, 136

Galas, Diamanda, 47, 48, 88; "Do You Take This Man" lyrics, 105–107
Garbage, 11
Gay rights, 34, 52–54
"Get Out the Map" (Indigo Girls), 122, 146–147
Girl groups, 3, 11
Goffin, Gerry, 3
"Good Enough" (McLachlan), 77, 96, 109–110
"Graffiti Limbo" (Shocked), 49
Grammy Awards, 10
Grant, Amy, 94
Gray, Macy, 20, 185
Griffith, Nanci, 46, 48, 76; "Down 'N' Outer" lyrics, 65
Gross, Larry, 176
Grossberg, Lawrence, 97, 177
"Groupie," 3

Hagar, Sammy, 24
Hailed. *See* Interpellation
Hall, Stuart, 177
"Hand in My Pocket" (Morissette), 75
Harris, Emmylou, 47, 131, 132
Harvey, P.J., 13, 40, 81, 167
Hate crimes, 7

Hatfield, Juliana, 80–81; "Nirvana" lyrics, 107–108
Hendrix, Jimi, 3
"Hey Jupiter" (Amos), 117, 138–139
Hill, Lauryn, 11, 185
History of women in music, 2–14
Hobson, Dorothy, 15, 181
"Hold On" (McLachlan), 96, 110–111
Hole, 2, 38, 71
HORDE (Horizons of Rock Developing Everywhere), 28, 152
Houston, Whitney, 19 n.1, 185
Hynde, Chrissie, 6, 8, 161

"I Am So Ordinary" (Cole), 85, 100–101
"I Am Woman" (as performed by Helen Reddy), 5, 74
Identifying with female artists' music, 28, 69–97
Identity development, 175
Idlewild (Everything But the Girl), 134
"I Honestly Love You" (as performed by Olivia Newton John), 24
"I Kissed a Girl" (Sobule and Eaton), 70, 97
"I'm No Heroine" (DiFranco), 1, 20–21, 160, 170–171
Independent record labels, 4
Indigo Girls: as affirming, 72, 74, 76, 78; appropriation of, 83, 89, 91, 93; bonding through, 124, 125; concerts, 129, 130, 131; favorite of, 24; feminist/political sensibility, 2, 7, 8, 47; "Get Out the Map" lyrics, 146–147; individual importance, 163–168; "It's Alright" lyrics, 65–67; les-

bian activism, 53; "Love Will Come to You" lyrics, 108–109; musical abilities, 42, 44; professional autonomy, 56; as reminder, 135; social importance of, 158, 162; substantive lyrics, 38; as used for expression, 122, 167; why included in study, 19 n.5
Industry's dismissive views, 2–3, 6, 150–158, 175, 185
"(I Never Promised You a) Rose Garden." *See* "Rose Garden"
In My Tribe (10,000 Maniacs), 117
"In or Out" (DiFranco), 90, 103–104
Instrumentalists, 5
Interpellation, 24, 27, 173, 176
Intimate relationships, 81–85
"I Only Want to Be with You" (as performed by Dusty Springfield), 4
"It's Alright" (Saliers), 53, 65–67

Jackson, Janet, 19 n.1
Jett, Joan, 6
Jewel: Grammy nomination, 11; as referred to by respondents, 45, 74, 121, 131, 150, 154, 158, 166; Woodstock experience, 13
Johnson, Janice Marie, 162
Jones, Rickie Lee, 10
Joplin, Janis, 5, 6, 37, 38, 39
Journey, 156

Keys, Alicia, 20, 185
Kidjo, Angelique, 8
Kid Rock, 12
"Killing Me Softly with His Song" (as performed by Roberta Flack), 149
Kimball, Jennifer, 42

King, Carole, 3, 5
Kittie, 13

lang, k.d., 71, 90, 91
Latifah, Queen, 8, 10, 55
Lauper, Cyndi, 6, 183
"Leader of the Pack" (as performed by the Shangri-Las), 4
"Leaving on a Jet Plane" (as performed by Peter, Paul & Mary), 23
Lee, Sara, 10
Lennox, Annie, 44
Lesbian: bonding, 124; Bradby study, 14, 27, 30–31, 183; coming out, 89–91; concerts, 128–130; "I Kissed a Girl," 70, 97; lesbian identities, 31; lesbian issues, 52–54; 1970s lesbian-themed lyrics, 4
Lewis, Lisa, 5, 127, 178, 181, 183
Lilith Fair: man-hating debate, 19 n.7, 152; as mentioned by respondents, 47, 52, 56, 69, 78–79, 130–132; motivation, description and criticisms, 2, 7–10, 155, 156; predominantly female-attended, 128; as transformative, 69, 77–79, 177
Limitations of study, 16–17
Limp Bizkit, 12
"Little Bird, The" (Lennox), 44
Loeb, Lisa, 8, 131, 132
Lois, 40
Lollapalooza, 28, 152
"Lost Woman Song" (DiFranco), 50, 62–63
Love, Courtney, 38–39
Love Deluxe (Sade), 71
"Love Will Come to You" (Indigo Girls), 83, 108–109
"Lucystoners" (Ray), 1, 21–22
Luscious Jackson, 8

Madonna, 5, 10, 11, 15, 51, 136, 183
"Make Me Stay" (DiFranco), 120, 140–141
Mann, Aimee, 8
McClary, Susan, 15, 19 n.2
McLachlan, Sarah: affinity with, 28; as affirming, 74, 77–79; appropriation of, 80, 84, 85–86, 94, 95; "Black" lyrics, 109; concerts, 131, 132; favorite of, 69, 150, 166; feminist/political sensibility, 2, 19 n.7, 52; "Good Enough" lyrics, 109–110; Grammy Awards, 11; "Hold On" lyrics, 110–111; Lilith Fair, 7–10, 155; musical abilities, 42, 45; professional autonomy, 56; as reminder, 136; social importance of, 158; stereotyped as, 154; as used for expression 117, 118
McRobbie, Angela. See Frith, Simon and Angela McRobbie
Memories, 18, 24, 90, 132–137, 166
Methodology, 16–17
Michigan Womyn's Music Festival, 2, 8
"Million You Never Made, The" (DiFranco), 47, 63–65
Misogyny in rock, 3, 19 n.3
"Missing" (Everything But the Girl), 87, 104–105
"Miss World" (Hole), 38
Mitchell, Joni, 5, 6, 131–132
Morissette, Alanis, 10, 13, 75, 153
"Mother" (Amos), 43
Ms. Magazine, 19 n.6
MTV, 5, 11, 33, 55, 159, 167
Musicianship, 40–46, 57–58
Music industry ideology, 150–158

Music industry sexism, 2–3, 150–158, 185
Music, vocal skills and musicianship, attraction to, 40–46, 57–58
"My Boyfriend's Back" (as performed by the Angels), 4
"My Little Sister" (Shocked), 49

National Women's Music Festival, 2, 8
Near, Holly, 4
New Order, 167
Newton John, Olivia, 24
98 Degrees, 12, 151
"Nirvana" (Hatfield), 80, 107–108
No Doubt, 11, 13
'N Sync, 12, 53

O'Connor, Sinead, 8
Olivia Records, 10
Osborne, Joan, 13

Paganism, 48
Payne, Hazel, 162
Peter, Paul & Mary, 23
Phair, Liz, 2, 8, 10, 74, 92, 153; "Fuck and Run" lyrics, 112–113
Poe, 13
Politics: attracted to, 46–54; Lilith Fair politics, 8–10; political discourse, 177–179; politically concious artists, 6–8
"Politics Aside" (Everything But the Girl), 134, 146
"Precious Things" (Amos), 75, 97–98
Pretenders, The, 8
Prodigy, The, 3
Professional autonomy. See Autonomy
Punk, 5, 127

Quiet Riot, 24

Racialized music, 17
Radway, Janice, 15, 181, 182, 183
Raincoats, The, 5
RAINN (Rape, Abuse and Incest National Network), 7, 9, 51
Raitt, Bonnie, 8
Rape, Abuse and Incest National Network. *See* RAINN
Ray, Amy: comments on industry, 13; Daemon Records, 10; "Lucystoners" lyrics, 1, 21–22; as mentioned by respondents, 42, 46, 47, 56, 93
Reception analyses, 180, 184
Reddy, Helen, 5, 74
Redwood Records, 10
Relationships, 81–85
Relevancy, 24, 28, 31, 96, 123, 173, 176
REM, 167
Respondent descriptions, 25–27
RIAA (Recording Industry Association of America), 24
Righteous Babe Records, 7, 10, 19, 55
Right On Records, 10
Rimes, LeAnn, 11
Riot grrrl bands, 15, 130, 178–179
Rise of women in rock, 1–13
Rites of Passage (Indigo Girls), 83, 167
ROCKRGRL magazine, 10, 57
Rock versus pop, 150–151
Rolling Stones, The, 150
Romance novels, 15, 85, 180, 182
Ronstadt, Linda, 136
"Rose Garden" (as performed by Lynn Anderson), 23
"Rush Hour" (DiFranco), 119, 141–142

Sade, 71
Sailers, Emily, 6, 42, 46, 47, 93, 125
Saint-Marie, Buffy, 47
Salt 'n Pepa, 50, 51, 55, 72, 73
Scott, Jill, 20, 185
Second wave of feminism, 4. *See also* Women's Liberation Movement
Seiter, Borchers, Kreutzner and Warth, 15, 180–182
Sexist music lyrics, 3, 13, 19 n.3
Sexual orientation, 52–54, 79, 89–91, 128–129
Shangri-Las, The, 4
Shirelles, The, 3, 4, 70
Shocked, Michelle, 10, 17, 41, 49
Short Sharp Shocked (Shocked), 41
Siberry, Jane, 10
"Silent All These Years" (Amos), 75, 92, 98–100, 160, 168–170
Simpson, Jessica, 12
Sinatra, Nancy, 149
Sister Sledge, 49
Skunk Anansie, 13
"Slant, The" (DiFranco), 119, 142–144
Sleater-Kinney, 80, 81
Slick, Grace, 5, 6
Slits, The, 5
Smith, Patti, 5, 8
Soap operas, 15, 85, 180, 181, 182
Sobule, Jill, 70, 97
Social allegiances, 25, 31, 96, 176
Social change, 2, 4, 10, 177
Social importance of female artists, 158–163
Solace (McLachlan), 45, 86
"Song of Sand" (Vega), 44, 67
Spears, Britney, 12, 13, 179, 185

Spice Girls, 12, 15, 19 n.8, 178, 179, 185
Springfield, Dusty, 4
Springsteen, Bruce, fans, 123
Stefani, Gwen, 13
Stewart, Alan, 19 n.1, 49, 185
Story, The, 42
Substantive lyrics, 17, 34–39, 46
"Suicide Alley" (Colvin), 86, 101–102
Surfacing (McLachlan), 154
Sweet Honey and the Rock, 29

Tapestry (King), 5
Taste of Honey, A, 162
10,000 Maniacs, 117, 135, 167
Texas Campfire Tapes, The (Shocked), 41
"These Boots Are Made for Walkin' " (as performed by Nancy Sinatra), 149
Tillis, Pam, 81; "All the Good Ones Are Gone" lyrics, 113–114
Transforming culture, 174–180
Transitions and challenges, 91–96
Turner, Tina, 6

Validation, 69–97, 137, 175–176, 179, 183
Van Zoonen, Liesbet, 15, 183
Vaughan, Sarah, 76
Vega, Suzanne, 8, 35, 44; "Song of Sand" lyrics, 67
"Verdi Cries" (10,000 Maniacs), 117
Vocal skills, 40–46, 57–58
Voice, provided by female artists, 116–120

"Walking on Broken Glass" (Lennox), 44
"Watching You" (Etheridge), 83
"We Are Family" (as performed by Sister Sledge), 49
"What If No One's Watching" (DiFranco), 119, 144–145
Wheeler, Cheryl, 46
"Where Have All the Cowboys Gone" (Cole), 135, 139–140
Williams, Dar, 46, 48
Williams, Lucinda, 11
Williams, Victoria, 8
Williamson, Cris, 4
"Will You Love Me Tomorrow" (as performed by the Shirelles), 3, 4, 70
Woman-identified artists and music, 4, 27, 53, 174
Women in rock in the 1990s, 6–14
Women's issues, 28, 46, 49–52, 54
Women's Liberation Movement, 4, 5, 70, 124
Women's movement. *See* Women's Liberation Movement
"Women's music," 4–5
Women's preference for female artists over male artists, 17, 27–32
Women's studies, 27–28
Women's use of media fare, 181
Women writing their own songs, 39–40
Woodstock 1999, 12, 128
Working through past abuse. *See* Abuse

Yes I Am (Etheridge), 89

About the Author

ANN M. SAVAGE is Assistant Professor in the Department of Telecommunication Arts at Butler University in Indianapolis, where she teaches subjects including television criticism, media studies, and women and music. She has also contributed entries to *Women and Music in America Since 1900: An Encyclopedia.*

DATE DUE